**Only A Woman's Heart**

You are holding a reproduction of an original work that is in the public domain in the United States of America, and possibly other countries.You may freely copy and distribute this work as no entity (individual or corporate) has a copyright on the body of the work.This book may contain prior copyright references, and library stamps (as most of these works were scanned from library copies).These have been scanned and retained as part of the historical artifact.

This book may have occasional imperfections such as missing or blurred pages, poor pictures, errant marks, etc. that were either part of the original artifact, or were introduced by the scanning process. We believe this work is culturally important, and despite the imperfections, have elected to bring it back into print as part of our continuing commitment to the preservation of printed works worldwide. We appreciate your understanding of the imperfections in the preservation process, and hope you enjoy this valuable book.

# ONLY A WOMAN'S HEART.

## BY ADA CLARE.

"If it be now, 'tis not to come; if it be not now, yet it will come: the readiness is all."—HAMLET.

NEW YORK:
M. DOOLADY, PUBLISHER,
448 BROOME STREET.
1866.

ENTERED, according to Act of Congress, in the year 1866, by
M. DOOLADY,
In the Clerk's Office of the United States District Court for the Southern District of New York.

JOHN J. REED, PRINTER,
43 Centre Street, N. Y.

# ONLY A WOMAN'S HEART.

## CHAPTER 1.

"LAURA, Laura, look where you are going. See, now, you have steered us up upon a bank, and I don't see how we are going to get off. I wish you would keep your eyes open when you take the rudder." The speaker, a girl of about eighteen, drew the oar, which she held out of the water, with a peevish jerk, and laid it across the boat.

Then all the girls in the boat, eight or ten in number, joined their voices in a confused hum of reproach against the one addressed as Laura, who, with a flush of mortification on her face, sprang up, seized an oar, and pushed against the shallow ground, on which the boat was stranded, with a vigor that revealed a muscular strength, strangely inconsistent with her slender frame. Fortunately, the boat was but lightly grounded; with Laura's vigorous exertions, it first swayed a little, then turned slowly round, as upon a pivot, and glided off into the stream.

"There, no harm done, you see, though you were all so cross about it," said Laura; and she sat down with anything but an amiable look on her face.

"Cross," said the first speaker; "*you* needn't say so; you're the crossest girl in school. You keep awake next time, and then there will be nothing to complain about."

"You know I was not asleep, Charley, I never go to sleep unless I try. I was thinking of something, and so I forgot all about the boat and the rudder and all of you."

The person addressed as Charley was a young girl, spite of the boyish cognomen, which for some reason, probably its inaptitude, had always clung to her. Her name was Charlotte, and she was elder half-sister to Laura.

"I don't know any thing about it; I know you are always thinking about something besides combing your hair and putting your collar on." The satire told, with Parthian effect, for Laura's brown gingham dress was destitute of any strip of white about the neck, and her dark hair was dragged off from her brow with a comb and allowed to straggle in rough curls about her neck, like a wild lion's mane.

"Laura's in love; I believe it as much as I believe anything;" and this third speaker fell to pulling at her oar, as though she were defending herself from the vengeance which this remark was sure to bring upon her.

"In love with whom, Julia Sydney?" cried Laura, her eyes kindling with that indignation a very young girl always feels when accused of harboring the tender passion in her breast.

"With a young man whose name begins with a V., who isn't a bit pretty and whose hair curls—when it is put in papers."

"You're a mean girl! you're in love with him yourself, and you know his hair curls without papers; gentlemen never wear curl-papers."

"Well, what do I care about his hair? I say you're

in love with him. If you are not, why do you make such great eyes at him when he is telling his long stories to your father? I say you're in love with him."

"Julia Sydney, if you say that again, I'll whip you the minute we get out of this boat!"

"Will you whip me, miss? I would like to see you do it. I can whip you any day; I'm bigger. I'll say it as often as I like; you're in love with a V., and what's more, I know what he thinks of you—that you are a cross, ugly school-girl."

Here such a skirmish of words ensued between the two girls, that, had not the boat arrived at a convenient spot for embarkation, a naval battle would certainly have convulsed the peaceful water of that shallow stream. But no sooner did it touch land than the brace of war-like spirits flew promiscuously at each other. The other girls, taking a boisterous interest in the affray, formed a ring and prepared to enjoy the sport. The plan of battle was a peculiar one; there were very few blows given, but the chief object seemed to be to ascertain which could squeeze the hardest, and drag the other about most unresistingly. In the course of events, Laura contrived to get hold of a handful of Julia's hair, and, by means of this, to pull her round and round, with no other view, apparently, than to make her describe involuntary circles. It was, however, considered a masterly piece of strategy by the spectators, and their expressions to that effect so maddened Julia, that she took her revenge by scratching Laura's throat from ear to ear, and then they tripped each other up, and rolled for at least ten minutes in the sand, in an entirely miscellaneous manner, after which both fiery spirits seemed quenched, and they quietly rose and equally claimed the victory. Charley, who was the young lady of the party, and therefore considered herself umpire in all questions, declared they were a pair of dunces, both of them; that they were all torn to pieces, looked like scarecrows, and the sooner they got out of the way of being seen the better. This opinion recalled them both to the realization of their disasters, one sleeve of Julia's dress being torn almost entirely out, and Laura's comb being left in fragments on the ground, while her dress displayed a great rent at the side. This consonance of misfortune caused an immediate reconciliation between the foes, and they helped each other most cheerfully to pin up the rents and fold over the holes.

In the meanwhile, the unconscious object of this contest was a hidden witness of it all. Just above and beyond them he sat with another young man, excessively amused by its ludicrous side, though it most rudely dispelled their former illusions about the young angels from the seminary, and shook their whole fair theory of gentle girlhood to its foundations. The being whose name has been mysteriously announced as beginning with a V., was a young man of partly foreign blood, pursuing the art of sculpture through ambition, that of the drama as a profession, and owning the euphonius name of Victor Doria, which, as to surname, the reader will perceive, was possessed of a most ancient and aristocratic flavor. Whether any of the blood of the house of the Dorias ran in his veins, he had not been heard to suggest, but from the peculiarities of his face and manner, popular opinion had already decided the question in the affirmative. At any rate, there he reclined on the grass, with his face in the shadow of a tree. It was a listless face, manifestly wanting in color and almost wanting in expression, unless a smile played over it, and then all the languid, apathetic features broke up into sunshine, and the whole face was irradiated as with an inward light. Something tender about the mouth and sorrowful about the eyes might easily have been the snares by which a woman's fancy could be caught and perhaps retained.

His companion was one of those blessed young men of the ordinary type, fair, blue-eyed, smiling and good-humored; no danger that through love of him any heart should be killed all the day long.

To say that they smiled at this scene would be to put it mildly indeed; they almost suffocated themselves with the attempt to laugh noiselessly. Perhaps, with Victor, astonishment would have conquered amusement had he known that this display of feminine ferocity was the result of indignation at being supposed to be interested in himself. Well, considering that ladies of finish and fashion had sighed for him and thrilled for him, this indignation on the part of an angular school-girl of fifteen, whose elbows were as sharp as nut-pickers, was a curiously scornful repudiation.

He had come down to this little village, a very pleasant watering-place in summer, but dreary enough in winter, expressly on business with Laura's father, and had seen both her and her sisters frequently with him, but had barely noticed Laura at all. On this occasion, he found himself singularly interested in her. He saw with a sculptor's eye those beauties of person, which to the ordinary sight would have been concealed under its lack of flesh. He marked the exceeding suppleness of the figure, and what lovely outlines were waiting to be created by the addition of a little fullness and roundness. He noted also the savage grace of the girl, her utter abandonment of herself to her impulses, as well as the large brown eyes that seemed to have a look both of sullenness and unrest in them. He took them all in at a glance, and resolved in the future to know the girl and "draw her out."

Meantime the girls all passed amicably on towards the spot where the sparkling bay curved into the white shore, and tempted bathers to taste of its delights. Though it was far too late in the fall to make bathing an actual pleasure, for it was verging towards the middle of November, these girls, all active and ambitious swimmers, in spite of the chill in the air, were soon battling about in the water, "ducking" each other with unparalleled rudeness, screaming shrilly, and indulging in boisterous exhibitions of animal spirits, which would have utterly shocked the proprieties of girls brought up in city schools.

## CHAPTER II.

The little village of Dorn founded its right to existence on possessing a "young ladies' seminary," and a tolerable summer hotel. All winter, the seminary kept the place from sinking into torpidity by its hundred bright noisy girls, and when the summer came, and that seminary slept the sleep of vacation, the hotel threw open its doors, and perhaps double that number of strangers galvanized the village into life till autumn.

Laura's father owned the seminary, and had an interest in the hotel. In the latter, he resided all the year, while his four daughters, of which Laura was the youngest, remained in the seminary, two of them as pupils and two as parlor boarders. During the summer season, when the seminary closed for vacation, he took all his girls to the hotel, and allowed them to be as wild as hares just out of a cage. He had been twice married, and was now for the second time a widower. He was one of those negative, characterless beings, whose whole nature cried out to be governed and shaped by some one. He had in turn submitted himself to his two wives, and after the death of the second, he contrived to be ruled by his daughters. Next to the pleasure of being governed by female influence, was the pleasure of protesting that he was about to throw off the yoke, and prove the strength of his manly will. But, as he had gone on in the same groove for forty-five years, no one believed that any such radical change could take place in him. Laura influenced him most and loved him best. She had always been his favorite, for he had early discovered a trait in her, most valuable to a man of his peculiar character—the fact that his yielding to her wishes did not diminish the warmth of her affection for him. His two elder daughters often showed for his pliant nature and weak kindness, something akin to contempt. Agnes, the third one, was too like her father to have any influence at all; but Laura, resolute to hardness and positive to obstinacy, never moulded her father to her views by her own will, without sealing her victory by a fervent demonstration of tenderness to the vanquished parent. She would throw her arms about his neck, covering his face with kisses, and indulging in every expression of affection and gratitude, as though he had been guided by his own sovereign will. What more could a naturally plastic nature desire than this— to be ruled and loved and petted and admired, all at the same time? No wonder that the weak, loving, soft-hearted gentleman set his fond, wilful daughter in his heart's core, and almost made an idol of her.

The seminary at Dorn was conducted on very mild and

exalted principles. Punishment was almost unknown, but such was not the case with reward. Everything was done to make study a delight and knowledge an honor. The road to learning was so strewn with flowers, that even the most stupid and frivolous girls found themselves eagerly walking in it, as though it had been solely the path of pleasure. What is called discipline was somewhat lax; the girls were allowed a great amount of liberty, such as the free enjoyment out of school and study hours, of the most boisterous and hoydenish games, as well as the roaming at large through the beautiful woodlands which surrounded the establishment. But all hypocrisy, malice, dishonesty and falsehood were crushed down with a firm hand. The consequence of such a mode of training was a set of scholars who were really the best educated in the State, who were about as honest and high-principled as their natures would allow them to be, who were, moreover, abounding in health and animal spirits, and yet who lacked all skill and coquetry and drawing-room graces. They were seldom of that flimsy, flabby texture too common with girls, but rather of a rich, solid and endurable fabric, but in a clumsy shape, ready to be cut out and formed by the world and its usages.

Nearly every Friday afternoon two of Mr. Milsland's daughters went over to the hotel to spend Saturday and Sunday with him, for he declared if he could not have them with him at least some days of the week, he would not undertake the exertion of living. Of these, Laura was always one, while the others came in turn. Mr. Milsland always said that as Laura was his youngest, he found it necessary to have her often under his eye; but satirical people said that he was oftener under her eye, than she was under his.

A short time before, Victor Doria had come down to this little place, accompanied by the fair-haired friend of the preceding chapter, Charley Oakford, on a visit to Mr. Milsland, who was trustee for some landed property in the neighborhood, that had been lately willed to him by a deceased uncle. The season at the hotel had closed long before his arrival. About a dozen permanent residents were there, only three of them being ladies, and these were entirely unsuited to his tastes by their dullness, indifference, and bigotry in religious sentiment. Poor Victor loving the society of women, as all fascinating men do, found the time that elapsed before his business could be settled, hang most wearily upon his hands. Had it not been for the good-natured offer of his friend to share his exile, it is impossible to say what mischief ennui might not have brought upon him. He had seen Mr. Milsland's daughters on the occasion of their last weekly visit to the hotel, had even been casually introduced to them, but had not hitherto felt the slightest interest in cultivating their acquaintance. Now the case was changed; he felt a sudden liking arise in him for the intrepid Laura, and he determined to make the study of her character his amusement for the remainder of his stay in Dorn.

## CHAPTER III.

"I am afraid you find life very dull here, Mr. Doria; I wish we had some interesting company for you. My daughters are nothing but country girls. I supposed you couldn't be amused with them. But stay; I have some company for you to-night—one of the heads of the seminary—my Laura's favorite teacher. She's a most fine woman; knows more about astronomy than any man in the county; and as for algebra, you should see her chalk out the blackboard! It's equal to a sermon. Oh! I promise you a treat in her conversation. Do you do much in algebra?"

Victor acknowledged that his doings in algebra were infinitessimal, and would have declined the honor of knowing this heroine of the blackboard altogether, had he not desired to question her on the subject of her pupil Laura. With this view, he expressed himself charmed with the prospect, and desired to know of Mr. Milsland where his daughters were.

"Taking tea in there. You can see them if you look in."

Victor did look in, and soon distinguished Laura, with her pretty sister Agnes. He stood for a minute, carefully scrutinizing the new object of his interest, and one thing he noted about her as most unquestionable, was, that she had an omnipotent appetite. Every minute she seemed to help herself from some new dish, and the next minute it was gone. After she had apparently consumed all the substantial viands, she calmly commenced a career on the sweets, and then pies and cakes vanished like stars before the breaking dawn. He stood there—this most refined and fastidious young man—in rapt astonishment, wondering that so young and slender a creature could appropriate such a quantity of the world's productions. If, as Sydney Smith states, we can never eat more than our natural share without taking it out of the mouths of others, how many human beings must have owed their death from inanition to her appetite. And yet there was nothing greedy about her manner. On the contrary, the gravity and aplomb with which she ministered to her rapacity, would have brought tears of envy to the eyes of an alderman. "Heavens!" murmured Victor to himself, "let me never lead her out of the immediate reach of provisions, for if I should, how short a time it would take her to eat me."

His meditations were finally interrupted by the rising of the two girls from the table. They swept out upon the porch, rushing past him as they came. He accosted them, and for the first time, joined them in their walk. A painful blush burned upon Laura's cheek when she perceived him, and she managed to keep her sister between them as they walked. Agnes was an affectionate, sentimental girl, ready to talk about the few simple things she knew, and quite flattered by the attention of this elegant young gentleman. She was more than a year older than Laura; yet, as the moonlight fell upon her golden hair and pearl-tinted skin, she looked much younger. Victor marked the contrast between the smiling blonde and her dark tawney sister, with her downcast head, and shy, sombre expression, who seemed not to listen to him, but to be wrapped up in some defiant, morose thought. But all his interest centered in Laura. She puzzled his will, and made him determine, at any trouble, to discover the key to her mystery. With this intention, he was not sorry when Mr. Milsland interrupted his conversation, by introducing to him Miss Marshall, the so much vaunted teacher. Victor expected, from Mr. Milsland's remarks about her, that she would, morally speaking, make a blackboard of him, and lay him out in algebraic propositions. But to his pleasant surprise, he found her a simple, interesting lady, and anything but pedantic. It did not take him long to get to the subject of the seminary, and to ask her which she considered the most promising pupil.

"If you mean, sir, as to scholarly promise, Laura Milsland is head and shoulders above them all. As far as other things are concerned, I scarcely know; she is very different from other girls; so strange—and yet we love her dearly."

"In what is she so strange?"

"Why, for one thing, it is impossible for any one to get the slightest authority over her. She seems to make up her mind to a certain course of conduct, and nothing one can do moves her from it. Yet I will do her the justice to say that she generally chooses the right course. But it is not pleasant to feel that you are only obeyed by a pupil because she chooses to obey, and not because you have the right to be obeyed."

"Is she very ill-tempered?"

"High tempered, but not at all malicious. When she first came to us, we mistook her displays of silent, abstracted spirit, for sullenness, but we soon found out that they were constitutional attacks of depression of the mind, very singular for one so young, and yet quite beyond her control."

"Is she always gloomy?"

"Oh dear, no, the merriest girl in the school more

than half the time! Since she came to us, she has effected a revolution in school; we never knew what fighting was before. But she brought it with her, and now it is a firmly rooted institution. Is it not strange that such an intellectual girl should decide every question by an appeal to blows? Would you believe it, she had a 'black eye' half of the time during the first year? Yet she effected a revolution on another side, which more than balanced the evils of this one. She seems to have entirely banished dissimulation and deceit from the seminary. Such a thing as a lie is almost entirely unknown; and secret midnight suppers, once the bane of our lives, are quite obsolete since she came."

"Is she quick at study?"

"She is quick in her ideas, not remarkably so in her study, but her perseverance is unequalled. When she began the study of geometry, she found it difficult, more so than any other she had ever attempted. After the first few lessons in it, she came upon a proposition which was puzzling to her. It even seemed to anger her, and I feared she would throw aside the book, and altogether refuse to study it. I was mistaken; that evening, when we all assembled for the regular two hours of study, I saw her open her book at that proposition, and for the entire evening her eyes remained fixed on its inch and a half of space. When I announced that the hours of study were ended, she shut the book with a smile, and from that day I don't recollect that she had much to contend with in the science of geometry."

"That proved a great power of concentration, surely; but you say she is lacking in the qualities of the heart?"

"Not at all; she loves me more, for instance, than any pupil we ever had. One day there was a dreadful noise in the garden. I looked out of the window, and saw Laura fighting like a cat brought to bay by a pack of dogs. In the course of the affray getting several new antagonists, some of whom she easily vanquished, and apparently receiving some hard usage from others, I called out to her to stop; but after I had spoken, she put Julia Sydney in a large box full of coal-dust, and you can imagine in what a state she came out. I called Laura up to my room. I did not know her as well then as I do now; so I sternly commanded her to tell me the reason of all this violence. She refused. I urged her. She would not tell. I asked her if she was sorry for her conduct; she said she was not sorry, and should the same provocation occur, would not change it. I was so shocked with her obstinacy, that I told her she should remain locked in that room until she did repent. I left her there until night, with no dinner and no tea, until I learned in the evening that I was the cause of the fight. A restriction I had recently imposed on the classes had awakened hostility to me, and several girls had called me a cross, ugly old maid. So Laura declared she would fight every one who expressed that opinion as long as she retained any life in her body. It was as my champion she had fought this battle, and that was why she had refused to acknowledge either its cause, or express penitence for it. I could not of course justify her conduct for that reason; but my heart yearned towards the poor, hungry, lonely child. Besides, I thought she had been sufficiently punished. I ran quickly up and opened the door, lit a lamp, and then I saw that she had fallen asleep in a great chair, with her head leaning over on one arm. She is not a pretty girl; indeed she is rather plain; but you would not have thought so if you had seen her that night. Her hair was all wild and tangled, and from the dark, swollen look under her eyes, I could see that she had been weeping; yet she looked like an angel—like a positive angel; I never saw such an expression on any human face. From that hour she has been so dear to me, that I sometimes fear my love for her is what they call doting. But here have I kept you all the evening, telling stories of a little school-girl that cannot possibly interest a gentleman like you."

"But it does interest me," said Victor; and he spoke truly. He was interested. That sleeping angel face, dimmed with tears, started vividly out before his imagination, mingled with some vague foreboding of the future, that held up a hand of solemn warning to him; but he put it aside, laughed his shallowest laugh, and begged Miss Marshall for some more scholastic anecdotes.

Not to-night; it is late (it was nearly nine), and I must say good-night to you."

"Good-night;" and he conducted Miss Marshall through the bare corridor to the stairway, then went back to the piazza, and found himself curiously speculating about the strange girl, who had taken such an unaccountable hold of his fancy.

## CHAPTER IV.

Long before Victor was up, next morning, he heard the voices of the girls in the garden, where they were evidently carrying on some exhilarating game. He could easily distinguish the shrill, penetrating tones of Laura's voice, as she romped with her sister. Her hilarity and talkativeness were in strong contrast to the shy monosyllables, and reluctant attention she had given to him the night before. He got out of bed, and standing behind the window-blinds, saw the two girls, without being seen by them. It was only a game of ball they were engaged in, but he could see that Laura was so brimming with animal spirits, so overflowing with vitality, that she could not help playing the romp to save her life. The amount of physical exercise she took while playing that simple game, would have exhausted a drill-officer. She jumped, she ran, she bounded, she almost flew in the air. "Heavens," Victor exclaimed, "what an appetite she will have for breakfast! Let me hasten down before her, for surely after her will come, if not the deluge, the seven years' famine!"

Later he learned that this was an after-breakfast amusement, a mere sportive way of keeping pace with the velocity of a robust digestion. As soon as he appeared upon the piazza, Agnes, with the instinctive coquetry of a young girl, became aware of his presence, and soon pleaded fatigue, as a motive for desisting from the game. A flimsy little bit of needle-work, opportunely drawn from her pocket, furnished a reasonable excuse for sitting down in a chair not very far from Victor's, while Laura seated herself, in not too good a humor, at her feet, on the highest of the stairs which led to the garden. Agnes' neat muslin dress and silk apron, together with her soft face and luxuriant golden hair, drawn in two picturesque rolls from her white brow, presented a striking contrast to Laura's moody face, and tangled, blousy curls, and distorted dress, which seemed to have been tossed on with a pitchfork. Yet he resolutely addressed his conversation to the latter, determined to make her converse with him, whether she wished it or not. From this conversation, he learned that she was one of the most arrogant and affected young creatures he had ever had the ill fortune to encounter. There was a mixture of pedantry, conceit, and pretension about her that was literally inconceivable. It was easy to see she considered herself immeasurably his intellectual superior, and looked upon all speech with him as a sacrifice to frivolity. No wonder, then, that the conversation soon drifted back to smiling Agnes, and Laura's old look of indifference returned to her face. Yet Victor's fancy, baffled in every effort to find some quality in her which should justify it, still clung to her, and as it slipped from point to point in her unaccountable character, it still caught at her great, restless, torrid eyes, in which slumbered such a world of infinite meanings.

A brilliant idea suddenly danced into his mind, to excite her interest by letting her see what emotions he had raised in the breasts of others. Out of this idea grew several romantic and mysterious anecdotes, which dimly pointed to himself as their hero, and were calculated to show the particular kind of blight he had been so fortunate as to cast upon other angelic and beautiful beings. Vain hope! these narratives only won for him a long, shy side glance, expressive partly of incredulity and partly of contempt. Possibly, however, he did not perceive this glance, for he really was satisfied that at least he was making an impression upon her, and when she rose and ran suddenly down the garden path, he imagined she retreated before the impossibility of hiding her interest. But scarcely two minutes had elapsed before her boisterous laughter came to his ear, mingled with the plaintive complainings of a cat. And then he saw the cat come scampering down the brick walk, mewing indignantly, and Laura following after and filling the air with resonant laughter. She had fled from the seductive efforts to please, on the part of the most polished and subtle young man she was ever destined to encounter, to abandon her whole mind to the delightful occupation of shoeing a cat with walnut-shells.

## CHAPTER V.

Strange as it may seem, Laura Milsland was more deeply interested in Victor than he was in herself. From the first moment that she looked in his face she felt herself attracted to him in some indefinable way. So new and peculiar was the feeling that she could not distinguish whether it was like or dislike that called her attention to him. An unusual share of intellect and independence in very young girls is apt to be coupled with an almost painful modesty and timidity on the subject of the tender passions. Thus, when she was accused by a schoolmate of loving this man, the idea burst into her mind with a kind of sickening thrill. The anticipation of a love for herself had long been entertained in Laura's imagination, but she had never dreamed of loving any one but some marble-featured hero, some grand, awful and commanding creature, whom she should worship with a solemn reverence and love, with a profound platonic esteem. In her most ambitious moments, he was pictured as a great general or statesman; in more religious moments, he resolved himself into a universal philanthropist or a grandly eloquent divine. But whatever his profession might be, he was always endowed with a towering form, a vast brow, a deep bass voice, and a manner that inspired overwhelming awe. And was this monstrous idol to be thrown down and crumbled into dust by the wings of a butterfly? for under that head she classified Victor. Then she would thrust the idea out of her mind, with fear and trembling, persuading herself that it was not attraction, not aversion, that she felt towards him. Had she been other than the strangely earnest creature she was, the idea that the affair would turn into a pleasant flirtation might have entered her mind. But it would no more have been possible for her to trifle with what she considered the momentous question of love than with her soul's salvation. Some blind animal instinct of self-preservation taught her to fly from him, and most conscientiously did she strive not to listen to his voice nor to look at his face. But what chance has ardent, earnest simplicity and crude youth against a subtle knowledge of the world and human nature, united to that insidious personal magnetism which coils itself softly round the whole nature, before it strikes the fatal blow. Doubtless the key to Victor's interest in her lay in this, for these magnetic natures are also strongly clairvoyant; that he perceived the desperately concealed and smouldering flame that quivered in the vestal bosom of this lion-hearted maid. The lack of vanity, of coquetry, of all temporizing with emotion, at once taught him that this was a nature utterly unlike the many sentimental maidens and more material matrons who had already paid tribute to his charms, and his interest in her almost grew into a passion.

When on Sunday he attended for the first time the village church, and watched her as she followed every word of the sermon with devout and reverent face, or when some pathetic reference to that great love which redeemed us from our sins and died for our regeneration, touched her heart, he saw the great tears soften the light in her luminous eyes, he could not believe that this was the morose, conceited girl of yesterday.

When Sunday evening came, he contrived to get her and Agnes out to walk with him, and Agnes being called away, she found herself reluctantly left alone in his company. But the sacred and softening influences of the day still hovered round her, and perhaps around him too, revealing themselves in more gentleness in her, more truthfulness in him. He ceased to act a part; he told her of his childhood, his ambitions, his studies, his mother's death, his failures, his successes, and his hopes. Insensibly she became interested in this account; she ceased to walk at an inconvenient distance from him; her large eyes, full of infinite questionings, fluttered timidly about his face, till all at once they dropped on his eyes and rested there. It was not very much longer before she accepted a seat beside him on a rustic bench among the trees. In seating herself, she struck against the bench her little brown hand, which was scarcely less hard than the wood itself. Sympathy for the bench might have been just as appropriate as for her hand, but the bench was not a young lady with eyes of the color of a lion's; so he caught up that little sun-browned hand, and caressed its stubby fingers with a soft exclamation of pity. Laura experienced such a shock when her hardy hand came into contact with his soft, warm palm, as might have smitten her had she thrust it into a nest of nettles. It was like that of a thousand stings, all throbbing away to an uneasy numbness. All these sensations ran through the tingling fibres of her flesh in the one or two seconds that elapsed before she snatched it from him and hid it in her pocket. Further, this little act of tender gallantry, offered with all the delicate grace its bestower was master of, filled her mind with astonishment. For nearly three years, she had incorporated a discolored eye as one of her features; she wore great scratches all over her, like honorable ribbons, as proof of the number of her battles, and her hands were generally outlined, like a map, with scars and cuts, and bruises, resulting from the incautious use of sharp-edged tools and the climbing of rough-stemmed trees. She was fearfully proud of being able to jump higher than any girl in her class, but in moments of too lofty ambition, while vaulting over the clothes-line, she occasionally tripped herself up and came down on the brick walk, subjecting herself to that painful process technically known as "barking" the knees; yet this mishap always called a shout of triumph from her rivals. Once from a cherry-tree where she was gathering cherries, and flinging them into a large basket below, she fell from a height of eighteen or twenty feet, raising a great lump on the side of her head, the size of a small gourd; but all the commiseration of her companions was expended on the cherries, which were reduced to a shapeless mass beneath her. And now to see a light blow on her hand calling forth caressive and tender sympathy, struck her dumb with amazement. In the meanwhile, she kept that hand clenched into a ball in her pocket, as though it were some rare and evanescent curiosity, which must be cautiously guarded for private scrutiny. To Victor's sentimental flow of talk, she listened as through a soft haze: for she was slowly gliding into the pathway of the sweet dreamland of manly tenderness and protection—that path that to the young mind seems the one of perfect peace, but which sometimes leads her to a quicksand in which she shall sink, never to rise again.

Nothing but meaningless monosylables and shy " I don't knows," could Victor draw from her after this, until Agnes came back, announcing it to be the very witching hour of eight, which, under ordinary circumstances, caused them to yawn, and their couches to give out such seductive attractions as they seldom thought of resisting. Agnes had no sooner mentioned the hour than Laura hurried, in fact almost dragged her off. Victor smiled as he saw Laura stride along the walk, while her heavy shoes ground down the gravel with a creaking noise, and one arm swang robustly in the air; but he noted that the other hand was still kept close in her pocket, and he was so puzzled by the circumstance, that he hardly knew whether to smile or not.

## CHAPTER VI.

The week following this Sunday included within its limits two holidays, the one set apart for thanksgiving, and the annual occurrence of Mr. Milsland's birth-day. As usual, the too indulgent father offered to give his daughters leave of absence from school for the whole week. To make such offers on the flimsiest pretences had always been his habit, but it was also Laura's to meet them with an unflinching refusal, for she was unwilling to lose the smallest opportunity of outstripping her class in every branch of study taken up by them. But this week she accepted his offer, complaining, for the first time in her life, of a pain about her head. Hitherto she had walked unscathed through all the contagion of bodily ailment. In early childhood, the whooping-cough had declined, on any terms, to locate itself in her system. At eight, she was put to sleep with an elder sister, with the delectable aim to contract the measles in a moderate form; but the measles, deeming that in equal contest with her they would get the worst of it, begged to be excused. A year later, the scarlet-fever had a chance at her, but such was the violence of her health, that the scarlet-fever quietly retreated, assuming discretion to be the better part of valor.

Thus, when she complained of headache, her father surmised that it was at least a brain-fever, and would have gathered in the village doctors for a formal consultation, had she not allayed his fears by opportunely remembering how in a moment of impetuous effort to allay thirst, her head had collided with the pump. This recollection also satisfied herself, for she did not yet comprehend that dull, wavering ache that crawls about the brain when one unremitting, unwelcome thought ever knocks for admission therein.

But, headache or no headache, she walked over every day to the seminary, took the sum of the lessons allotted to her class, and committed them conscientiously to memory. This scholarly energy and perseverance did but work the more completely to her heart's undoing. Victor, ever on the alert, watched her out of the gate, immediately joined her in the roadway, walked over with her to the gate of the seminary, and, waiting for her among the trees beyond, accompanied her home again. The first time he thus attended her, she walked the whole way before him, striding along like a peripatetic champion, and giving him hard work to keep up with her. But, afterwards, she ceased to resent his keeping by her side, and soon laughed heartily at his wit, and sighed at his sentiment. Seeing there was nothing to be got from her in conversation but spiritless monosyllables on his own ground, and a stream of stilted school-girl pedantry on hers, he wisely occupied her as a listener, and found that she eclipsed her whole sex in that capacity. Here, in the open air, with her straw-hat swinging on her arm—for she had no more fear of freckles than a sun-flower has—and with her bounding step, she was at home and in perfect harmony with her surroundings, while in a drawing-room she seemed as out of place as an ostrich. Victor noted this, and his inexplicable interest in her was strengthened by it.

It is patent enough how cultivated men of the world succeed in impressing themselves on natures utterly irresponsive to their own. It is easy to see, then, how such a man as this could stir a nature to its depths, which was as consonant to his own as life is to the human soul, which was his perfectly adjusted counterpart, and could no more refuse its response to him than the true notes of the keyboard can refuse to give out their harmonies to the touch of the wise and cunning hand.

Before the week was over, she hung on every word from his lips, with rapt eagerness, and the half-veiled glances that streamed up to his face from her questioning eyes, told of the unutterable depths of fond disquiet from which they came. Like one long, dizzy, sweet, uneasy dream the week sped by, and lapsed into another Sunday, till in its hushed and holy twilight she was taking her last walk with him through the garden grounds. She knew that on the morrow, he was to take the early stage away from Dorn. By force of thinking of it all day, her mind wavered between nervous depression and angry excitability. Even in church, the old devout spirit would not take possession of her; the sweet hymns floated by, unnoticed by her insensible ear; the tender, reverent words of the pastor, who preached emphatically a gospel of grace, no longer moved her heart, but dropped like hollow echoes, the mere shadows of sound. Some trick of *his* voice, some quaint gesture, some half-sad, half-wildering play of the eyes filled her mind, and made all other things look colorless and dead. Even the precious Book of books faded dimly away before her, while she was thus, for the first time, opening the book of her own heart and turning over its crimson leaves with a frightened, feverish flutter. The wavering pain in her head returned upon her, and, while it saddened and wearied her, the thought stole warily into her mind, that it would never be at rest till it lay upon his breast. The idea brought such a burning blush to her cheek that she thrust it out of her mind in positive terror. It was succeeded by a sensation of remorse and utter self-disgust, which could not have been greater, had she broken every commandment in the decalogue.

Her half-sister, Charlotte, who came over to spend the day in place of Agnes, perceived there was something wrong with Laura, and by sly, irritating questions soon exasperated her into violent invectives and taunts, resulting in a succession of quarrels, so that altogether they had a turbulent day.

After the early tea, when the long twilight began to set in, Charlotte found a chance to give her father a detailed account of Laura's wickedness, while Victor, availing himself of the opportunity to get the latter to himself, immediately took her off for a ramble. In the course of this walk, he told her that, feeling an absolute necessity for the beauties of rustic scenery during the warm months of the year, he had concluded to come in the summer time to Dorn, for a much longer stay. At this announcement her heart, which all day had been sickening in her breast, gave a sudden bound, as though it would burst the confines of her bosom—then sunk slowly back, heavy with unspeakable content.

Victor had long since learned that this young savage was not to be approached like more civilized members of her sex. A dual contemplation of the setting sun would never justify to her the clasping of hands; and if under the melting rays of the moon he should allow his arm to glide about her waist, there was no telling what effect that moon might have in calling forth lunatic demonstrations of indignation on her part. He had seriously considered whether the moment of parting might not render appropriate a very evanescent kiss on the cheek or brow, but on further thought he surrendered it as an undertaking fraught with danger. He even cut short this interview by a less ambitious attempt at tenderness. While slowly drifting about the garden, he asked her if she would try to remember him until his return, and she faltered out a low, trembling "yes." Then he stooped and gathered a branch of heliotrope, bidding her keep it as a token of remembrance. She would have taken it, but he bent forward and attempted to fasten it in the bosom of her dress, at which she sprang from him with a terrified look, and flew swiftly back to the house.

She fled regretting, with a stinging blush, that she had promised to remember him.

Ah! that memory already stood behind her, like the angel with the flaming sword, to divide her from all return to the peacefulness and the simple interest of her former life; it followed noiselessly, ready to deal its fiery wound, whenever her feet should falter, or seek to turn into the placid paths of oblivion.

## CHAPTER VII.

WHEN Victor arrived in the great Atlantic city for which he was destined, he began to prepare himself for the important object, which was the main aim of his visit there, namely, to make an appearance on the English stage and in English drama. For four or five years, he had been tolerably popular as an actor in Italy. But several considerations had determined him to leave his native country, and woo fame on the English stage. In the first place, he considered the narrow field, either for the attainment of fame or riches, afforded in his own country: then he was conscious of too little physical power among a people where luxurious development is the rule rather than the exception. Many other actors had finer voices, more striking faces, and much more commanding forms than his. So, because his voice lacked boisterousness, and his face was pale, and his person slender, he found himself set down as being intended by nature for a comedian, while everything within him cried out for the pathetic, the romantic, and the passionate. He was not without a liberal supply of other talents; he was a fair painter, and had not been unsuccessful as a sculptor.

On one occasion he had introduced on the stage the modelling of a figure in clay, which his skill and dexterity made very effective, and that was really his only genuine success in Italian drama.

He was the child of highly cultivated parents, and had himself received a thorough education in the solid departments of learning as well as in the more subtle arena of art. None of the coarse and illiterate influences which unhappily so often surround the childhood of men and women of talents, were the lot of his early years. His parents were possessed of education, gentle blood and high breeding, and though a comparative narrowness of means caused them to live in strict retirement, they brought up their son as carefully as though he had been a prince. Every advantage of a solid education was early bestowed upon him, and when at a later age he exhibited a talent for pretty nearly all of the fine arts, he was encouraged in the cultivation of them. He went into the studio of a sculptor, exhibited considerable talent for that art, then gave himself up for a time to wooing the muse of painting, till finally his true talent, the dramatic one, seized him by the heart and bore him away to the stage. To the circumstance of his mother's having been an American, he owed his knowledge of the English language, which he spoke without perceptible foreign accent, unless it were the southern softness and sonority of speech, which lent it a new charm.

After the death of both father and mother, he concluded to visit America, both with a social and professional view, for several brothers and sisters of his mother were living there, and were desirous of seeing him. He found them well situated as to fortune and position, and with this foundation, he soon had no lack of acquaintances—his own elegant and winning address and strangely attractive person left him with no lack of admirers.

Like many sensitive and highly-strung natures, decision of character was not one of his mental traits; indeed a versatility of determinations was as noted in him as a versatility of talents. After his arrival in America, he hesitated for some time as to which of his professions he would follow. At one moment, he came to the conclusion that he would pursue the art of sculpture as more respectable than the drama; at another, that he would devote himself entirely to painting as less arduous than either; finally, he came to the conclusion that he might engage himself in a more immediately profitable art than either, that of marrying an heiress.

He went up to Dorn, under the impression that the piece of property left to him by his uncle, would make him rich enough to lead a life of voluptuous leisure for the short time that might elapse before the merchant princess and her dowry should be obtained. After a few days' residence in the village, he perceived that his legacy was of little or no available value. But his stay there benefitted him in one respect ; it completely dissipated his doubts as to a future profession, sharpened up his ambition and hope, and crystalized them about the drama. The new life he led there, with its almost pastoral simplicity, strengthened the tone of his system, insensibly rubbed away the artificialities he had been gathering in the last few months of drawing-room success, and in making him more natural, made more desirable to him the life that nature designed him for.

He left Dorn with a resolution to appear on the English stage as soon as he could obtain a hearing. The peculiar circumstances of his artistic and social life made that easy of attainment, and he speedily made a two-weeks' engagement at a first-class metropolitan theatre. He prepared himself for a debut in "Romeo," with several other similar rôles to follow it. For a first appearance, he could not have selected a part more calculated to win him applause than " Romeo," combining in itself a mixture of sentiment, sensuousness, romance, tenderness and youthful impulse, entirely in unison with his own peculiar talents. It is a question whether he could utterly have failed in it, had he tried ; a certain measure of success was inevitable. Everything worked to his advantage ; he had all the excitement of a first appearance, with none of its disadvantages. His years of dramatic experience on the Italian stage gave him the self-possession, self-control, cultivation and remembrance of former successes, while the entrance into a new field of action agitated him only to infuse into his spirit an unusual amount of nervous power and expression.

Perhaps a shade of healthier color in the cheek, a touch more of animal spirits, a slightly less plaintive echo in the voice, might have been more consonant with the character of the fiery "Romeo;" but Victor had youth, unspeakable grace, characteristic intelligence, pathos, personal magnetism, a thrilling voice, an audience favorably disposed, even to blindness, on his side; and these worked together to win for him an overwhelming success. After every act, and even after certain scenes, he was recalled before the curtain, and steeped to the lips in acclamations of delight; while his singularly modest and seductive manner in receiving these honors, only exaggerated the admiration, which gained him the recall.

The four or five other parts which he had studied to succeed "Romeo," were not for the time called into requisition, for that play alone gathered into the theatre as many spectators as it could contain alive, and continued to do so, until his second week drew to a close. This finished his engagement, but to the public was promised his speedy return, as soon as the theatre could find time for him from the midst of its inevitable engagements.

Victor, in the meanwhile, covered with dramatic glory, and happy in that unapproachable satisfaction which a genuine artist may experience when able to act out his highest impulses, and please the public at the same time, went off to gather new laurels and fortunes in other leading cities.

Ah me! happy are those whose desires, talents, and powers to please all flow harmoniously in the same channel. They are the blessed elect, who already possess the earth.

## CHAPTER VIII.

The same morning that Victor took leave of Dorn, Laura returned to her school, and applied herself to her scholastic labors with a vigor that was remarkable even for her. Already in the foremost class, she soon outstripped her classmates, and her teachers began to fear that she would also pass them on the road to knowledge. The distribution of prizes ceased to be a matter of speculation; it was a foregone conclusion. Historic, geometric, scientific, orthographic rewards she swept down before her as though the whole duties of a school were a game of bowls, and she were forever making a ten-strike. That new power with which her attraction to Victor had endowed her, expressed itself only in a new, untiring energy, a strong propelling force, which drove her along the path of intellectual acquirements, because it was the only way of progress open to her. It was clear to her that she must always be doing something now, and doing it with all her might. She felt like a ship pursued by a pirate, which must strain to the wind every inch of its canvas, counting all her hopes on the mere chance of running away. That shadowy, undefined passion, which pursued her like a spectre, she was always fleeing from. Did she cease to labor for a moment, it seemed to be gaining on her, and her strange soul was filled with terror. To other young girls the first ideal of love is a sweet, seductive one, but to her it was one of fear and trembling.

This intense application to study both pleased and distressed her teachers, for they saw that with it her temper had not its former geniality. On the contrary, she was peevish, fretful, and sometimes her face would from a gloomy reverie flush into an expression of defiant anger, that no surrounding circumstance would even suggest, much less justify. Then she had evidently acquired a dislike to children. Formerly she loved to romp with the little ones, who loved her for it; now she fled from their approach, as though their presence even was intolerable to her. Not three months before, she used to be held up as a model of repose, during class-hours. Her power to keep entirely quiet was not one of the least of her virtues in the opinion of her teachers. But suddenly she had grown to be the very embodiment of restlessness. Even in hours of study, she would forget herself, spring up with her book in her hand, and begin walking rapidly up and down the room; at other times she was turning over her book, or tearing her writing-papers, or biting the end of her pencil. While in class, although her closest mental attention was given to the lesson, her uneasy fingers were never at rest, but ever twisted her dress, or plucked at her apron, or twisted a bit of thread, or were knawed at by an equally restless mouth. Yet this continual fidgeting passed away when she had anything really difficult to overcome, whether in physical or mental labor. A very knotty geometric problem, or a game involving violent bodily energy, equally absorbed her restlessness, and swept the shadows from her face.

The proprietors of the school were very much puzzled by the phase of character she now exhibited. It was entirely new to them, and they had, in fact, many a secret and anxious discussion over it. Like wise young ladies, the daughters came to the conclusion that she was suffering from some nervous disturbance of the system, but was doing her utmost to subdue it, and therefore the less notice taken of her disquietude the better.

The mother of these two ladies, the nominal head of the school, differed from them, and considered it a fitting occasion to exert her authority. "I do not," she said, "understand this Laura Milsland. I don't like all this learning and independent spirit, without any of the graces of modesty, submission and piety which we are taught are woman's highest attributes. I am decided I at least will govern her; I will let her see that she owes me implicit obedience, as well as the other pupils."

"But how," said Miss Julia, "are you to exert authority over her, when she never disputes it? Who is actually more obedient and faithful to her duties than she? Why, mother, we will never have such another scholar in the world."

"Do you think, that should you give her an order without a reason for it, she would obey you?"

"I am afraid not; but then would it be fair to give an unreasoning order to intelligent conscientiousness like hers?"

"You give such orders to others."

"But she is so different from others, it is quite another question."

"How is she different from others? She has no more senses, faculties, features than the other girls."

"I know that; yet you must see the great difference. And then she really loves Rachel and myself, and we dearly love her."

"That's what I can't understand. Julia Sydney, sweet creature, is worth a dozen of her. I believe she has bewitched you both. But she shall learn she must bow to my will."

Poor Mrs. Marshall took the first opportunity to

attempt to give this lesson, calling Laura to her room, immediately after dinner that very day. Arrived there, she fixed her eyes upon her with a look that was meant to be imposing, but was only cross, and began.

"Laura, why do you curl your hair?"

"I don't, it curls itself."

"I don't like it;" and as this was met with no reply from Laura, but a perfectly indifferent look, she went on in a querrulous tone: "It looks untidy, very untidy; it is quite disgusting. Could you not fix it in some other way?"

"Not very well, it is too short; besides it is easier to curl it, and I like it so."

"That is of no consequence; it is neither decent nor becoming. I insist on your combing it out entirely straight, and twisting it up at the back. Do you hear me?"

"Perfectly."

"And do you mean to obey me?"

"Not in the least."

"I never heard of such disgraceful conduct. Are you not, as a pupil of this seminary, under my control?"

"I suppose so; I haven't thought much about it, but I don't mean to allow you to extend your control to my personal privileges; therefore, I shall continue to wear my own hair in the way most convenient and pleasing to myself. Have you anything more to say to me?"

Completely cowed by the manner, in fact the wicked manner, of the girl, Mrs. Marshall could only mutter something about "severely punishing her, and speaking to her father," trying to gather up the tattered fragments of her dignity, which Laura again swept away by a glance from her incomparable eyes, in which was mingled such complete defiance and baleful contempt, that the elder lady was only too glad to motion her out of the room.

Strange what an amount of contempt a young, bright, keenly intellectual girl often feels for a silly, elderly woman, when there are no ties of affection between them to modify the sense of superiority. Later in life, when the temper and self-esteem of such girls are modified by circumstances, they are gentler and far more lenient in their judgments than women of a less intellectual type.

Mrs. Marshall remained for some time in her room, very angry with Laura, and secretly vexed with herself. After all, the girl had always chosen to obey all the rules of the school, as well in spirit as in letter. This was her first act of insubordination, and she herself had forced her into a posture of defiance, driven her into a rebellious position, for which she really deserved punishment, if implicit obedience meant anything. And yet, how to get her punished—it was plain that neither of the younger teachers would undertake it. The difficulty between them was one in which Laura evidently had the right; so what would be the use of appealing to her father? After much deliberation she concluded not to mention, on her own part—and Laura, being reticent by nature, kept it to herself—so the interview which had taken place remained a secret between them.

Mrs. Marshall, however, did not pardon Laura for her contempt; she cherished a lingering dislike of her, convincing herself that Laura's strange ways proceeded from innate wickedness. She determined to discover what her peculiar form of wickedness was; and it was not long before she persuaded herself this discovery was made, and the guilt consisted in the reading of forbidden books—dreadful French novels, or something of the kind. More than once she saw Laura, at the approach of others, quickly put in her pocket a book she had been reading. At such times she burned to go out and demand the book of Laura; but she knew what a savage the girl was, and dare not accuse her openly. But, one afternoon, fortune favored Mrs. Marshall. When the other girls were at play, Laura stole quietly into a half-ruined, vine-covered arbor at the end of the garden, with a book in her hand. There was nothing dangerous in looking in upon this retreat, so she followed her, and, peeping softly in, saw the wicked girl bending over a short, chubby, black volume, which, to her suspicious eyes, had a very ominous and evil look. Heaven! how she would have enjoyed going in and snatching the volume from her, and dragging her forth to universal condemnation, yet she wisely considered discretion the better part of valor. But, as before remarked, fortune favored her, by some voice which called, "Laura, Laura, come here!"

To the delight of the old lady, Laura hid the book under some dead leaves and left the arbor, and not three seconds after, Mrs. Marshall heard her clear, ringing laughter, which told that she was already absorbed in the merry-makings of her school-mates. Fortified by this knowledge, Mrs. Marshall rushed in and pounced upon the hidden book—it was a Bible, a little dark, frowsy, ill-printed Bible, and on its dingy pages were several small, oblong blisters, not to be mistaken for anything but tears.

Mrs. Marshall placed the book back in the concealment from which she took it, and retraced her way to the house, utterly bewildered and confounded. On her way thither, she passed Laura, who was deep in the mazes of some hoydenish game, laughing sonorously, and with all her lustrous hair blown wildly about her face. The contrast between this sport and the neglected arbor and its tear-stained Bible, went still farther to confuse the teacher's mind, till she ended by summing up Laura's case as one of madness, and looking forward to her future incarceration in Bedlam with something like a sensation of pity.

Mrs. Marshall, like many others of a like calibre, could not understand the mysteries of the religious temperament. Religion to her was a surface demonstration, principally expressed in joining the church, donating the missionaries, talking in a lugubrious, canting way, and losing all relish for natural pleasures. The blending of silent, inward struggles, in a heart swayed by unspeakable yearnings after spiritual things, with high animal spirits and vivid senses, presented a new character quite out of her depth. Thus, being quite unable to understand such a nature, she settled the whole matter to her satisfaction by adopting the theory of madness, and looked down upon Laura from the height of her own conformity to all the common-places in the universe.

Laura went on in her own way for the remainder of the term, only one circumstance occurring during that time, that made any impression on her. One day, about three months after Victor's departure, she received a letter, in a mincing, contracted hand, bearing the postmark of a distant city upon it. When she opened it, there was no signature appended to it, and it consisted of these few lines, in an evidently disguised hand:

"An unknown friend to Laura Milsland cautions her against a strange young man, with whom she became acquainted last summer, whose name it will be needless to mention. That young man is possessed of a dangerous fascination, which it would not be wise for an inexperienced young lady to tamper with. Any communication between Miss Milsland and a man of such strong personal magnetism (not always used to a good purpose) would be imprudent in the extreme. A friend, who has her interests at heart, though taking a rude way to further them, entreats her not to submit herself to his influences, but rather to refuse all acquaintance with him, should she encounter him on any future occasion."

This mistaken piece of kindness had an influence upon its recipient, very different from what was intended; it raised her fancy for Victor, which lately had been growing less and less prominent, at once to a bad eminence.

Was this true, then; was he so fascinating and so dangerous? Then, he was a man of character and power. He was not a mere frivolous creature, as she had feared; nay, perhaps he was a hero. It might be her fate, after all, to love him. Then, why should she fight against it?

The receipt of this letter was the unluckiest circumstance that could befall a young girl of Laura's temperament. Hating the common-place as she did, it at once clothed the man in a garb of romance. It gave him a strength and positiveness over other men. As for the danger that might accrue from association with him, it only sharpened her desire to know more of him, for each young girl is persuaded that there can be no danger for her. Others may suffer, but in her lies a power to resist temptations, beyond all her sex. Others may dash themselves headlong into an abyss, but unseen angels are detailed to guard her footsteps, so that she cannot even stumble by the way.

After the receipt of this letter, of which no one but her sister Agnes knew, her eccentricities and mental disturbances increased, and finally resolved themselves into a morbid, nervous intensity. Her teachers noticed this, and would have persuaded themselves she was developing some latent disease—consumption perhaps—had it not been patent that her immeasurable appetite neither diminished nor dwindled away. Neither did her muscular strength diminish. On one occasion it was necessary to move a small chest of drawers, from a lower to an upper dormitory; the man-servant objected to undertaking it alone, on the ground that he had not come there " to murder his back," for any body. Thereupon Laura, in a moment of irritation, first took out the drawers, and then carried it up stairs herself, without an instant's hesitation. This feat accomplished, without apparent effort, convinced all observers that she was certainly not suffering from physical enervation.

The letter, which unfortunately came into Laura's hands, was, in fact, the composition of Charles Oakford, that friend of Victor's, who had accompanied him to Dorn. Just before this foolish letter was written, Oakford talked with Victor of their visit to the village, and the latter had remarked that Laura Milsland was a sweet little girl, and he intended to revisit the place, simply to see her. Nor did he deny himself the indulgence of throwing out several innuendoes as to the impression he had created on her youthful fancy.

Charles Oakford, having seen so many female heads completely "turned" by Victor's fascinations, had almost come to the conclusion he bore about with him some secret charm like a black-snake.

Nobody, Oakford reflected, broke her heart for himself, nobody was jealous of him, and yet he was stalwart, finely-formed, handsome, and rich. Whereas, Victor, in his opinion, was an insignificant fellow, slight, pale, and with a dash of effeminacy; yet eyes might be seen to blaze and cheeks turn to marble at this man's approach.

Thinking of this, he could not help pitying the simple, green, country girl, who might be subjected to such an ordeal, and so he wrote her that letter, which was meant to warn, and only served to encourage.

Young girls are not apt to be frightened by a prospect of disappointment in love; in fact there is something secretly seductive in the idea. If they are at all ambitious, their future lives look so narrow, they would willingly woo a heart-sorrow, as a means of widening the vista. It is only by experience they learn that instead of giving breadth to life, it straightens and cramps it like a winding-sheet. That despair, which, to the eye of youth, seems but a species of voluptuous grief, is then seen to be the seed of a life-long monotony and tedious self-disgust.

Laura would have been terrified at the idea of being drawn into a mutual attachment with a common-place, insignificant being—but the prospect of enjoying the stormy delights of a broken heart, quite raised her spirits to enthusiasm.

The time slipped away so quickly, it seemed but a few days after this, before the close of the term arrived, popularly known as examination day. All the pupils who had parents within a reasonable distance summoned them to witness their individual passage through the exciting ordeal. Laura's father always considered that day as of more importance than the day which brought them in a new governor, or some trifle of that kind. Of all these great days this was the most momentous, for it beheld the graduation of his two daughters, one of whom was the great star of the occasion. Of course he was one of the judgest, though innocent, soft-hearted creature, he was not capable of asking a question that would puzzle a canary. It was a pleasure to look at him, as he gazed down the long rows of young figures, all spotless in purest white, until his eyes dropped caressingly upon the dark, bright face of his girl. It was well known, by both teachers and scholars, that Laura was the show-piece of the display, on which was to hang the visible glory of the Dorn mode of education. Dorn, forgetting all its back-ground of girlish inanities, brought her forth as a simple specimen of its manufacture, and defied its rivals to produce a finer sample.

Much geography, and history, and natural philosophy, and arithmetic rippled up and down those shining rows of sweet faces, but when it came to Laura's turn to exhibit, an immediate hush prevailed.

Then to hear the parents and judges asking questions —generally absurdly easy ones, because they were careful to select only such as they could answer themselves. Most of the men appeared very timid in questioning Laura, she looked them so directly in the eyes, and smiling with a disdainful indifference at the questions, answered them with a manner that showed she despised them as trash. Generally the fathers and judges were thankful she could not turn upon them and question them. A slim chance their literate reputation would have had of it, they secretly surmised. But then, they much preferred the modest backwardness of their own daughters, they thought, and were even beginning to pity Mr. Milsland very much, until he began to question Laura himself, and she answered his contemptibly weak queries so gently, while a sweet little tender smile crept around her mouth, smoothing out all the disdain and indifference; then they saw that he was not an object of compassion, after all. By the time that he had asked her who discovered America, and who built the Ark, and how many months there were in a year, and she had answered these inquiries with gentle gravity, they began to think that as a daughter, she could not be looked on as an affliction.

Then came the moment for the reading of the selected "compositions,"—as the literary effusions of the schoolroom were called. They contained, as such productions always do, flowery sentimentalism, mingled with hackneyed classical allusions, bursts of oracular statement as to all the virtues, and a degree of assumption as to the certain means to conquer and subdue the world, which is only found in those who know nothing of it. Laura's disquisition passed for a marvel, as might have been expected, for it was really the worst thing that appeared on the occasion. It lauded the claims of ancient classical Rome to admiration and reverence, as above all other earthly interests; suggested a number of expedients for revenging Lucretia and Virginia, and righting Coriolanus; breathed sanguinary vengeance against the Goths and Vandals; urged for the Parthenon and other reverent ruins, that place in the thoughts of her hearers that was now occupied by mere modern families and property; closing with the addition of her personal threat to the world if it did not leave off minding its own business, and go to glorify "Rome, my country, city of the soul," immediately. As it contained a vast number of ideas rifled from the older writers, as well as the author of "Childe Harold," all distorted and aggravated by passing through the excitable current of the writer's mind, as every sentence was inflamed with about seven shrieking adjectives, and nearly every one began with "then, then," or "thou, thou," and ended with "godlike immortality," it was considered by the scholars a masterpiece of eloquence. Even the fathers, when they saw her fold up the formidable manuscript, after reading it in a fierce, high, fluttering tone, with a flushed cheek and palpitating throat, concluded there must be something in it, though it did not seem to be any thing very practical.

Last of all, came what to Mr. Milsland was the crowning glory of all, the performances, geometric and algebraic, on the blackboard. He leaned back in his chair, his fat face crowded with smiles, and wringing his own hands with painful cordiality. To him the scraping of the chalk on the shining ebony board was the highest form of music, and as the obedient angles whizzed about under the hands of his Laura, and the equally plastic alphabet sprinkled itself about them, and the rapid explanation gushed from her unabashed lips, he was as nearly niched in Elysium as it is possible for mortal to be.

After the legitimate scholastic ceremonies, the spectators were requested to remain for a few moments longer. In the midst of the hush which followed this announcement, a young girl arose, requested Laura to do the same, and after faltering out a few spasmodic words, which expressed the concentrated pride of the seminary in this its gifted pupil, hinted at mental powers in her which a little exceeded those of Socrates and Isaac Newton, but not much; and ended by assuring her that in the academic halls of Dorn she should ever hang on memory's walls. At the last touching allusion, Laura burst into tears, and so did many of her class-mates, carried away by the recollection that, though Laura had willfully dominated them all, yet many were the times she had scrambled herself into rags, climbing trees to get apples for the general benefit; and though she had been wont in aggravated moments, to bump their heads, and scratch their faces, yet in the matter of ruling their composition books, and helping them with their sums, she was never deaf to the appeal of the troubled pupil. As for Laura, she wept because she liked, her school and her studies, and her companions, and had not the common desire of her sex to turn her back upon them.

When the speech and the tears were both quenched, the speaker produced a crown of artificial green leaves, supposed to resemble bays, and it was lodged with considerable difficulty on the top of Laura's head, after the shaking hand of the crowner, had contrived to pinch her ear and drag some of her hair out by the roots.

Then the great day was over, and people crowded around the graduating class to congratulate its proud members; while Mr. Milsland, whom the last scene had reduced to complete debility, could only stumble up to his daughter, with fat tears tumbling down his chubby cheeks, and violently shake her hands, until all the other fathers were looking at them. Of course Laura felt ashamed of this display of paternal affection—every immature nature does in the like situation—but she was a brave girl and did not show it. Only she reminded her father that he had another daughter to congratulate—that Agnes also had her diploma.

The day closed with an exceptional dinner to the

pupils, to which a few also of the favored parents were invited. There was an unlimited quantity of roast beef, and veal pie, and apple dumplings, and plumb cake. Laura immediately descended from her high Roman and classic platform, at the sight of these viands, and fell upon them like a Harpy, much to the secret mortification of her teachers.

Thus were a class of some thirty young girls tided over the education stream, and supposed to be landed on the brink of life. They were then technically announced to begin life, as though there was a very broad and varied path open to them thenceforward. And yet nothing in the ordinary woman's existence more resembles life than the boarding-school era. There is a reality and distinctiveness in her ways and aims there, that her future life necessarily lacks. It is a very little world, but she is a being, an entity, not a shadow there. Action and not passivity is the virtue of her life. To get the greatest number of "merit marks," to unravel the knotty strands of algebra, to have hydrogen gas, hydraulic presses, and exhausted receivers at her fingers' ends, may not be very stupendous objects of living, but they at least are definite in themselves, and honorable in the seeking. But the getting of husbands after school-days is a very indistinct aim. You must get one, and you must not make any efforts for it—you must secure him by running away from him; it is your duty to get him, and yet you must not want him, till in fact, this whole female duty of making wives of themselves becomes a very mystic, spectral affair.

Many was the time in her after life, when Laura looked back upon her school days, as the only period of her existence which she had worked to an end; nay, the only one in which her existence meant anything. She thought of these days of keen, young conscientiousness and honorable industry, in the after perfection of her nature, when her senses, powers, perceptions were worked up to the roundest harmony and beauty, and then thrown over by stern fate to rust and inaction; she thought of them in the days when all her beauty, intellect, and brilliancy were in vain, and she stood outside of the gates of Hope as they closed upon her, and heard their adamantine clang echo down all the inexorable vista of her years.

## CHAPTER IX.

As soon as Laura was settled at the hotel with her father, she experienced, for the first time in her life, a period of repose. Her books she laid by for the time, and even seemed to avoid very violent physical exercise. Often she would lie upon the grass, for hour after hour, of the still, sunny, June days, engaged in such earnest thought that even the ringing of the dinner-bell did not stir her nature to its depths.

Strangers, by no means very fashionable, though some of them were refined, agreeable ones, began gradually to fill up the newly-painted hotel. Then, Mr. Milsland observed that Laura attracted considerable attention. Her face and manners were improving every day, and even the obtuse parent saw that she had that form of animal spirits, which is generally attractive to the other sex. At school, Agnes, with her pink and white skin, dove-like eyes, and massive rolls of golden hair, was accounted far more beautiful than Laura; but with young gentlemen, the large, lustrous eyes and moist, sparkling lip of the brunette, made a more vivid impression than the blonde charms of her sister.

Things were going on in this pleasant way at Dorn, when Victor suddenly concluded to keep his word to Laura, and visit that quaint little village. He played a great number of engagements in various cities after his debût, each of them only serving to advance him further on the bright road to fame and fortune. The press was unanimously in his favor; the most scholarly and refined minds offered him a perpetual incense of eulogies, and, what was still more to him, he was cherished by a large number of refined and attractive ladies. Whenever he was disengaged, he spent his time in the most luxurious private houses, where delicately-bred ladies made a pet of him, listening to all he said with a smile of approbation, choosing seats by him in preference to others, and giving him little soft pressures of the hand when parting. His autograph was very much in demand for albums, and little as it was in keeping with his disposition, it was a sound, majestic, elegantly precise autograph, instead of the lurid scratches which most men of genius indulge in. Though he had some trouble with the affections he managed to call out, and then knew not what to do with, yet somehow he managed to get rid of them, and taking really a pleasure in flirting, for its own sake, the balance was struck rather on the side of enjoyment than otherwise. To a man of a sensitive and delicately strung nature, like his, such an atmosphere of female tenderness, was the one best calculated to foster and elevate his talents. But, in doing this for him, they did too much, they tempted him out too often at nights, and prepared too many dainty suppers for him, the end of which was, that they gave him back to poor, simple, earnest little Laura. He was attacked with a very disagreeable form of dyspepsia, that made him misanthropic, and that, also, made him long to leave all that hitherto had given him pleasure, and, finally, that made him think of Dorn and of Laura. True, when he saw Laura, he attributed his return to memory and faith, and this was literal, if those words are duplicates for pheasant "pateés" and anything "aux truffles."

The sober reality was, that out of the dyspepsia came forth the blues, and memory wafted back to him the early hours, pastoral simplicity, and sturdy appetites of Dorn. Laura was an after-thought, which came in dimly along with the corn-cakes, and long after the eggs.

And yet, would one believe it, our poor little fool had no more doubt that he would keep his promise and return, than that the river would remain water and not turn into fire. This was the secret of the growing gentleness and beauty, and of the long, dreamy hours spent on the grass under the drowsy trees.

Victor arrived at Dorn in the early afternoon, but he did not see Laura until after tea time. He had spent about eight hours in the horrible, springless stage that conveyed him there, and he was not a man to shine under disagreeable physical circumstances. Getting up at five in the morning was a disgusting sacrifice to begin with, then rattling and battling all day in a rough, rickety, dusty, beastly old coach, seated in the middle of the middle seat (for coming last he had the last choice), between a fat farmer, in a grey woolen suit covered with smudges, on one side, and a distressed and distressing poitrinary invalid on the other, combined with a breakfast (after two hours of this infliction), composed of the grossest kind of fried pork, and coffee that tasted like a combination of soot and tallow, were cir-

cumstances to rasp the temper of a cherub, not to speak
of a fretful, nervous young man, sorely tried with the
dyspepsia. After breakfast, when the sun began to get
very warm and all the passengers very sleepy, his case
was hardly improved. Overcome with a feverish drow-
siness, he continually fell into troubled dozes, from
which he was always awakening in a nightmare to find
that his dreadful corpulant neighbor, snoring wildly and
bathed in agricultural perspiration, was sprawling over
his breast; or a hollow cough and pulmonic, rasping
wheeze would weave itself up in his ugly dreams, till
he awoke to find the ghostly head of his consumptive
neighbor, jammed between his cravat and his dainty ear.
No wonder, then—considering the texture of his nature
—that when he arrived at Dorn, half stupified with unre-
freshing sleep, wilted by heat, covered with dust until
his clothes looked like the refuse of a second-hand slop-
shop, his hair mottled and frowsy, and his face elaborately tattooed with "blacks," and distressed by that
knawing dyspeptic hunger that sickens at the thought
of food, his state of mind was one of savage irritation.
As is the case with all physically fastidious persons, the
realization that he was dirty and shabby brought a
sense of self-depreciation that actually hurt him like
material pain. As he traveled up the narrow hotel
stairs, that in his present mood looked particularly forlorn and cheap, with his pale, greenish face and pinch-
ed, disgusted features, thinking, with a shudder, that
he could never touch the clothes he wore again, except
with the tongs to throw them out of the window, he
formed a ludicrous contrast to the late darling of metropolitan parlors.

When he had washed off, in an abundance of fresh
water, all the plebeian contact which he had encoun-

tered in the stage, and thoroughly changed his clothes, he threw himself upon the bed, and the pillow which he noticed (such things never escaped him) was cased in linen, and very white linen, he found sufficient leisure to notice that the room was well-sized, better furnished than one expects to find in a summer hotel, and that on a little table under the glass stood an inartistic but luxuriant bouquet of fragrant flowers, highly-scented roses, tender heliotropes, scented verbena, and nodding flower-branches of the locust tree, which, with its strange, insidious perfume, found its way to the senses in advance of all the others. It immediately suggested itself to Victor that this room had been prepared for him by the faithful Laura, who, by some inexplicable means, had been led to expect him at Dorn. The room had been specially prepared by Laura, but for the hoped for advent of her step-grandmother, who had been threatening all summer to visit them. Much, however, to her disappointment—for she was a great favorite with the old lady—she never did appear there, until she was brought to be laid at rest in the village churchyard, several months afterwards. But Victor was put into the choice, comfortable room by some mistake, and remained under the impression that Laura designed it for him.

After an hour of gentle sleep on the white bed, with the gentle breeze rustling in upon him, laden with fragrance and the soft hum of peaceful country life, the sound of the tea-bell awoke him, refreshed in body and restored to complete equanimity of spirits. He dressed himself calmly, arranged in the most enticing way his dark, wavy hair, and went down to the tea-table, prepared to drive Laura to distraction before he looked at her.

Just a little to his disappointment, she was not there. He glanced with a rapid glance up the length of both tables, of which half the seats were now empty, and his eyes encountered no Laura, but they did encounter a display of genuine country delicacies, including an abundance of fruit, which at once buried the young lady in temporary oblivion. The dyspeptic appetite, recently prostrated by high-seasoned delicacies, and the elaborate sumptuosities of ambitious French kitchens, which had recoiled with such abhorrence from the abominable fried pork of the stage route, in the sight of this simple fare, rose from its despondency like a convalescent from the sick bed, hopeful, and with a naive interest in little things, that else had never attracted the most passing attention.

In the meanwhile Laura, who had finished her evening meal, and resorted to her reveries in the garden, was busy stringing, on a long grass stem, a quantity of red and yellow flowers, peculiarly fragile in fibre, and sickly in perfume, bearing the mysterious title of " four-o'clocks," which all school-girls love to bind around their heads. Just as she had finished the wreath, and attached it about her head, a step on the gravel startled her, and she looked up and saw Victor, pale and captivating, dressed in the most subdued and exquisite taste, coming through the garden bushes, shaking down upon himself the crimson rose leaves and scented shrubs, as he parted them with his slender hands, and smiling like a perfectly ravishing and irresistible Adonis. Laura did not advance a step to meet him, but, as her eyes caught him in sight, a deep, settled content sprang from them and inundated her whole earnest young face. The first thing that struck Victor on approaching her, was the very slight change that had taken place in her figure and features, and yet some vital alteration in her expression gave an entirely diffcrent meaning to them. However she might have been lacking in physical loveliness before, his practised eye at once settled that she was beautiful now. True, her skin was almost as swarthy as a gipsey's, but it was lighted up with a rich, peachy bloom, that was perpetual in the cheeks, and flowed all over her face, when touched with feeling or excitement. The always brilliant eyes shone with a softer brightness than ever, and the humid, sparkling lips seemed to reflect back their lustrousness. As for her figure, in some respects it was worse than when he left, for she had grown taller without acquiring additional roundness. It was still nothing but a sketch, or a mere suggestion for a figure, in which the joints, and the angles, and the muscles stood prominently out, and defied concealment, though heaven knows Laura had never dreamed of concealing them, or in fact of the necessity for modifying them.

"How is my dear little friend?" he said, grasping her two hands; "and did she believe I would return to her?"

"Certainly; you said you would come back."

Victor blushed as nearly as he could, to hear this positive expression of faith, and compare it with his own past forgetfulness and utter indifference; but he said gaily enough, "And have you been impatient to see me?"

"No; I had to study all winter, and since the close of school I have been very happy waiting for you."

For a moment he almost wavered in his intention to prosecute his suit, not that the innocence and youth of the girl moved him, but an indefinable something in her awed him. A certain natural dignity that, in con trast with her childishness, almost took on an air of solemnity. He wished she had not believed him so faithfully, or had not been so happy waiting for him; and the lack of all coquetry, of all attempt to conceal the absorbing interest his coming bore for her, sobered his light and fleeting admiration. For an infinitesimal part of a second he thought of returning next day whence he came, and pulling up the snares he had set for this rural dove, who showed some symptoms of turning out an eagle as well as a dove. Alas! in the way of hardened consciences, there is none so utterly seared as that of the man who pursues the conquest of the other sex, simply for vanity and amusement. The "still small voice" may reach somehow the conscience of the murderer, the bigot, the miser; but the fascinator sweeps it away with a sigh, hushes it with a bound of the ardent pulse, drowns it with a surge of the warm and eager blood.

Thus the momentary better impulses of the young man fell almost still-born from his heart, and he devoted himself to the conquest of the deep-hearted maid, with a carefulness that was quite thrown away on the occasion, for he had only to be himself and remain in her company, to draw out her entire possibility of love.

"And you did not think I might forget my promise?"

"No; why should you? I did not ask you to come; it was your own wish."

"I have had much to occupy my mind since I last saw you; I made a successful appearance on the English stage, and played a continuous series of superb engagements. So you see my time has been occupied with important events.

"So has mine; I passed through my final examination, and took a diploma." This said with an air of ingenuous triumph, which showed she considered the two events as being equally conspicuous and equally momentous in their bearings.

"Ah, then, I trust that you found more in your triumph to satisfy your inward yearning than I did in mine," retorted Victor, discovering that he could not get any sympathy from her on the ground of public glory, and so falling back on that debilitated sentiment which is the safest tone to take towards a perfectly inexperienced girl.

"And were you not satisfied with a complete success on the stage?"

"Ah, no; it is dreadful to play before the cold, unsympathetic world" (the one that had exploded its gloves and rasped its voice in applauding him), "it seems like showing your sensitive heart to the unappreciative multitude. Now, if I could play my parts, play them like confidences, to one tender heart," and he ceased abruptly, with a lingering, languishing look into her eyes, which were deep with wonder. Ten chances to one if he had performed his "Hamlet" to Laura alone, her rustic mind would have immediately come to the conclusion that his sojourn in Dorn was to be credited to an escape from Bedlam; the kind, enthusiastic audiences of the metropolis thought it the perfection of art, and he knew it, for such is almost always the difference between ripe, mellow cultivation, and crude, green inexperience. But he went on elaboratrly to explain to her, with much languishing eye-language to aid him, how necessary it was, for the development of happiness in an artist, that he should get away from the great, heartless, splendid world, and shut himself up to one congenial mind, till Laura began to remember with excessive mortification, that she had never found out the superiority of demonstrating problems on the blackboard (her fine art), to sad, sentimental audiences of one, rather than to a covey of cheerful, if not over literate fathers.

In such talk as this the evening wore away softly, until the great hall-clock struck nine, and then Laura felt that the time had come for her to retire.

"Good night," she said, springing suddenly up from the bench on which they had been sitting, and she passed out among the rose bushes to the walk, while Victor guarded them from coming in contact with her, as though she were not used to running through the underbrush like a squirrel. Then he parted from her, by raising her hand to his lips, impressing upon it a warm, soft kiss, and it was all done with a tender gallantry as new and as winning to Laura as any of the marvels that might, in her dreams, sweep down on golden wings from the realms of Fairy Land.

## CHAPTER X.

BEYOND the garden, near the brink of the stream on which the girls were so fond of rowing their boats, Victor found a small, one-roomed cottage, which, whatever its original intention might have been, did not then serve for anything. So he determined to appropriate it for a studio, having discovered in the neighborhood some beautiful clay for modelling. Thither he pressed Agnes and Laura to come and permit him to copy their heads. Agnes consulted her father, and he said, "Yes, of course, and if the young gentleman can make good figures of you, he may name his price," never stopping to think whether it would be prudent to submit young girls like his daughters, to unrestrained communication with a fine young man from the gayest of gay worlds. Wonderful, indeed, is the culpable indulgence of the American father towards daughters of a tender age! It thrusts them into temptations, which they are expected to resist with the sobriety and self-poise of a philosopher. It would be easy to understand this indulgence if fathers were a set of spotless creatures, selected from an upper arcadia of innocents, and set in full-blown dignity at the heads of families; but when we reflect that they have been young men, and sometimes heartless, scheming ones, before arriving at the patriarchal majesty, to comprehend it is far more difficult. So, Agnes and Laura went for several days in succession, and Victor, in a black, velvet coat (decidedly a member of his theatrical wardrobe), patted and plastered and slapped about a considerable quantity of wet clay, patting them into things he called Agnes and Laura, but wherein the likeness was not visible to the naked eye. After a week of this, Agnes got tired of seeing herself represented with a Grecian nose (she had a lovely pug) and eyes that looked like spoons, so she ceased to come, and thus Laura was left to go alone. On her Victor continued to repeat his daily libels, from time to time, between which would come walks through the trees and excursions down the stream, in the little boat which was the property of the Milsland girls.

These were Laura's halcyon days. She would have been almost entirely happy had she not possessed a species of Nemesis in her eldest sister, Charley.

Charley was always sneering at her about her fancy for Victor, and saying such things both in private and public, as were calculated to bring out Laura's worst qualities, and display her in the most disadvantageous light. Charley had considerable personal attractions herself, though of a very peculiar type. Her hair was very black and glossy, more like black satin than like hair; her eyebrows were also black, as well as heavy, but her eyes were blue; her teeth were fine, but her lips extremely thick, and coarse in texture; her skin was of a very rich olive hue, without a particle of color; her forehead was both low and narrow, and entirely flat over the eyebrows. Her figure was really very fine; she was rather inclined to be tall, but was firmly and roundly developed.

Of Laura she had always been absurdly jealous— jealous of Laura's superior influence over a father, whose love she cared little for and to whose happiness she was indifferent; and jealous of Laura's superior intellect, though she really looked with contempt upon all intellect. She had the serpent's wisdom, the wisdom which works to the evil of others; and, besides, she was as suspicious as a spaniel. Being of this disposition, she enjoyed a great unpopularity in school; while impulsive, wayward, arrogant, but generous and affectionate Laura was the best beloved girl there. But the possession of this nature did not prevent Charley from being a universal favorite with the youths of the other sex; whereas, Laura, until she saw Victor, was an object of terror to them. Not a boy in the village, of her size, had escaped a fight with her, and some of them had been worsted in combat. After Laura met Victor, and the soft influence of the tender passion had unbound some of the hard knots in her character, she gradually ceased to be a horror to the youths, and ended by being particularly attractive to them.

When Charley saw that her sister was interested in Victor—a discovery which she made at an early stage, for she had that low cunning so often developed in shallow minds, which enables them to get at a secret which would be hidden from broader intelligence—she determined to annoy her in every possible way connected with the subject. Frequently she gave out hints, which Laura did not resent, because she did not understand them. But her favorite amusement was forcing Laura to display herself in the worst light in Victor's presence. She would cunningly sting Laura into an irritation of mind that made her seem ill-tempered, selfish, and abusive, while she herself preserved an angelic appearance of amiability. Then she would reproach her with her untidiness before him, pointing out the rents in her gown, and referring to it as though it were not only a want of order but of personal cleanliness, a confounding of two different faults, which occurs to many persons. But as Laura was almost a monomaniac on personal neatness, as her undergarments were always of immaculate purity, however torn and ill used her outer dress was, this reproach, before the man she loved, enraged her beyond anything else.

Then, Charley loved to bring out Laura's defects of figure by throwing them into contrast with her own beauties. She would lay her own soft, white, round arm against the brown and muscular arm of her sister; or she would put her own dimpled shoulder beside the acute-angled triangle that stood for that member in Laura's anatomy. Not, however, that this affected Laura in the least; she was quite unaware that a lesser or greater amount of flesh was of any consequence to attractiveness, or that it could possibly be even noticed by gentlemen. Indeed, like most school-girls, she despised all tendency to fleshiness, and considered leanness a thing to be rejoiced in.

To Victor this was the most effectual way of depreciating Laura, though she was so utterly unconscious of it. He used to look, at such moments, on the muscular frame of his adorer with something like a cold shudder, and then the blandishments of Charley were not altogether ineffective. If she had possessed the most ordinary conversational powers, it is probable his allegiance had been transferred to her. But her conversation consisted of the most dreary platitudes, and she never or seldom finished a sentence. Before she came to the end her ideas seemed to feebly evaporate, until she would mumble her words in an inaudible tone, and leave you to fill her sentence up as you liked. When she was stating facts, especially those to the disadvantage of others, she could be direct and forcible enough; but outside of these, in the world of thought, her views resembled the jelly-fish, which, at the slightest examination, dissolves itself into a slimy moisture and disappears.

Victor tried her, also, as a listener, talking to her in his most thrilling way, but her attention would slip away in a few seconds, and her eyes wandered down to the contemplation of her own lovely shoulders. In these moments of wounded vanity he always turned and addressed himself to Laura, with increased tenderness of tone, at which her shadowy eyes would light up with an almost heavenly joy. Thus would his vanity be healed, and in the radiance of those eyes would be lost both the color and the angularity of her shoulders.

As for the muscular arms, sometimes they assumed the beauty of usefulness—for instance, when they rowed him up and down the stream. A diminutive awning served to protect him from the sun, but she sat under its most piercing rays, in the hottest hours of the day, working her oars like a professional bargeman, and shooting up and down stream with the celerity of an arrow. Some compunctions of conscience used to visit him when he saw her hair hanging wet around her face, and the always reddening flush on her cheeks, at which he would offer to take the oars from her and let her rest. But she met his offers with a laugh, declared she didn't believe he could row, and vowed she wouldn't have him spread his hands for all the trees in Dorn.

"My hands," she would jokingly say, "have been baked; I put them in the brick-kiln and took them out perfect bricks, so I would like to see the sun or any oar making an impression on them."

"But why, dear Laura, do you permit your hands to get so dark and hard—why don't you take care of them, and make them soft and white, like your sister's?"

"Why, what use is there in soft hands? you can't do half as much with them."

"Oh, but they look so much prettier!"

"But who in the world would look at my hands?"

"I do, and it would please me to see them whiter. I want you to wear gloves whenever you go in the sun; will you?"

"Yes, if you wish it; but, indeed, I'd tear them to pieces every minute. Even in church I take my gloves off, because, when I have them on, I feel as if I couldn't take hold of anything."

"Will you tie your curls back with ribbons too?"

"Yes; but if the bushes pull them off?"

"Keep clear of the bushes; you can look where you are going."

"I might, but I never do. For, you see, I love to catch a horse for myself, 'specially if he gives me a good run."

Victor laughed, and went back into silence, and she rowed on, so far from being tired, that she wished he needed to be rowed straight through life, and she might have the delight of working the oars.

## CHAPTER XI.

AGNES MILSLAND was at this time the recipient also of very particular attentions from one of the other sex. Her admirer had been in his life a man of many trades, the dramatic stage having had its share of his attentions; but when he came up to Dorn he was in the business of manufacturing musical gold pens, an invention of his own. The stems of these pens were quite bulky, and contained within themselves the apparatus for making melody, like infinitesimal musical boxes. Each pen was warranted to play three tunes, all the composition of the inventor. The pen was not a success eventually, owing to the circumstances that it would not write and that it would not play. The ink ran up and drowned out the works, and the works ran down and cluttered up the nibs. After the failure of the musical pen he was forced to begin his circuit of trades, and run regularly through them, like the sun through the signs of the Zodiac. But during the time he first made his court to Agnes, he represented himself in all the glories of an æsthetic inventor and a prospective millionaire.

From the stage he had brought away all its vices, and

not in anywise profited by its discipline and training. He used artificial intonations, and kept his features on display like circus horses. His dress was eccentric, his hair curled in ambrosial curls, his eyes rolled about like wheel-barrows, and his whole manner had a kind of imitation fascination, that passed as genuine in the eyes of the susceptible Agnes. At any rate, he was an Apollo compared to the bashful, awkward youths who had hitherto been her only experience of manhood. When she first saw Victor her sensibilities were stirred by him, but detecting the superior interest which he created in Laura, like a good sister she retired from the field at once. Now she thought herself rewarded by the preference of the entrancing Willister, whom she considered as far more desirable than Victor, for was not his voice louder, his figure larger, his cheeks redder, his eyes blacker? So, on the whole, she rather looked down on the slender frame and pale face of her sister's ideal.

In the meanwhile Mr. Milsland was living lazily through his favorite summer days, with the usual fatherly obtuseness and blind partiality. Agnes' love affair progressed with great rapidity, so that before she had been acquainted with her admired Willister for four weeks, she announced to her papa that she was engaged to "dear Joseph." Papa scolded, and grumbled, and growled for several days, but finally he was obliged to yield to the tearful entreaties of his child. Luckily for her, he only knew him as a gold pen maker; had he dreamed that the pen was a successor with him to the buskin and sock, never had she gained the paternal consent.

As for Laura's romance, *that* he never became aware of until it was too late to censure. He was aware of the "degradation" of Victor's professions, the drama, sculpture, and painting, all seeming to him to be so many forms of vagabondage, beyond which shiftlessness could not go. A gentleman farmer now, or a dealer in general hardware, or a commercial dispenser of oils, paints and putty, might naturally lay siege to the heart of his idol, and capture her honorably. But for a showman, (thus he denominated the inimitable representative of Shakspeare), to expect to make an impression on the heart of the child of a respectable owner of real estate— clearly it never entered his wildest imagination. Thus, Laura, thrown entirely on her own responsibility, passed all her days in the little rustic studio, on the brink of the water, and all the change that her father noted in her, was a gradually increasing gentleness of look and manner.

Victor marvelled that she did not improve more rapidly; the change was so gradual to him, that she seemed almost as unformed and crude, except in the beauty of her face, as when he first began to notice her. Laura, spite of her impulsive and violent manner at times, was by no means a nature to mature rapidly. The process of development was a slow one with her, because her changes were not from the surface, but from within, and gradually working outwardly.

The half shy, half defiant manner still clung to her, but in his presence she followed him with troubled, tremulous eyes that were not at all in keeping with her character. To Victor, those eyes seemed to cling to him with ceaseless questionings, which he could not or dared not answer. When he first met Laura, and wondered at that strange, intense, abstracted nature, he was smitten with an ardent curiosity to know how such a nature would work, when under the influence of love. He had partly tested it, and now felt an uneasy desire to undo the profound impression created in her. He began to feel satisfied it was likely to prove an annoyance, so he was daily casting about for a way to escape from its consequences. There are many more such "Frankensteins" in the world, who set their most vital energies to work out exceptional creations, which, when they have accomplished, they fly from, leaving them in all the plenitude of lonely and unsatisfied life. Ah, me! how many such loves have been skillfully "worked up," and then thrown upon a world to which they were alien, in which they could find neither their place nor meaning. Thus are they doomed to stalk through life, lonely and incomprehensible spectres, objects of ridicule to most, or at best of curious pity. Did not some of these lie under the altar, who had come up out of great tribulation, whom God has promised to lead to the fount of living waters, and that all tears shall be wiped from their eyes!

As was natural, Victor found his work far easier to accomplish than to undo. He tried neglecting her, and flirting with other young ladies, but he found the symptoms of jealousy developing themselves in a dumb, dreadful appearance of physical pain that was an ugly sight to look upon. He tried allusions to his speedy departure, with suppositions that they would probably never meet again, and they also only produced that dreadful look. If she had but remonstrated with him, reproached him, wept, quarrelled, anything but this proud, silent despair, he could have finished up the case with ease and despatch. But how to deal with this Spartan girl, who, having taken an insidious passion into her heart, would fold her arms over it, and let it slowly consume her, fairly puzzled him. Do you think the boy of history, who suffered the stolen fox to eat its way to his vital organs, could have been at the time a pleasant companion, or have worn a cheerful face to look upon? But how do you think he would have looked to you, if you had put the fox there, and were compelled to see him tortured by it?

Besides, Victor was not by any means a man without heart or conscience, only he had a reckless way of rushing into anything that offered him amusement for the moment, and feeling distressed about it afterwards. He was so fitful and inconsistent in his resolutions, that a determination to discover to Laura the indifference of his own feelings to her, generally resulted in a short period of harshness, succeeded by increased tenderness, when her grieved look had called out his pity. It is no wonder, if under these circumstances the state of her mind changed for the worse. Nothing in the world can bear the effect of continual sudden transitions of temperature, without serious deterioration, if not ruin, except comets, and upon them we look with anything but a brotherly feeling.

Many times in his little studio, he commenced a strain of conversation intended to make her open hostilities on her own part, and would end it by taking her frightened face in his hands and spangling it all over with kisses, for the surging blood followed the contact of his lips, like bursts of crimson flame.

Every day he became more and more convinced he had never loved the girl, and even the superficial influence she exercised over him by her beauty and her love, having lost the charms of strangeness, little by little, lost its hold on him. What most astonished him, was the amount of time he had wasted in the society of a young person who had not even the charm of simplicity; for though crude and undeveloped, she was not simple. She was a mixture of womanly precosity and boyish roughness. Now that the illusion was over, he began to think of her rough ways and strange habits, so different from those of other girls, with a feeling of dismay. He thought himself a double-dyed fool to have taken all this strong, fiercely positive material and impressed an image of himself upon it. He could not look upon her as a conquest, but rather as a Nemesis, destined to come up in a troublesome shape in after life. Sometimes he felt very angry with her, for presuming to suppose she could absorb the love of a man of the world like himself. He forgot that if she had a wish or a hope beyond the school-room or the play-ground, he had taught them to her.

But the summer was nearly all gone, coming engagements began to beckon him, and Laura was getting decidedly tedious. Finally he made up his mind one morning, that before the next dawn he would be in the abominable Dorn stage, with his back turned to that village in which would remain two nightmares of his past—Laura and the dyspepsia. Not ten minutes after this resolution, she came down to his studio, with her sun hat as usual dangling over her arm, but her curls were tied back with a fillet of pink ribbons, and a branch of locust flowers was wreathed across them, in a tolerably graceful way. Victor saw her from the window as she bounded down the pathway, and at sight of the ribbons and flowers, his heart smote him with a mingled thrill of pain and pity. These piteous little attempts at ornament were to please him, and now they were only to adorn the lamb for the sacrifice. With a feeling of great compassion he met her at the door, led her in and placed her in a chair, with that air of graceful homage, which was the most enchanting phase of his manner.

By way of breaking the news to her, he proposed to read some passages from Shakspeare—" Hamlet " and " Romeo," principally. Taking advantage of the retirement, he rendered them with full force and effectiveness, and with all the passion of which he was capable. Laura listened with a shy, perplexed restlessness, till finally an expression settled on her face which indicated that she was ashamed of him, and blushed to see him make such a fool of himself. With his customary inconsistency, he was enraged at her want of appreciation, rather than glad he had disgusted her with one phase of his life. In revenge, he took occasion to make himself as dreadfully fascinating as possible for the rest of the morning, until the poor child went home to dinner, with her whole nature wrought up to a morbid extremity of sensibility. At dinner Victor told her he should sleep till tea, and after that he wished particularly to see her, down on the river-bank, alone. But sleep he did not; he went immediately to the stage-office, engaged a passage in the stage that started at twelve o'clock that night, then for the rest of the afternoon he busied himself with getting his trunks packed for his departure. Tea was a very uncomfortable meal to him that evening; he hurried nervously away from the table to the trysting spot, with a troubled, beating heart, longing to have the interview over; and yet dreading it with an aching sense of remorse. After ten or fifteen minutes' delay, Laura appeared, looking so fluttered and so happy, that she evidently thought some very delightful communication awaited her.

"Why did you keep me waiting so long? I have been here more than an hour already," he said, trying to encourage a feeling of irritation against her, in hope so to beat back the growing sense of self reproach which her bright, trusting face was only increasing.

"An hour, Victor! it is not a half-hour since the tea-bell rang, and I came the moment I finished my tea, only I ran upstairs twice to wash my hands, because you are so particular about them."

"You astonish me. What reason have I to be particular about your hands? I shouldn't take the liberty of remarking upon a young lady's hands."

"Oh, but you did tell me to take care of them, and make them white like Charley's; do you mean to say I don't speak the truth?"

"No, miss; no. Very probably you are right."

"But what have you got to tell me, please?"

"Don't you think this a dull place; wouldn't you like to go to Italy?"

"Oh, yes, yes; I would be willing to die if I could go there once. Italy is my dream, my land of promise. Oh, Rome, my country, city of the "—

"Yes, it's a fine olive country. I know a countess there with the prettiest foot in the world. I adored her for that foot."

Laura gave a dreadful wince at these words, but she kept her courage up bravely, and vowed "I would glory in giving up my existence in the ruins of the coliseum, that incomparable monument before which all others must bow with "—

"Dear me, those ruins are favorable to romantic love-making. I remember once taking the most delicious little woman out to see a mass of ruins by moonlight; the ride was exquisite, in a close carriage of course; it made such an impression on her warm little heart that she became "——

4

A crash and a splash here cut him short, the crash being occasioned by the branch of a tree broken fiercely off by Laura, and the splash by its being hurled angrily into the stream. She knew he was relating circumstances and attempting to use words he had no right to do in her presence; and, fired by this conviction, indignation entirely overmastered pain in her breast.

Victor continued, hastily, " Would you not like to see me play, Laura ?"

" I suppose so ; I never saw a play. Is it wicked ?"

" No, you foolish child ; how can the acting of a play be more wicked than the reading of it ? You have read Shakspeare, have you not ?"

" No ; I've read all of Byron and Moore, but I do adore ' Childe Harold ' and ' Manfred.' "

" If you ever come to the city, will you come to see me play ?"

" If my father will let me, but I don't expect to go there."

" Well, at any rate, I trust we shall have the pleasure of meeting again, some time in our future lives."

" What do you mean ? Meet again ! Will you leave me ?"

" Oh dear, Miss Laura, don't put on that look of misery ; you know you will be glad to get rid of me. I feel that I have intruded long enough."

" What can you mean ? what have I done ? I would rather die than lose you."

" Indeed you flatter me too much, but you must be joking ;" and he gazed into her scared, pleading face with a slight sneer and the most irritating little laugh in the world.

She did not reply, only her face grew paler and paler, and the angry tears started hotly out of her eyes.

"Don't cry, my poor little girl," trying to take her hand, but she struck his fiercely from her, and kept snapping off the small branches from the trees, which hung over her head, stripping them roughly of their leaves and casting them into the stream.

"You see I was right, Miss Laura, when I said you did not love me; I understood the joke."

"What joke? what joke? I am a foolish girl; you are a man of the world, and you know so well how to plague me and make me utterly ridiculous. You know I love you; what am I to do to prove it?"

"Let that wretched tree alone, and come here; you have a queer way of loving; you won't even allow me to take your hand."

"Because you don't want it to please yourself, but only as a means of teasing me."

"Oh, what a cunning little philosopher!" and again that aggravating, fiendishly pretty little laugh.

"No, I am not a philosopher; I'm a fool, or I never should have cared for you. I must have been a crazy fool—not a girl in the primary department would have been such a dunce. I took every prize in school; they said I knew more than all the rest of the scholars put together, and the first man who makes an effort, leads me by the nose, like a blind puppy, makes me adore him, and then pretends its a joke. Stop laughing at me, I tell you; it makes me love you and hate you at the same time, you look so heartless and so beautiful; stop laughing at me, or I believe I am capable of flinging you into the river."

"No, Laura, no, you won't do that, for I can't swim, and you'd have to jump in yourself and fish me out. But don't be cross; let us talk calmly."

"How can I talk calmly with this pain in my heart—

I wish it would break, I do; I shall never be happy again."

"Oh, yes, you will; the world lies all before you. With your beauty and talents "——

"They are nothing if I am to lose you. I thought in school I could accomplish anything, by putting my mind to it and never giving up. If you were only a lesson, a whole book full of horribly difficult lessons, that I could study night and day until I had mastered them all, oh, how happy I should be! I should soon have you, or die with the book in my hand. But you are a man, and I know no more how to please you than to take off my shoes and stockings and walk straight into heaven! But you know everything; you taught me how to love you; teach me how to unlove you."

"Give me your hand, then; there, that's right; now be quiet, and let me talk to you," all the while he was drawing her to him with a soft, insinuating perseverance, until her flushed, throbbing head lay on his breast. He could not see her face; he could only feel the deep, deep sighs which shook his breast with their passionate sadness, and told the excess of agitation under which she labored. He felt them, and yet he felt them not, for the locust flowers in her hair sent up their weird, languishing odor to wrap him in a cloud, through whose dim haze his mind gazed back on former loves, on other women who had loved and suffered, and the whole subject looked so hollow and ghastly that he shuddered to think of it, and clutched Laura still closer to his breast, with an involuntary motion, as though he were surrounded by ghosts and found comfort in the close contact of something human.

Laura broke the silence with, "I know I should not be here; I ought to hate you. Many and many a time

I was admonished in school for my pride; they said it was my great fault, the evil spot in my nature; where is it now—what have you done with my pride? I want it back, for I feel as though I were putting myself in the dust, and begging you to trample on me."

"Child, foolish child—but you are not used to stay out so late. Laura, I must tell you good night and—good bye."

"When shall I see you again!"

"Perhaps never; I am going to leave Dorn to-night" (showing her his stage ticket), "and before the spring I must leave for England and Italy. Tell me good bye, Laura, for you will never see me again."

She flung him off from her, at these words, with such a sudden violence, that he nearly fell to the ground: "Then, what am I to do? tell me what am I to do? you have taken my soul from me, and you leave me to live without it. I ought to kill you, and if you were ugly I would. My God, have pity on me! this is too much. I looked down upon the other scholars; I thought myself better than they; I thought every one must give way to me; I was wicked, but the punishment is too great; it hurts me too much; pity me a little!"

"Laura, my child, try to restrain yourself."

"I will not try; I have tried long enough; I don't care who knows I love you; if the whole world knows it, what do I care? I shall always love you and always be miserable. I wish I were dead. I would go home and cut my throat if I were not afraid. I ask you, for the last time, will you leave me forever?"

"I must say yes."

"Then, remember this, you will never get rid of me as long as you live. When you are whispering your lying words of love to other fools, I shall come between you like a spectre; I shall haunt you till I die, and after. Oh, but I am afraid to die; it all looks so black and full of wrath. I believe in the infernal torments, for I feel them now."

She turned to go. Victor tried to hold her, but she struck him in the breast with her clenched fist, and, breaking out into hoarse and dreadful weeping, ran straight into the thickest of the woods, tearing her dress and scratching her flesh at every step. For a little while, after he lost sight of her, he still heard those ugly moans, but they gradually grew fainter and fainter, and died out, and then all was painfully still.

Victor stood for some time quite motionless, with his heart beating heavily in his breast. With all his experience of the world he had never met any woman like this one. The mingling of immaturity and precocity, the child's want of dignity and cultivation mingled with this violent, crazy, ravening phase of love, made a most repulsive contrast. Not a woman at all, he thought, but a baby and a man, blended in one, "Othello" and "Desdemona" fused together, and it shocked and startled him beyond measure. He reproached himself for having caused all this suffering, and he almost hated himself for being the object of her love. He could only console himself with the thought that she was too young not to be soon cured, and with the hope of speedily getting away from her.

Several hours would elapse before the stage started, but he went immediately, paid his bill, and had his baggage removed to the stage office. After what seemed days, instead of hours, midnight came and the stage started. Troubled thoughts, and the after-effects of fourteen consecutive cigars made him anything but a comfortable companion that night. He kept opening and shutting the windows, turning and twisting about in his seat, grinding his teeth, and trampling about the bottom of the stage, until the only lady present told him, with tears in her eyes, that he had given her an additional corn. He changed his seat for one outside, where he fidgeted so, that the driver asked him if he had ever had the delirium tremens, and hinted something about the antidotal effects of potash and flaxseed. Thus, he fumed and fretted till daylight, when the stage stopped for the morning meal, and he fell asleep at the breakfast table, dropping the ravishing countenance, which had undermined Laura's heart, into a deep dish of Indian meal (fortunately not very hot), from which it was with difficulty extricated.

## CHAPTER XII.

An hour after her usual bed-time, when Agnes was getting alarmed about her, Laura ran into her father's room, with her dress in rags, her hair flying like a lion's mane, her face and hands scratched and bleeding, and panting like one who had been running from a mad bull. Mr. Milsland, unaware of her absence, was quietly taking his last smoke. At her extraordinary appearance, he threw his pipe out of the window (though it was his most cherished meerschaum), and caught her in his arms, with an exclamation of fright and surprise. "What is it, what is it, my Laura? has the prize bull got out of its pen? It must be killed to-morrow; it should be if it had cost me five thousand dollars. Cheer up, and be yourself again, I'll get rid of all the live stock, if you wish it."

"Let me sit down; I am weary, nothing has chased me, I ran from myself. I want a glass of water. Oh! call Agnes."

In a half a dozen seconds Agnes was with her, and not only Agnes but her half-sisters Miriam and Charley. Agnes threw her arms around Laura's neck and burst into tears, and Laura laid her head on her bosom, and closed her eyes with a less wretched expression on her features. Miriam mixed a little Cologne with some water, and, dipping her handkerchief in it, washed the blood gently off from her face and hands, and smoothed out her tangled hair. Under this skillful mode of treatment she was fast calming down; but Charley, who meant to be kind, acted as an irritant on her, by exclaiming—

"Papa, I know what it is, it is that deceitful actor; he left the village to-night; I saw them taking his trunks away. He has been behaving shamefully to Laura, and that's the cause of her distress."

At these indiscreet words Laura bounded out of Agnes' arms, with the former wild look in her face, and almost shrieked to Charley not to mention his name.

"You see, papa, I was right. She loves him, and he cares nothing for her, the mean, ill-looking villain."

"He is not ill-looking," cried Laura, resenting this slight to her taste, "and I love him, I believe I worship him. I believe I am almost crazy, I love him so."

"Oh, Laura," said gentle Agnes, with a blush on her sweet face, "do not tell it, oh please keep silent, you will be so sorry to-morrow for what you say to-night."

"No, I shall not; my hope of happiness is gone for ever. What does it matter whether I keep my pride or not."

Mr. Milsland, who was recovering from the astonishment and consternation which had completely extinguished him for the time, burst out with—"What does this mean? Have you disgraced yourself and us all? If you have, I never will forgive you. Tell me the truth; what is there between you?"

"Oh, papa," cried dear Agnes, "she loves him, and he has only been flirting with her, what else could there be? Don't insult her, when you see how she suffers. How dare you speak so to the best girl in the world?"

Laura almost smiled at this ebulition of spirit in her timid sister, and papa was so cowed by it that he immediately begged Laura's pardon. "I didn't mean it, my Laura. I knew better, but that villain must answer to me for his conduct to you. I will kill him."

"No use. I could have strangled him, but I did not. You can't punish him without punishing me, for you see I love every square inch in him," said she, unconsciously falling into an arithmetical form of speech, the field of study in which she was most at home.

"Oh, Laura, if you love me, if you care for your Agnes at all, you will not talk any more, it is so dreadful to hear you expose a feeling, that you should hide from every eye. Won't you go to bed?"

"I will;" and with a sudden show of self-restraint she arose, and kissing her father and elder sisters, went with Agnes to bed, but not to sleep. Oh no! but to shiver and toss from side to side, and to feel as if she had grown old since the last sweet sleep of the night before. In vain! a gulf never to be recrossed divided her from that sleep, and never more should the old sound slumber come to her again. Henceforth one sweet fatal face would rise between her soul and unconsciousness, and keep it ever toiling and struggling with agitating dreams.

## CHAPTER XIII.

Agnes arose softly in the morning, dressed herself without opening the blinds, and crept softly out, leaving Laura muttering in a troubled sleep, which only visited her at daybreak. Agnes went down to the kitchen as soon as she had breakfasted, and caused to be prepared for Laura a meal, composed of all her favorite dishes, to be ready for her when she should awaken. Then she went up softly to her room to see whether Laura was up, knowing her to be naturally an early riser. But the poor girl still slept, and turned from side to side, and muttered as she slept. Agnes went down again, seated herself on the piazza under their window, feeling sure that Laura would throw it open as soon as she got out of bed. After the lapse of two hours she went up again, and Laura was still wrapped in the same uneasy slumber. Dinner came and went, the afternoon slipped by, the tea bell rang, and yet Laura slept. Before this her father had been in several times to see her, said he was glad she could sleep so, begged Agnes not to disturb her, but finally feared she was ill, became alarmed, and sent for the doctor. This medical party on arriving acted with far more humanity than such parties generally do: he felt Laura's pulse, looked at her face, pressed his hands upon her temples, tried to awaken her, but, not succeeding, said she was a little feverish, and that sleep was the best medicine for her. Some physicians would have injected a few grains of calomel into a vein, or forced a blue pill down her throat, if they had to blow it down with a pea-shooter, rather than let her off from the absorption of that abominable drug. But this particular doctor was not at any time a violent druggist. He believed in nature, and let her have her own way whenever she seemed inclined to take it. So he let the exhausted girl alone, and when Agnes came up to bed she still slept, and continued to sleep until their usual time for getting up the next morning. At six o'clock she opened her eyes, and looked vaguely about the room. Agnes kissed her tenderly, and asked if she felt better.

"Better, have I been ill?"

"You were; you were not very ill, you were in trouble, you know."

"Ah! yes. I remember it now, let me think." And she sat up in bed, with her head bowed upon her breast, her eyes cast down, and not a shade of motion in any feature. She looked as if turned into stone. But Agnes could not see her thus, and tried to divert her attention by begging to be allowed to bring her breakfast up to her.

"No, Agnes, I had rather go down; I am not very hungry. Aggy, I think I shall take my horse, and go for a long ride to-morrow."

"Laura, to-morrow is Sunday, wait till next day."

"How can to-morrow be Sunday, when yesterday was Thursday? I went to bed the same night that the stage left, did I not?"

"But, dear, you have slept right through another day and night."

"A whole day slid right out of my life. I wish they would all crumble away so."

"Don't talk so, you make me unhappy. Come down to breakfast; make haste to dress yourself."

Laura assented, and her simple toilet being soon made, she accompanied Agnes down to the breakfast table. Mr. Milsland and the elder girls were not down yet, and when they did come Laura was so composed, that they concluded her heart trouble was only a temporary affair after all.

Thenceforward Laura lived her old life, sewed, read, ate and meditated, so that a casual observer would not have dreamed that any change had taken place in her. For all that, her whole nature was revolutionized; but the change was in her heart's core, and more than a day or month was necessary before it would work itself through perceptibly to the surface.

Charley, with her usual cunning, shrewdly guessed, from her knowledge of Laura's persistence, that her feeling was not dead, but only valiantly buried, and therefore she made every effort to dig it up as often as possible. On one of these occasions she involuntarily suggested an idea that immediately brought forward all of Laura's innate energy.

"What a little fool you were," she said, "to suppose an elegant man like him could really love you! You are bright about some things, but dull about others. Haven't you the least idea what kind of appearance you make? Of course you haven't been much in society, but just compare yourself with some of the young ladies you have seen in the hotel, and think of the difference. What pretty silk and muslin dresses they wear, and how gracefully they dance, and walk and talk, while your dresses always look as if they had come out of the hay-press, and you walk like a fireman, and dance like a dervish. Perhaps if you had been elegantly dressed and polished, like the young ladies in the big cities, he might have cared for you; but being such a rough hoyden, how could you expect it?"

"Do you think so, indeed, Charley? Yes, yes, I

know you speak truly. As I am now, I could not help offending his fastidious tastes. I have always been too wild. I see it now; I must, I will improve."

From that day all Laura's strong, willful and persevering nature set itself to one intense aim—to induce her father to leave Dorn, and make his home in that great metropolis, where Victor's first successes as an English actor had been won, and would in future be the reservoir into which his personal presence would flow when freed from any detaining influence elsewhere. At first Mr. Milsland flouted the idea indignantly; but while Laura had a breath of life in her body, it was not possible for her to renounce the desire, so she continued to return to the attack, until accident put in her way the means of accomplishing her designs. That fortunate chance grew out of her first offer of marriage.

## CHAPTER XIII.

WHEN Laura passed so triumphantly through her graduatory examination, she frequently noticed the eyes of a stalwart young man fixed evidently upon her, which fact she resented as far as sharp and forbidding looks could do it. Nothing daunted by these looks, he asked her father to introduce him after the ceremonies, and in spite of her apparent displeasure, shook her hand with a crushing squeeze, that would have caused serious pain to any hand that was less hale and hearty than Laura's. He also complimented her by "allowing" that she recited "beautiful," and he "never saw" anything so complete in his life." This Mr. Brockwell lost sight of from that moment, suddenly appeared at the

Dorn hotel, to obtain a little rest after the hard summer labors on his farm. He bought a new suit of dark blue clothes, got his hair cut by the village barber, washed his hands in citric acid, and commenced to pay honorable attention to Laura. She was not at all flattered by his preference, in fact snubbed him unmercifully. But he cared nothing for that, indeed he seemed to like it, he thought it a part of womanly modesty, and that it only made her the more " complete."

About this time a very scientific old gentleman, accompanied by his scientific daughter, came over to Dorn, to examine its mineralogical and geological peculiarities, by way of an annual recreation. In these two quaint and amiable bodies, Laura at once took a great interest, accompanying Miss Mix on many of her explorations.

One afternoon, not long after the arrival of this learned pair, Laura happened to wander out alone to the village cemetery. Brockell being in sight, took advantage of her loneliness, cornered her on a tombstone, and immediately spread his matrimonial projects before her. He was not a man to dally about an idea, so he immediately said, "Miss Laura, ever since I saw you at the examination, I have made up my mind to marry you, if I could; and I will tell you why. You see, I never had any education gave me; what I have, I stole. You must have noticed that I don't know anything, haven't been anywhere, haven't seen anything, haven't heard anything, don't know how to say anything, and haven't got anything to say. Now you see, I value education and learning more than anything; I am too old to learn—twenty-seven yesterday—so my only chance is to get a wife who has them, and then as she would be mine, they would be mine too, don't you see?"

"Yes, I see you want a piece of educated property, a learned chattel, not a companion to love and esteem."

"No, I don't; I love you dreadful. You could have your own way in everything, and nothing to do but to talk beautiful, and teach me a little bit."

"You must allow me to decline; I have no intention of marrying."

"Come now, that's a little too much, such a fine girl as you to be an old maid. Think twice before you refuse me complete. Don't you think you could be happy with a man who wouldn't contradict you, and who would buy you all the books in the store? I am not a very rich man, but I've got a fine farm, and more property coming to me. Say the word, and I'll make it yours and myself yours, faithfully, till death us do part. Say, will you?"

Laura, even at her worst phases, always had a sense of humor, so before this her anger had given way to good-natured amusement.

"Indeed Mr. Brockell," she replied, "I cannot accept the honor you offer me; but then so many of the other girls in the village have education, why not think of others?"

"Not one of them but you, has any more sense than she can spare. I want a regular out and out learner, with more brains than her share; and I allow I don't know any but you that stands up to that description."

"But I do, Mr. Brockell; there is a lady in the village now that knows everything; she is a little older than I am, do you mind that?" (she wasn't much more than double Laura's age).

"Well, I can't say I do mind the age much, but I'd rather have you."

"But you can't have me; and as you are that rare being, a man with a taste for blue-stockings, Miss Mix is your only chance. Come, let me introduce you to her."

Before she finished the last sentence she was rapidly walking away, her discarded swain following her very reluctantly.

"You will be very happy, Mr. Brockell, she will tell you exactly what your land is made of; you'll have to dig holes in the ground for her every day, and catch every bug that you ever meet."

"Is it so? but I don't know whether I would like her; I'd rather have you. Won't you think better of it? You see, I know your family, which is agreeable, and your father, who is a man I take by the hand and say there is none better."

"But you can't have me, I tell you; never, never, never. There is the lady I'm going to make you acquainted with, and you needn't be alarmed, perhaps she won't have you."

By this time they had come within some fifty feet of Miss Mix, who was a short, plump lady, about thirty-four, with limp, flaxen ringlets dangling down her fat cheeks, fine teeth, and a plenty of them, and brown eyes, which would have been pretty if one of them had not been disfigured by a "cast," as it is called. At the moment they approached her, she was hovering over a lot of rubbish, composed of stones, bits of rocks, and hard earth, like a hen over her first brood of chickens. Laura questioned her about her labors, introduced Mr. Brockell, and quickly made an excuse for leaving them together. Naturally chivalrous, he soon found himself offering little services to her, which she in her capacity of inveterate blue-stocking, was quite unused to. He broke her rocks for her, poked out a colossal lump of earth in a spot where she thought there were mineral properties, captured a bug with an unprecedented streak on his tail, and when the twilight began to deepen he took up her bag, and offered her his arm. He found her much easier to talk to than Laura, he knew a great many things that interested her, and she was not to be wearied of talking herself, with such a listener. He had always found it impossible to make Laura talk to him, but he modestly concluded that he was ignorant of those subjects calculated to interest her. So he was, but in a different sense from the one in which he imagined ; because he was not acquainted with Victor Doria, he could not hope to interest Laura. If he could have told her in what street Victor lived, at what hour he went to bed and got up in the morning, who his tailor was, and the size of his clothes, where he got his hair cut, and how his boots were made, and who he associated with, he would have absorbed her attention down to its depths. These were the questions that interested her untiring mind, and literature, science, and all knowledge, whether earthly or heavenly, seemed tame and lifeless in comparison.

By Miss Mix he found himself appreciated. She was unaccustomed to the male gallantries of stalwart, wholesome, good-looking twenty-seven, and made the most of them. On the other hand, Brockell was alive to the advantages of education, language and affability combined, and determined to win a mineralogical bride at the shortest possible notice. Things progressed so well that by the end of a month this amiable but incongruous couple were united in what proved to be the happy bonds of wedlock. This did not occur, however, until Miss Mix had accidentally rendered Laura a service which opened the way to the accomplishment of the fixed purpose of her life, that of removing to the metropolis, which loomed up in her imagination as the Paradise of this ill-regulated globe. Accompanying Miss

Mix on most of her scientific expeditions, Laura once told her that there were some very curious spots on the ground which surrounded the seminary, and suggested she should examine them. Miss Mix was delighted with the idea, and Laura conducted her to the eccentric spots. Nothing came of it that day, though the geologist looked very grave and interested. The next day she brought her father, and they burrowed in the earth like two moles just escaped from Bedlam. The third day she asked Laura, "How much land is there included in the seminary grounds?"

"About six acres."

"Is the spot where we have been trying experiments situated on its border?"

"Not far from the middle, I should think."

"Then your father is a richer man than he thinks. That piece of land is permeated with a perfect shoal of mineral springs. We found water strongly impregnated with iron, sulphur, potassium, and in fact all sorts of mineral properties, capable of being developed, I should think, in sufficient quantities to feed inexhaustible drinking springs, as well as baths. Your father has only to engage the proper persons to explore and develop, and he has as fine a resort for health-seekers as could well be found. Were there no mineral springs known before in the land?"

"The water has always been very bad there. All the water we drank was collected from a tin roof into a cistern, the pump water was so mean."

"No wonder, it was brackish with the faint simmerings of minerals; very much like water poured in an unrinsed glass which has contained liquor."

"Will you, my dear Miss Mix, speak to my father about it, and urge him to action?"

"Indeed I will, I feel quite proud of our discovery."

Miss Mix did speak to Mr. Milsland about it. At first he received the idea very coolly, said he always knew there were mineral properties in the land; it was very poor land; there were a half a dozen places where the water oozed up and actually rusted the earth, leaving it a deep red, but that was common to a great many places, it never would amount to anything.

It might have died out so, if Laura had not been continually beside him with her sleepless vigilance. If the constant dropping of water will actually wear away a stone, how can a daughter's incessant soft pleadings fail to hollow out a loving father's heart!

In a short time the mineral springs were subjected to the closest tests, and proved to be more varied in kind, and more positive in degree, than Miss Mix had predicted. One particular spring was composed of sixteen distinct disagreeable drugs; its taste was so pungent, and its effervescence (when all these separate substances were uncaged in the air) so ferocious, that it bid fair to become a perfect idol with the mineral-water drinkers. Accounts of this discovery, coupled with the facts that the village was picturesque, healthy, and near enough to the shores of a bay to make salt water bathing daily practicable, soon found their way into the journals of the nearest large cities, and before the new year came Mr. Milsland received from a couple of sanguine capitalists an offer to lease the land at what seemed to him a perfectly Utopian valuation. With these means at his command, he yielded to Laura's ceaseless urgings, to which were joined those of his other three daughters, and finally went to the city to reside for an indefinite time. The hotel at Dorn having also risen in valuation, from its contiguity to the future great mineral baths, he sold his interest in it for about double its original value, and with these properties set out to provide himself a home in the wilderness of civilization. When Laura threw her arms about his neck, and thanked him for thus gratifying her dearest wish, he told her he was glad to be able to prove how near her happiness lay to his heart, as he felt he owed her some reparation for " a question—a suspicion, on a certain night, unlike any other in your life, I need not say which night, when I feel that by a doubt I insulted my own child, and I have never forgiven myself for harboring it a moment."

He put this in the form of an apology, but in spite of himself the faintest tinge of anxious inquiry showed through his manner. Laura answered him very quietly that she never supposed for an instant he would really doubt her, and looked into his face with such an unflinching expression, that he thought if this were not the most supernal proof of innocence, what could be!

So the family gathered up its effects, and departed to the new life. Charley, Miriam and Agnes felt all the delight that young girls experience when going from a dull country place to a city, in which all the enjoyments of youth are to be had at every turn.

But to Laura the allurements of the gay city were nothing. She went forth only in the hope of seeing Victor again. It would have been the same to her, if she had been setting forth to cross the great Australian desert, with the prospect of a sight of him, for a recompense on the other side. For her this planet was divided into two parts, one the particular spot where *he* was!— the other, all the rest where he was not. The latter stretched like a vast void of emptiness before her mind; but the former was alive with all the aspirations, resolves, joys, agonies and passions that can saturate, ravish, torture, purify and elevate a human soul.

# PART SECOND.

## CHAPTER I.

THREE years after Victor Doria parted with Laura by the river-side in Dorn, he again arrived in that city, where he first seized the laurels of the English stage. In the meantime the civilized world had justified the verdict of that generous city, and, steeped in honors to the lips, he came back to it with a gratitude that was almost filial. He remained in town a week, before he learned that Mr. Milsland and his family were permanently residing there, "and," added Charles Oakford, who imparted the information, "this is their evening at home, and you had better go up and call. They have a fine place, and that Laura is grown to be a stunner, in fact a perfect smasher."

Victor, urged by curiosity, determined to take his advice and go. So he dressed himself in his best clothes (and beyond them mortal tailor could not go), caused the barber to give an additional roll to his already too captivating hair, and at once proceeded to the address furnished him by Oakford. It was a fine double house, surrounded by a lawn, diversified by many flower beds, and it looked so imposing by moonlight, that Victor, comparing it with the former situation of the Milsland family, concluded he was mistaken in the number.

But he touched the bell, and the door being opened by a dignified and lugubrious looking man-servant, he learned that Mr. Milsland there did dwell, and the young ladies would receive him up stairs. The hall in which Victor stood was slightly oval in its contour, paved in white and colored marble, the ceiling was pale blue, relieved with gold; and the stairs, which turned once before they arrived at the second story, were so wide, so polished and so stately, that he fancied himself transported into some palace of his native country. He wondered exceedingly how Laura could fit herself to such a stately earthly tabernacle, she that ran over the trees like a creeping vine at Dorn, and otherwise outraged all forms of composure necessary to a well bred young person. While he was thinking of this, he arrived at the top of the stairs in another beautiful hall, out of which three spacious rooms invitingly opened. Soft music, the ripple of sweet laughter and gay voices fell upon his ear, subtle perfumes floated about, and the whole scene was directly in consonance with his delicate, refined, and sensuous nature. He entered one room, looking with an eager curiosity for Laura, and his eyes fell dizzy with astonishment on a figure at the very end of a second room, which was only divided from this with a velvet curtain, now looped back in the centre. Yes, surely that was Laura; the unmistakable eyes were there. But was it possible from that rough hawk of the village, had come forth this bird of Paradise? It seemed like a transformation scene in a burletta, when the squalid home of persecuted virtue suddenly bursts into a burnished, lily-decked lake, with tinted lights glancing up, and ambrosial naids floating down, and a golden glory hanging over all. The last time he saw Laura she was in a dress of brown lawn, too short in the skirt, and too long in the waist; her figure looked like a patent geometrical chart for the demonstration of angles; and she was running through the trees and bushes, tearing her absurd outer garments to pieces, and acting like a panther crazed by the moon. Now she was certainly the most perfectly beautiful creature, both as to form and face, his eyes had ever looked upon. She was dressed in a white watered silk, gored as to pattern, cut low in the corsage, so as to display the living marble of those superb shoulders and perfectly modeled arms. It was buttoned up, from the neck to the floor, with blue turquoise buttons, set in an antique rim of gold, a narrow strip of sumptuous stuff, turquoise-colored, finished off the skirt, and her little white boots fitting so perfectly the little foot, gleamed with a double row of the same turquoise buttons. Her abundant black hair was bound in heavy bands from the brow, a few thick Grecian rolls surmounted her brow, and around them a stream of turquoise ornaments wound like a cerulian river, till they were lost in the heavy curls at the back. Her face most excited the astonishment of Victor. He always thought it remarkably pretty, even when it had a long diagonal scratch across its nose: but who could have dreamed that a flower like this would expand from such a bud! The low wide brow was framed so well in its mass of black hair, the finely cut nose, and the firm, yet elastic mouth, together with the great, soft, dreamily radiant eyes, over which the eyebrows curved like a crown, and the whole being set in so perfect a contour as the shape of the face gave, which again was so admirably poised on the neck, that it was in itself the perfect realization of an artist's most sublimated dream. True the face was rather too dark in its tint, but it was a clear darkness, and the skin was so transparent that you could

almost see the pure blood coursing through her proud
cheek. And then the form, of which this resplendent
face was the crown—how admirably soft were the
lines which bound it, from the wide shoulders sloping
down to the shapely waist, the firmly rounded chest,
and the round arms, softly tapering down to the dimpled
wrists and hands. To Victor she seemed too
tall, and framed on a little too large a scale for womanly
beauty; but he acknowledged to himself that that
fault might arise from her very stately bearing, rather
than from actual excess of size. He stood for a few seconds
watching her, with just the sentiment a living
statue of incomparable beauty might inspire, and then
he saw a sudden tremor strike through her whole body,
and he knew she saw and recognized him. She came
forward instantly, with a step so light and graceful that
she seemed rather to float than to walk. While Victor
was advancing to meet her. half-way he was wondering
desperately whether the former fancy for himself was
still extant in that stately breast. The moment she
spoke to him the doubt was settled; there was the old,
old questioning look in those hungry eyes, and even in
the few words she spoke there was the faintest echo of a
sob, which lay in ambush behind them, to betray her
from her assumed indifference and composure. Her
eyes seemed distinctly to ask, " what do you mean to
make of me?" and his eyes, having no answer to that
uncomfortable question, at once shrank from their gaze,
and fell before them. He took the hand she offered him
with the kind of hesitation one might show at taking up
a beautiful but dangerous reptile, and having touched
it he dropped it suddenly, as though it had stung him.
A few unmeaning words passed falteringly between
them, then he expressed a desire to present himself to

her sisters. He accosted both Charley and Miriam in the most friendly manner, and to Agnes, now Mrs. Willister, his greeting was almost affectionate. Why then did he feel that instinctive repugnance to Laura, whose earthly beauty was so resplendent that it blotted out the prettiness of her sisters, and made them look like peasants beside her? He asked himself that question, and could not answer it; he only knew that he almost loved her sisters, especially Agnes, for being so unlike her.

Laura passed on from him as he stood talking to Agnes, and sailing like a white lily down a swaying stream, entered among the other guests, and did all she could to appear composed, and did succeed in being unusually gracious and cordial. Victor, while talking to Agnes, accidentally remembered that she had a father, and identified him with a certain amiable, sleepy-looking gentleman not very far off from themselves. He crossed the room and spoke to the latter, recalling himself by name, when he found that his face was not recollected, and he received from Mr. Milsland a very cool reception indeed. He was not disconcerted by that, however; being accustomed to antagonism from the fathers of pretty girls, he had long since forgotten that such was not the normal state of the paternal parent.

Victor told Mr. Milsland he was very glad to see him; Mr. Millsland replied that he would like to see him on business next day; Victor rejoined that he would do himself the pleasure of calling; to which Mr. Milsland dryly answered that it was a matter which would not necessitate a very long interview, with a final sniff that so plainly intimated a desire to terminate the conversation, that Victor immediately gathered up his fascinations and took them to a sex and an age where they were likely to be better appreciated. A few more remarks to Agnes, an introduction to one or two young ladies, and he concluded to leave, for he found it impossible to make himself entirely at home in a place where Laura was evidently the ruling spirit. So he promised to call again, dropped a delicate flattery into the ear of each of the elder sisters, and then approached Laura to bid her good night. She seated herself at his approach, evidently expecting him to follow her example; but he would not be caught so, he only wished her a very civil good evening, and passed directly out of the room.

After his departure she remained sitting in the same position, her eyes fixed on vacancy, and wearing a weary, drowsy look, until a servant tapped to enter the room, when she rose and said, " Let us have more light; it has grown dark here."

## CHAPTER II.

WHEN Mr. Milsland first arrived in the city, three years before the evening just alluded to, he felt so entirely out of his element, he gave himself up to the direction of Laura, like a huge lumbering ship to its helm. And if worldly prosperity and success mean anything, it was lucky for him that he did so. The family went first to a hotel, to remain until a house could be found to suit them. The morning after they arrived, Laura said :

" Papa, have you not an elder brother living here ?"

" Yes ; but we are not on good terms. I have not spoken to him for many years."

"Then I should think the sooner you enter into a conversation with him now, the better."

"I will not seek him; he was entirely at fault in our quarrel, and I will not make the first advances."

"Then I will; I fancy a bachelor uncle above all things. Let me know where he lives and I'll call this very day."

"I know nothing about his address, and I trust you will have more pride than to intrude yourself where you are not wanted."

"Your trust is vain. I don't see how you are to know wheter I am wanted or not till I put it to the test; and you need not think I am to be put off by ignorance of his address. I know the value of a directory, though I was brought up in the country."

Mr. Milsland made no further opposition to her purpose; indeed he felt so lonely in the great city that his heart warmed towards his estranged brother, so he was secretly glad Laura was going to seek him, and she knew it.

"Papa," she said, when she was ready to go, "do you think I should have a carriage?"

"Certainly; and you don't look fit to walk in the streets, your clothes are not in the fashion at all. Your uncle will be ashamed of you."

"Oh no, he will not; he knows I am nothing but a country girl."

Having given the coachman the address found in the directory, he speedily drove her to the same house in which Victor afterwards found her. She ordered the coachman to wait, rang the bell, and asked if Mr. Milsland were in, and being replied to in the affirmative, told the servant to say that Miss Laura Milsland desired to see him. She was ushered into the reception parlor, while the servant went to deliver her message. Her uncle was surprised at the name, concluded it must be one of the daughters of his brother in the country, wondered whether she wanted to ask a favor of him, concluded not to grant it, and preceded the servant to the parlor, actuated as much out of curiosity as any motive. There he found a young girl, dressed in the plainest manner, in a pink muslin dress, and a straw bonnet, with hands almost as brown as the carved oak furniture, for she had already drawn off her gloves, with her usual dislike to them. And yet she did not look at all meanly attired; youth and beauty combined are generally utterly independent of costume. She was looking at the pictures and other pretty things when he opened the door, and his sudden entry seemed to confuse her beyond the power of speech at first. The natural instincts of a gentleman, of course, urged him to set her at ease at once, so he made her sit down, saying gently, "You sent in the name of Laura Milsland; are you the daughter of my brother Charles, from Dorn?"

"Yes, sir; I'm his youngest daughter. My father said he was not on speaking terms with you, but I thought as you had never seen me, you would not be angry with me. So I thought I'd come to see you, if you didn't mind?"

"Mind, certainly not; I'm very glad to see you. You look like your mother. I was very fond of your mother."

"Were you? I'm glad of that."

"Have you come to make a visit, my dear?"

"Oh no, we have left Dorn entirely; you see it's so dull there, and I wanted to come to the city, and learn to be a fine lady, and I think I will ask you how to commence."

"Not a very difficult thing to learn, I should say, but for my part I prefer you as you are."

"Is that so?" beaming with astonishment, "why, everybody frets because I'm so wild. They used to call me a hoyden in school. But do you know, as old as I am, past sixteen, I love to play as much as ever! Do you think I shall ever get over liking to climb trees, I'm so fond of it?"

"Very likely, though at your antiquated age, it is not easy to say."

"I believe you are laughing at me. But tell me, uncle, have you any daughters?"

"Fortunately not; it would be awkward if I had. I'm not married."

"How foolish of me; papa told me you were a bachelor."

"Indeed," with a rising sneer, "he ought to know; he made me so."

"What in the world do you mean by that?"

"Laura, I may as well tell you now, as any other time, for I like you. Your father and myself both loved your mother, and she married him."

"Is that so? Well now, do you know, that if you had both been courting me, I would have chosen you?"

"Indeed, now tell me why."

"Because you are slender, and you have a soft voice, and such white hands," lifting one of them as she spoke, and comparing it with her own brown fingers.

He smiled at this, but it must have pleased him, for he took that rough hand in his, and stroked it gently and silently.

"Well, uncle," she said, "do you think you could be friendly with my father now? you know my mother is dead."

"I know; does your father wish it?"

"Indeed he does, though he will not say so. Now brothers ought to be friends, for there is so much trouble in the world, is there not?" and, unconsciously referring to her own only trouble, her face grew sad and stern for the moment.

"Yes, I think that brothers ought not to be enemies. If your father wishes to be reconciled with me, he could not send a better envoy than you, Laura."

"Indeed, he did not send me; I would come."

"Tell me, my child, what are your father's circumstances? Has he the means to enable him to live here?"

"Yes, indeed, we are rich," naming the amount of her father's income, which seemed a great sum to her, though very insignificant to her wealthy uncle.

"I think your father *is* rich. I wish you were my daughter."

"I am delighted to hear you say so; but don't you think me a little *queer?* they say so in the country."

"Do they? I rather think the city people will find some other word to describe you with, than queer. You will please everywhere, when you are polished up a little in dress. You seem to speak like a well educated girl. Did you study hard in school?"

"So hard that I took every prize in the academy. I was the best scholar in mathematics they ever had," she replied, at once dropping the simple naturalness which had so captivated her uncle, and returning to that disagreeable arrogance of manner, which usually characterized her when speaking of her school affairs.

"Indeed! Then we have only to teach this famous mathematician a few frivolous ceremonies, and she is prepared to take all our hearts by storm."

"I don't want any hearts; I want to improve myself,

and grow to be perfectly splendid. But, uncle, I like your house; won't you show me some more of it?"

"That I will, and leave it to you when I die. You need not look so shocked. I'm a wretched invalid; but come and let us take a look at the house."

He led her from room to room, and was rather astonished to see that, though pleased, she was not at all awed by its splendors. Laura's was not that type of nature, to feel itself belittled by mere artificial luxury. After the grand classical dreams she had fed herself upon, and the sublime architectural glories with which she had dignified the realms of ancient story, it was not a mere fashionable brown stone house that was going to awe her. The girl who in spirit had traveled through Italy with "Childe Harold," drowned herself with "Hinda," crossed the "Bridge of Sighs" with the younger "Faliero," and ascended the mystic mountains with "Manfred," was not to be abashed by mere upholstery.

When she was satisfied with her explorations, she told her uncle "I must go home; and since you are ready to be friendly to my father, why not go home and see him now?"

"I will call some other time; next week, or the day after to-morrow."

"I am not going to let you off so long, I tell you once for all; so just put on your hat, and come along." Saying which she took him around the shoulders, and almost carried him across the room. The action was not very elegant, it was even unrefined; but it was so hearty and so affectionate, that he was carried away by it mentally, as well as physically.

"Well, if you insist, I suppose I shall have to come."

"Of course you will; I don't find an uncle every day, to let you go, when I do."

"But are you sure Charles will be glad to see me?"

"That I am. I should like to see anybody who would not be glad to see such a fine gentleman. When it comes to have such a fine gentleman for a brother, it is better than ever. Will you come?"

"I'm a captive, lead on."

When they arrived at the hotel, Laura held his hand tightly until they came in sight of their parlor, then she could restrain herself no longer, but rushed wildly in. "Oh, papa, I've brought him, such a nice gentleman! doesn't think me very queer at all. He is all ready to make friends with you, and I told him you were very anxious to see him. Come in, uncle. Here he is, isn't he beautiful? What do you think of that for an uncle, Aggy? Isn't he fine?"

All these exclamations covered the awkwardness of the first meeting of the brothers, and in the midst of the tumult they were able to shake hands cordially. Now that they were face to face, it seemed impossible they could have lived as strangers so long, and all because they both happened to love the same woman.

The elder brother was much pleased with Mr. Milsland's other daughters. They were not so pretty, but they were far more presentable than Laura. Yet the youngest one, with all her faults, crept into the warmest place in his heart, and stayed there as long as he lived.

Before the termination of that visit he had insisted that his brother and the girls should come up to his house, and remain there until they could make suitable arrangements for themselves.

## CHAPTER III.

So it fell out that after the lapse of two days, they all removed to the elder brother's house, and never left it again. At the expiration of a week, he was taken ill, or rather an incipient malady came to light, and he never really got better of it, before he died, which was nearly a year afterwards. It did not, by any means, confine him to his room all the time. There were consecutive weeks, when he was able to go about the streets as usual. But he never was willing to allow his brother's family to leave him; after being nursed through a week's severe illness by the girls, he would not consent to be at the mercy of a housekeeper again. He declared that he could not manage to live without his neices, and took such pains to introduce them properly into society, that the younger brother was finally persuaded to remain with him permanently.

As soon as he recovered from his first attack, he gave an evening party, to bring forward the claims of his neices to recognition. He took care that they should be perfectly well dressed, invited the choicest people he knew, caused all the appointments of the occasion (especially the supper), to be all that wealth and taste could make them, and then left the girls to their own wits to teach them how to behave. He knew very well that girls well educated and with gentle blood in their veins, if only well dressed, and placed in elegant surroundings, will be sure to show nothing incongruous in their manners, however unused they may be to society. The girls' justified his conviction, and passed through the ordeal with triumph. After this evening he gave a very large dinner party, and was glad to see that they acquitted themselves with equal propriety on that occasion. Laura, who had already learned that the extent of her appetite was vulgar, took care to indulge in an immoderate lunch, so that at the dinner table she did not consume any more than her neighbors.

The girls were so pretty, so fresh, so interested in everything, so ready to talk with everybody, that the most indifferent gentlemen were pleased with them, especially when it was intimated that they were to inherit Mr. Milsland's large property. Invitations in return flowed in to them, and in a short time they were seldom at home any other evening, except the one which their uncle had fixed upon to receive company himself. In the meanwhile, Laura had set out on the work of self-improvement, with all the vigor of eager and undaunted youth. A dancing teacher was engaged to come to the house every day: the other girls thought three times a week often enough, but Laura would have him daily. But the taking of dancing lessons was only a very small fraction of Laura's vast plan of self-development. Perceiving that leanness of figure was not a beauty, she determined to fill out the hollows, and cushion the angles of her own body, by determined attention to physical exercises, and not to wait for the slower process of natural development. She joined a gymnasium, learned to fence, took boxing lessons, studied vocalization, acquainted herself with the game of billiards, and persuaded her uncle to add a bowling alley to the treasures of his house. Throwing herself into all these exercises with an energy and spirit that convinced her teachers she was slightly crazy, it was no wonder that her chest began to round itself out, and her muscular arms to slowly fill up their cavities, and acquire the curve of beauty. Her hair she delivered into the hands of a skillful hair-dresser who came to the house every day; the most tasteful dressmaker fitted her dresses; for her bonnets she went to the dayspring of millinery inspiration, the French modiste; she coated her face with cold cream every night, to bleach out the sunburn, and her poor little hands folded themselves on her breast for sleep, saturated with almond paste and caged in kid gloves. With all these efforts, her days were entirely filled up; morning visitors seldom saw her, and reading was a luxury not often indulged in, except when the hair-dresser was in command of her tresses. Nothing escaped her. There was no form of physical cultivation, of which she was not nervously ready to avail herself. She did not consider it too much to spend an hour every day, in the development of one of her least fingers. If her foot could have been beautified by hopping up and down stairs, every day of her life, she would have hopped from garret to basement and from basement to garret, until the end was gained. Fortunately her foot did not need improvement, for there nature had done her best.

Though without a general taste for reading, there was one department of literature that she did attend to as a duty,—that was the class of books treating of hygenic methods of preserving the health and beautifying the person. Not an atom of food would she consume calculated to tax the digestion and fret the stomach. She regulated her diet by rules as stern as those of mathematics, and took her baths in algebraic conformity to the standard of health.

All this she did with a simple earnestness that partook of the nature of religion. Not a particle of vanity, conceit, or coquetry tinged her method of self-culture.

She was like the philosopher working out some hidden law of nature, or the devotee concentrating his whole soul on his faith. What wonder if nature, already lying in wait with the richest stores of physical beauty, melted before all this fervent wooing, and yielded them to her before the fullness of time! What wonder, with all this fruitful soil, and the seed of loveliness lying fallow in its depths, that such a warmth of culture hastened the outgrowing of the plant, and spread forth all the glory of its fragrant, radiant bloom! Yes, before the very eyes of her friends, Laura grew and blossomed, like a flower in a torrid clime. And even as she grew in charms, she told them off like sacred beads, that were symbols of worship to one imperishable idol. She watched her own beauties with eager eyes, but vanity had no part in that eagerness; it was a tribute to him, and him only

Ah, poor, fond, idolizing heart! you have yet to learn that no measure of toil will bring you nearer to Love; that it will be blind to your merits, though you should make yourself thrice worthy of it; it will be deaf to you, though you plead to it while your heart drops tears of blood at its feet; though you should come to it in the guise of an angel clad in heavenly robes, it would fly from you, and leave you alone in all your sorrowful splendor. For it comes only like that Holy Spirit, which in the form of a dove descends out of heaven, flutters into the unexpectant heart, and nestling there, folds its wings in trembling joy and hope!

## CHAPTER IV.

The elder Mr. Milsland grew weaker as the days wore on, until even the girls began to see that his temporal accounts were fast closing up. They accompanied him to Saratoga, to Newport, to Cape May, to Long Branch, to Niagara, for he was determined they should experience a complete round of watering-place life. Nor would he allow them to forego any of the usual pleasures of such places, even when his own health prevented his leaving his room. Laura's beauty, grace and intelligence won her so much admiration, he was afraid she would be spirited away from him before the close of the season. But Laura seemed perfectly insensible to the manly attractions which disported themselves around her.

It was useless to flatter her; she seemed pleased to know that she was charming, but she did not connect that satisfaction at all with the suit of the flatterer. All the compliments that flowed into her ear, only made her say to herself with a secret thrill of exultation, "They cannot all combine to deceive me; I must be beautiful. Will he not find me so, and can he fail to love me, if I do credit to his taste and love him so well ?"—unconsciously leaning her strongest hope upon the frailest reed of all, the extremity of her own love.

Thus in every place they visited, she grew to be a mystery with her admirers. They saw how charmingly she danced, how gallantly she mounted a horse, how expert she was in the bowling alley, how gorgeously she dressed, and yet how little she seemed interested in the scene about her. Always striving to excel, and yet taking no note of her triumphs, so careful to seize every advantage to shine in the firmament of her daily life, and yet living as far away from it as any star that blazes lonely and distant in the sky. Here was material for a mystery indeed; and what stranger could know that the key, by which all these weird characters resolved themselves into a simple, touching story—was one sweet face, whose lovely, languid, dreamy eyes went before her like sacred stars, and drew her soul ever on through the dark of the visible world.

But one young man found her the most eager listener in the world;- in fact he never knew any young lady to be so absorbed in his conversation, since he entered on his earthly pilgrimage. He spoke of the theatres: "Are you fond of places of amusement, Miss Milsland?"

"Yes, in a measure, though it seems to me there is always something lacking; every time I see a play, I feel as though I had only read a preface, and the story was yet to come."

"Indeed," of course not understanding this, "I never remarked that; who have you seen?"

"Pretty nearly all of the celebrities."

"You have seen Victor Doria then?"

"What—who do you mean?—yes, I understand—no, I have not seen him play. Have you?"

"Oh, yes, frequently. He's a fine actor. The girls go crazy about him."

"Do they?" with the most gushing interest, "and how does he play?"

"Beautifully, beautifully; he has such a sweet voice."

"Oh, yes, yes, but how does he look?"

"He makes up well, in fact excellently. He brings out his eyes admirably on the stage."

"Does he? Is he fiery in his action?"

"Oh, yes, pretty lively; his style is very taking. He's not a bad fellow in private either. I met him one evening at a party; was introduced to him just before leaving; and as we were going the same way, we walked home together."

"Is it so? What did he say?"

"Well, he said he thought the oysters very fine in this country."

"What else?"

"I think he said something about the Baptists."

"Was that all?"

"I scarcely remember now; he mentioned about being unlucky in a square game of cards. Something about three-handed euchre—but excuse me, that cannot interest a young lady."

"Oh, yes, I think I should delight in three-handed euchre. What is it?"

He was beginning a scientific explanation of that game, but he had hardly got beyond his prologue, when she interrupted him with:

"Oh, yes, thank you, I understand. Did he wear a dress-coat, or something else less formal?"

"I really cannot tell, but I think it was the former; he has a good figure, and looks well in a dress-coat."

"Then you think it was a dress-coat? white cravat?"

"Possibly, I have entirely forgotten. By the way, have you heard Adelina Patti?"

"I have; she has a fine voice—is Mr. Doria's voice on the stage anything like hers?"

"It is almost impossible to compare a singing and a speaking voice. Do you live near the Academy?"

"Farther up town. You were speaking just now of a walk you took; what part of the city was it in?"

"In Tenth street. Have you visited Paris?"

"Not yet. Did Mr. Doria mention to you in that walk whether he was going there, or where he was going?"

"He did not."

"What, did it take all the way going home to like oysters, and refer to the Baptists, and three—I think you said three-handed euchre?"

"Yes, I said so, but the fact is, he said he was afraid of getting hoarse, so he tied his scarf over his mouth and nose, and left me to do all the talking. Now, I told him my opinion of art at length, and as you seem to be interested, I think I can repeat every word I said, while he was muffled in that scarf."

"Can you indeed; what kind of scarf was it?"

"Something woolen, it seems to me; but, as I was saying, I gave him my opinion quite at length, and he listened most attentively to it."

"Did he? How very kind of him! Are you quite sure that it was a woolen scarf?"

"I won't be positive. It might have been silk."

"Very likely. Did you notice whether the color was anything like blue?" and so she continued to walk him up and down that bit of pavement in Tenth-street, like a policeman on his beat—nay, like a detective policeman, for she seemed to be trying to make him reveal the faintest clue of that conversation, as though it were a thread leading to some stupendous discovery.

"What!" said he to a friend on the piazza the next morning. "Do you call that girl absent-minded, and say it's hard to interest her? Why, I never saw such curiosity in my life. She questioned me out of my senses almost; I had to repeat the least thing over and over to her, and she seemed to be very unwilling to close the conversation, when her sister called her to go to bed. Talk about Eve; why, she was nothing, compared to that girl. Think of it, she wanted me to explain three-handed euchre to her, and to give my opinion on art, and on dress-coats and scarfs. She asked me too, how long it took to discuss oysters and Baptists; think of that!"

"I do think of it, my boy; and I think you are either drawing a very elongated bow out of the quiver of your imagination, or else you have made a conquest."

"Well, she didn't seem to be smitten with me, I must say; but you ought to have seen her eyes sparkle when I talked to her about the theatres—she fell into my views immediately. She has a wonderful thirst for information, that girl."

## CHAPTER V.

NOTWITHSTANDING the gradual failing of the elder Mr. Milsland's powers, and the long premonition he had of his summons to the undiscovered country, that summons came at last, with all the shock and surprise of sudden death. In the latter part of September, shortly after their return from the summer tour, his long waning life, abruptly went out. For a week before he never left his room, and his four neices were, one or the other, almost continually with him. He lay with his beautiful, old face, clothed in perfect content, while the girls fluttered about him, nursing him, smoothing his hair, beating up his pillows, making his tea, and ministering to his wants in a generally delightful way. Upon Laura, principally, devolved the task of reading to him; it amused him and touched him at the same time, to hear the earnest way in which she enunciated even the most common-place language, and the air of importance with which she would pause and trace pencil-marks and mystic letters, against passages particularly sympathetic to her. Besides, her voice, if not exactly sweet, had no affected nor hollow tones in it; it indicated, in every intonation, the strict sincerity and faithfulness of the reader. To her uncle, passing from the world, and drifting out of the way of all that can be gained by artificiality, his young neice, in her sturdy realness, seemed to him, among so many of his acquaintances whom custom had long since robbed of nature, a warm, living creature, in an assemblage of brilliant but evanescent spectres. One evening she was reading to him a volume of poems new to her, and made so to him, by the thrilling interest they awoke in her breast. Long after the other girls had retired, she sat there reading, until her uncle told her to put down the book and talk to him, which she did, wondering that any one could prefer her conversation to the pathetic words of the poet.

"Tell me, dear Laura," taking her full, firm hand in his wan fingers, " tell me something about your life before you came here, for I have long seen there are thoughts lying heavy on your mind, of which you do not speak. Tell me what has occurred to make this impression on you?"

"I hardly know what you mean, uncle; is it because I'm fond of study?"

"No; but you are so abstracted, my child, from your daily life; yet you never lose a chance to perfect yourself in its duties and accomplishments. I have been watching you ever since you came here, and every day you are becoming more and more of a puzzle to me. Why do you subject yourself to such unflinching discipline; why do you never let yourself alone for a moment ?"

"I am trying to improve myself; and I never could do anything unless I threw myself into it with all my soul."

"I see that; but why this intense desire to improve yourself? What are you aiming at? I see very clearly that you are not scheming for a great match; you do not seem to care for the admiration of those around you, except as it affords you evidence of progress in your cherished hopes. Is it not so?"

"It is so, uncle."

"I wish you would make a confidant of me, my sweet; I have been noting the peculiarity of your life and character for many months, and I am satisfied there is more than appears to the superficial observer. You are not a common girl; your individualities are marked; your feelings dangerously strong, and I own I scarcely like to see so much concentrativeness, both of power and action, in such a young nature as yours. What is it governs your mind, my dear? What are you striving for, with this fixed intensity of purpose?"

"I don't know how to answer you, uncle."

"Answer me by opening your heart to me. I do not question you from any idle curiosity, but from my deep interest in you. If you have any serious views in life, I may be able to further them. If you have any trouble, I may be able to relieve it. I want you to trust me, and, my child, you have no time to lose; I shall not stay much longer with you."

"Oh, do not talk so. You are getting better every day."

"Why, my child, it is but a matter of a few months at best, and I may not be alive next week. Would you not like to confide in me, Laura?"

"Yes. uncle, if I could."

"Ah, then I was right; you have something to confide. I can only imagine one thing likely to produce the symptoms I see in you. It may be very difficult for you to make statements, but not to answer questions. Tell me truly, Laura, are you in love?"

"Oh, uncle, how can I talk about it?"

"Well, I see you are. Now, will you tell me, is it with any one you have left behind you in Dorn?"

"No, indeed;" with a visible expression of pride rising in her face.

"I might have known better. No man, in ordinary life, or of an ordinary character, could have stirred that strange nature of yours to its depths. Well, I see it was with some stranger, who happened to visit the village. Now, I want you to tell me all about it, for I know something of the world; I love you, and perhaps I could help you. Who is so fortunate as to have won my Laura's heart?"

"Why, uncle, he didn't think himself fortunate at all. In fact, he didn't love me; but then he knows so much, is so charming, and so beautiful, that I couldn't expect him to love a rough, awkward school-girl like me; could I?"

"That depends on himself. And so all this self-cultivation is to put yourself in a position wherein you *could* expect him to love you!"

"I am afraid you will be displeased with me if I tell you, yes."

"Not displeased, my child, but amazed. And so you are cultivating yourself up to the level of his tastes.

But, Laura, I am afraid you are sowing the seeds of future sorrow for yourself; simply making yourself worthy of a man's love, is by no means a certain way of obtaining it. Besides, my dear, he may be married before this."

"No, no; if that were so, I should have read it in the newspapers."

"Aha, then, this gentleman is known to the public; an object of general interest?"

"Yes, uncle; he is an actor."

"Oh, my girl, you grieve me. How did you make his acquaintance? Who is it?"

"His name is Victor Doria—oh, uncle, I wish I hadn't told you, I feel so troubled."

"What! because you're making a friend of your uncle? Why, your secret is known to him, is it not?"

"It is; but I couldn't help it. Oh, I could not help it. He is so different from other people, he could just draw anything out of me. Then he knew without my telling him, how I loved him, so what was the use of my trying to hide it? He could read what was passing in my mind; it was like a scroll spread out before him, and, indeed I could not deceive him."

"I do not doubt it. I know the young man, and have seen him play. Nothing could be more winning than his address; besides, he has a subtle power, delicately concealed in his softness and gentle manner. Laura, I am very, very sorry you ever met him. I can augur no good from this. Don't you think that, by exerting all your strength of mind on this attachment, like a good and brave girl, you could overcome it?"

"Never while I live in this world, and I believe never in any other. You may think I speak thoughtlessly, extravagantly, foolishly; but I tell you, my dearest uncle, my dearest friend, I never shall overcome it. I shall love him straight on to the end. Do you know, the first moment I looked at him, long before I knew who he was, I felt something pierce right into my heart like an arrow; it is there yet? Do you know, it made me feel at first as if I had been swinging very high, till I was dizzy? Oh, no, I know just as well as if I had read it in God's book, I shall never cease to love him. Is it so wicked?"

"Not wicked, but very, very unfortunate."

"Why is it unfortunate? Am I such a fright no man could love me, even if I improve myself ever, ever so much?"

"It is not that. But men like Doria seldom love, in the true sense of the word. They generally shrink from anything serious. I am afraid you are not capable of piquing him into loving you. If you could seem to be perfectly indifferent, we might accomplish something."

"Seem to be indifferent to a man like that, impossible! I should be ashamed of my taste, if I did not appreciate him."

"I thought so. Well, money may do much. I will perhaps thank you for this confidence in my last will, my child. Perhaps that may charm the subtle fascinater, after all."

"How can you talk so? You make me hate the world I am living in. I wish I had leave to go into another one. Yes, your foreboding is right; I am going to be miserable."

"Do not distress yourself; it may be all for the best. God's ways are mysterious, but He knows best; let us leave it to Him. I feel that you are a good girl, and want you always to talk freely to me now. It will be a relief to you. Now tell me good night, and go to bed.

To-morrow I am going to give proof of how dear your welfare is to me. God bless you, my precious, blessed child."

## CHAPTER VI.

It was always a consolation to Laura to remember these words, for they were the last her uncle ever spoke to her. He was found next morning in the same position in which she left him, lying quietly on the sofa, with his head resting on his hand. There seemed to have been no struggle, no pain. His face had a peaceful expression on it, but he had evidently been dead many hours when they discovered him. According to the belief of the physician called in, he must have died shortly after Laura left him, a little before twelve o'clock. At first she supposed the conversation he held with her had been the means of hastening his death, but she learned from her father, that he had seen his brother after she left him, who had expressed a desire to make his will in the morning, at the same time announcing what his intentions were in regard to that will.

"He desired that the greater part of his fortune should go to you, Laura," said her father. "He said you were perhaps fated to suffer many things in this world, (what could he have meant by that?) but at least a lack of abundant means should not be one of them. He told me he had been talking very seriously to you, my dear, and that your happiness was his dearest earthly wish. He did not live to accomplish that wish, but I hold it as my sacred charge to fulfill it. Your uncle's fortune is now mine, for, dying without a will, it descends to me, and from me it shall nearly all pass to you."

Laura took little notice of this; few young girls, if left to themselves, do. She liked to live in a fine house, luxuriously appointed, and to be able to indulge all her tastes; but to the superior advantages of property in her own right, she was not at all alive.

Mr. Milsland's death caused very genuine grief in his household. His younger brother had found it so agreeable to be governed by him, that he even preferred the fraternal to the filial dominion. As for the girls, they were all sincerely attached to their uncle, often striving among themselves for the pleasure of remaining at home with him, when it was considered necessary that some of them should accept an evening invitation. They looked upon him not only as the most superior being in himself, but as the benefactor to whom they owed their present pleasures and future prospects. A shrewd judge of human nature, he perceived the extreme tenderness with which they regarded him, and it made him a happier man, during the last few months of his life, than during the many brilliant but egotistical years of his previous existence.

So at his death nothing but the most sincere sorrow prevailed in his household. None of the girls ever lamented either the time that must elapse before they could again enjoy the gaieties of life, or the necessity to lay by their beautiful wardrobes, and clothe themselves in sombre black. Indeed, they all wished to attire themselves in the deepest mourning that could be devised, but their dressmaker had a character to sustain, and would not allow it.

Laura missed her uncle very much, but her grief was softened by the one-absorbing idea which had her mind in possession, making everything else, however important and however solemn, a secondary object. Sometimes, when she went into that room where she last sat beside him, a feeling of unutterable grief came over her, and she felt as if she never could sufficiently regret the loss of that kind friend; then she would think over every word he said to her, and her mind would incessantly come back to that last conversation, when they spoke of her love. What he said, and what she said, were as easy to retrace as though she read the words from a printed page; and, in consequence of this, her uncle's memory became mixed with future hopes regarding Victor, and took a greatly heightened value from that cause.

After the first few weeks of mourning were over, she returned with renewed zeal to her labor of self-cultivation. The very fact of seclusion and privacy gave her all the more time and opportunity to prosecute her studies, if they may be called by that name. The lessons in all manner of physical accomplishments and exercises were more frequent than ever, for there was now no call to attend evening entertainments of any kind. She could slip off to bed before ten, and be up by six in the morning, a habit she had read of as being greatly conducive to beauty. She was always getting herself weighed, and measured in all possible directions, to find out whether she was approaching the exact lines of beauty. If she visited any collection of sculpture or paintings, she looked at them simply with the eyes of one who seeks to wrest from them the secret of their charms, and to learn how to become like them. With this entirely personal view, she became a keen student of the fine arts. Indeed she was, in some sense of the word, herself an artist, and her own body was the material out of which she was fashioning an image, fit to be shrined on the altar of love.

It may seem that this excessive concentration of thought upon herself would naturally tend to make her both egotistical and selfish. It did, in a manner. But her aim reached so far out of herself, that it gave to her self-concentration a tone almost of self-abnegation.

She was selfish, in so far as she never allowed anything to stand between her and the one great personal object; and she was egotistical, only inasmuch as her intense self-consciousness extended, which did not allow her to raise her little finger without intensely watching herself, to see that it was done according to the rules of artistic grace. It did not create the kind of selfishness that is allied with conceit, and requires to be nourished by admiration and flattery. Indeed, she was so constantly under her own observation, that she did not feel it necessary to secure the attention even of others.

## CHAPTER VII.

During all the time that had intervened since the exodus of the Milsland family from Dorn, a certain young man, to whom the heart of Agnes was given, has not been mentioned. But Willister had by no means retired from the scene; on the contrary, after the adoption of Mr. Milsland's family by his elder brother, his devotion to Agnes became stronger than ever. Agnes had engaged herself to him, but neither father, uncle nor sisters approved of the marriage. Together they persuaded her to wait one year before consummating the union, for her uncle hoped that before that time, some worthier image would be impressed on her heart. As is usually the case, the wish was hopeless; at the end of the year Agnes was more in love with him and more determined to marry him than ever. Finding it useless to oppose it, her father reluctantly consented and allowed them to be married, simply in the presence of the family, in his own house. He had told her, after her marriage, that her uncle had intended to leave her twenty thousand dollars, and desiring religiously to fulfill all his dead brother's wishes, he would give her that amount, hoping it might enable her husband to set himself up in some safe and respectable business. This he promised most faithfully to do, but declared that imperative duty called him to Europe, before he could settle down for life. He took his wife and sailed in a few days for Paris, where he remained for nearly two years, and then returned suddenly with his wife, without notifying her family. The first intimation they received of this arrival, was a note addressed to Laura from Agnes, begging the former to call on her at a hotel where she had arrived. Laura went, without speaking to her elder sisters, as the note seemed to intimate a desire to see her alone. When she returned, she said to her father:—

"Agnes has come back, and she has a baby, about three months old."

"Why did she not come here to see us at once?"

"Because there is something wrong there; I fear she is not happy with her husband, and what is more, I believe he has spent every cent you gave her."

"Why do you think so?"

"Because she has no proper clothes; she is obliged to have her meals sent to her room, for lack of the wardrobe adapted to the table of a fashionable hotel. She asked me to lend her some money, and I gave her all I had, nearly a hundred dollars, and when I came home I sent her a large trunk full of my clothes. I am quite sure she was even scantily supplied with linen, so I sent her an abundance of mine. I was rather glad, for it gave me a chance to buy some new things for myself. That reminds me, you will have some bills to pay for them to-night."

"Have you any idea of how much they amount to, Laura?"

"Close upon seven hundred dollars."

"Why, my child, don't you think you are unnecessarily extravagant?"

"Why, no, papa; you see I was obliged to replace the things I gave to Agnes. You will see how necessary the articles were to me when the bills come home."

Even while they were talking, the bills arrived. Laura handed them to her papa, who began to examine them with rather a dubious expression of face. After a few minutes he looked up and said, "Why, Laura, is this item genuine—four night-dresses, ninety dollars?"

"Yes, that's just right. They are lovely things, and, considering what they are, they were very cheap."

"Considering what they are—what are they?"

"Why, they are elaborately trimmed with fine embroidery and valencian insertings and edgings."

"And can't you sleep without being covered with embroidery? Do you fancy yourself the Sleeping Beauty of the Fairy Tale, fated to be wakened from your slumbers by a king's son, in the presence of a court?"

"Of course not, but you know I do love elegance in my under-garments—what I wear outside I care much less for, in fact very little."

"So I perceive—item, one bonnet, fifty-one dollars;

one velvet sacque, one hundred and eighty-seven dollars; one dress-pattern of watered-silk, ninety-eight dollars; one set, collar, sleeves and handkerchief in point d'aiguille, a hundred and twelve dollars; and sixty dollars for miscellaneous articles of under-clothing. Yes, I perceive you care nothing for your outer-garments."

"Now, papa, don't be sarcastic; don't you want your Laura to be dressed as well as other people? Besides, I want another dress soon, and at least three handsome morning-robes; besides, I am to have a complete set of ermine, long cape, muff and cuffs, you know, as soon as the fall sets in. And, by the way, I ordered a lace cape in point d'aiguille, to wear with low dresses; they hadn't one to suit me, so I told them to send to Paris for one. I hope you are not going to scold me."

"My child, I don't want to scold you, but use your good sense, and reflect how much such extravagant purchases will amount to at the end of a year."

"But, papa, I thought you said my uncle's fortune nearly all belonged to me?"

"So it does; but the income arising from it will not support such an establishment as ours, if you are to add to it such extravagant outlays on dress. A thousand dollars seems to be a trifle in your hands, when you go on a shopping expedition."

"I know it, papa, but you cannot imagine how little one gets for that sum, and you know I must appear as well as possible."

"I don't understand the change that has come over you. You never thought of your appearance at Dorn. I recollect how hard it was to get you to go over to Sydney's store and choose a dress, and invariably you came home with some sober stuff that would have besuited a Quaker. And then the dressmaker used to complain of you; you would not suffer her to try your dress on; and when you did, how impatient you were, and vowed you didn't care whether it fitted or not; and how, when obliged, by the sad imperfections of your figure, she justly insinuated a proper amount of wadding into the waist, you indignantly pulled it out, and flung it into the fire."

"Exactly so," she cried, laughing heartily, "but you see I do not need such aid and comfort now."

"Oh, you have a fine figure, my girl; no one will deny that you have a glorious figure; but couldn't you contrive to spend a little less in future?"

"Papa, I promise you I will try; only let me have the things I have mentioned, and I will promise you to economize—a little. But won't you go to see Agnes? don't you want to see her?"

"Certainly I do. Agnes is a very dear daughter to me, but I have an unconquerable aversion to her husband. Did you see him?"

"No, he was out all day."

"Bring Agnes here to-morrow morning, and don't forget the baby, my first grand-child. Let her husband come to dinner at six."

## CHAPTER VIII.

LAURA started off before nine the next morning, while her elder sisters were breakfasting, and brought a carriage-full home with her, consisting of Agnes, Agnes' baby, and baby's nurse. Mr. Milsland and the girls received them warmly, and, after an hour of general converse, while the young aunts were cherishing their neice,

Agnes' father took her off for conversation in his private room. Then it all came out, what her present situation was, and how she came to be dressed at the very moment in Laura's clothes. Mr. Willister and herself had proceeded directly to Paris, in which city she supposed the pressing business of which he spoke was to be transacted. After a short time, spent at a fine hotel, Mr. Willister sought a furnished apartment, and, as he could not find one to suit his exalted views, he hired an unfurnished one, consisting of a modest compliment of eleven rooms. These he fitted up in a very showy and costly manner, without being discouraged at all by Agnes, as she confessed. So fine an apartment necessitated a suitable *menage*, entailing a carriage and pair for Agnes, and a horse for himself—which necessary luxuries drew with them the retention of at least seven servants. A box at the imperial opera, one at the "Italiens," and another at "Les Francais," followed in natural order, together with all the necessary suppers, dinners, fêtes, &c., which an inferior actor of provincial theatres could not for a moment be expected to exist without. Twenty thousand dollars seemed a very large sum to Agnes, and yet, marvellous to relate, not more than a year elapsed before it had dwindled away as if by magic. To this fact even her not unloving Joseph had finally opened his big black eyes, and vowed within himself to restore the sum to its pristine completeness. So, taking what remained, he repaired with it to work out a stupendous scheme of his own for breaking the bank of a famous institution of play. At the end of a very few days he returned, looking very gloomy, and with just three francs in his pockets. A great part of the fine furniture was sold, the grand apartment given up, and they removed to another of about half its size and splendor. Here Agnes received into her welcoming arms her first-born, a little girl, which event, in the clumsy management of the young couple, soon swallowed up the money obtained from the sale of their furniture. Agnes' jewels went next, and, being soon consumed, the furniture remaining to them was sold, which, from the circumstance of Willister having a few debts at large, was not at all sufficient to take them from Paris to New York. So everything of value in Agnes' wardrobe was turned into specie, by the means of which they were able to return to their dear papa, in the hope he would forgive, and vouchsafe them one more trial.

All this Mr. Milsland easily elicited from Agnes, not without some severe comments of his own, as the narrative progressed. Like an indulgent parent, he could find no reproof for his child, but he was most severe upon her Joseph; while Agnes, like an indulgent wife, pleaded most eloquently that the whole blame rested with her.

"And oh, papa," she cried, with her arm around his neck, her fair soft cheek resting against his, "will you not give us just one chance more? you won't let us starve."

"I don't see the necessity for your starving; your husband is not at all decrepit, let him earn his living."

"But, dear papa, with only just one thousand dollars, Josey sees his way to a comfortable position for the rest of his life."

"He sees his way to some abominable foolery, no doubt."

"You are very unkind to talk so of my husband, and I see you don't love me at all."

"It is just because I do love you, that I am vexed to see you thrown away on such a man. It is just another proof of the depravity of actors; I detest the whole race of them more than ever. I allowed my daughter to disgrace herself and me when she married one."

"And if you don't help us, he'll be obliged to continue disgracing you, by going on the stage again. In an inferior position too, papa, for the other actors are so jealous of him, they have combined together to keep him down. The press too will fiendishly strive to crush him, because he will neither cringe to, bribe, nor flatter it. Don't you see?"

"I see nothing except the absurd conceit and folly of your husband. What is this thing he can accomplish by the aid of a thousand dollars?"

"He will not tell me, but I know he must leave the city to accomplish it, and he hoped that during his absence you would keep me."

"I only wish I could keep you for the rest of my life. Tell your husband he shall have the money. I don't want to see my daughter's husband parading himself as an actor before the public, and an atrocious one at that."

"Oh, papa, how unjust! if they would only give him a chance to play 'Hamlet,' he would—"

"Make me wish the last scene were a reality, I've no doubt. You can come here with your baby to-morrow, and your husband shall be provided with the money to leave the city before night."

"Thank you, dearest papa, I shall be so happy to come to you and my kind sisters for a time. Now I'll go and tell Laura all about it."

Next day she arrived with her baby, to the delight of her sisters, and she was still staying there some months afterwards, at the time of the opening of book second.

## CHAPTER IX.

The morning after Victor's visit, Laura came down to breakfast, with an indifferent, abstracted look, that to a superficial observer, might have only indicated a haughty, self-sufficiency of nature. Even her sisters, who were accustomed to her strong-willed ascendency over the whole family, were amazed at the amount of scorn and cold pride her manner exhibited. Miriam was puzzled, Charley irritated, and Agnes grieved by it. After breakfast she went into the reception parlor, whither sympathetic Agnes followed her. She took a book, turned over the pages restlessly, let it fall finally into her lap, and closing her eyes, would have seemed to sleep, if Agnes had not seen a pulse from time to time quiver about her mouth, which was quickly repressed with stern energy. Agnes watched her, not daring to speak, and yet longing to try to comfort her. Suddenly the street-door bell rang,—no sign of animation from Laura; a servant was heard to open it, and a man's step to fall upon the marble floor,—utter petrefaction still on the part of Laura; then a sweet, vibrant voice was to be distinguished inquiring for Mr. Milsland—all at once the statue of stone into which Laura had hardened, starts up, its eyes all aflame, its breast travailing with deep throes, its nostrils dilated, its mouth burning with a crimson pulsation. It was Victor's voice; (no one who once heard it ever forgot its peculiar temper), Agnes recognized it, and instantly she understood the spirit that possessed her sister's soul.

By an almost superhuman effort, Laura commanded her agitation, and was externally calm and dignified before Victor was ushered into the room. He came in with that graceful, elastic step that was peculiar to him, smiled when he saw the ladies, and, taking a seat, began to talk to them, while around his whole presence, hung that air of delicate elegance, that caused everything to swim before the eyes of Laura, like incense swung in the thrilling pauses of some grandly effective Catholic ceremony.

After a few minutes, Mr. Milsland sent to inform Mr. Doria that the latter would receive him in his library, as he called it, though newspapery would have been the name most in accordance with the only branch of literature with which he consorted.

Before Victor left the room, Laura, with a cold exactness of manner that amounted to a command, requested him to allow her an interview before his departure from the house, with which request, of course, he was forced to acquiesce.

Mr. Milsland met Victor's frank greeting very coolly, and then stated that he would proceed to business at once. He said the piece of landed property, left in his hands more than three years ago, as not being available, had, in consqueence of its contiguity to the mineral springs on his own estate, risen greatly in value, so that when the excitement was at its height, it was sold, by advice of his daughter Laura, and the proceeds were so well invested, as to have now amounted to the sum of ten thousand dollars, which he desired to pay over at once to its owner.

Victor expressed his gratitude, which the elder gentleman seemed not to notice, and then left the room, thinking that this parent was even sterner to him than parents were wont to be.

On his way out, he returned to the reception room, to hold that interview with Laura, the thought of which at once excited his curiosity and his repugnance. He entered and found Laura there, pale, quiet, and rigid. He took a seat (at as great a distance from her as possible), expressed his acknowledgments of her father's kindness, and then invited her to explain the object of this interview.

She said, with a great pang in her breast, which nearly choked her, "Victor, you seem to have forgotten me, and our life at Dorn."

"Forgotten you? no. How could I have forgotten such an elegant and beautiful lady? I remember with pleasure your graciousness to a stranger, whom you never expected, and probably never wished to see again. How could I forget it?"

"I say you have forgotten it, but I have not."

"You honor me too much, my dear Miss Milsland."

"Look at me; am I changed at all since I last saw you?"

"Wonderfully, superbly changed!"

"Well, this change, accomplished by years of incessant toil, and an unflinching resolution to which I have sacrificed every natural pleasure, every wish, will, hope, is the work of one man—that man is you."

"I do not understand you," getting nervous, and consequently lapsing into his irritating little laugh.

"Then I will teach you. Four years ago you came to the village, where I was a simple and happy schoolgirl. Man of the world as you were, possessed of all the fascinations calculated to steep a girl's whole nature in love for you, of all that subtle knowledge of human feeling which enabled you to strip her heart of its outer coverings, and read it, as though you held it naked in your hand; I yet fled from and resisted you with all the strength that belonged to my poor, foolish young life. You followed me like a destroying angel; you shut up every avenue of escape for me; you tangled my feet in soft, soothing tenderness, and blinded me with your false, delusive caressess, till no longer struggling in the hopeless toils, but staggering beneath a burden of love greater than I could bear, I sank down on my knees and yielded up my whole heart to you. What did you do with my love when you had won it—what with my heart, when you had plucked it out of my breast? What did you do with them, I say? Why, you flung back the love like a bruised reed, and my heart like an empty cup, which had been drained and dropped apart and forgotten. Victor Doria, what have you to answer to this? What do you mean to make of me? For you I have cultivated my manners, my tastes; for you I have melted myself into a new mould, fitted to please your artistic eye; for you I have considered myself but as so much senseless soil in which to plant the seeds of beauty; the harvest is up and waving in the sun—look to it! You could not love a rough, angular, unformed country girl; I am now worldly-minded, self-satisfied, accomplished, and an acknowledged beauty—what do you mean to do with me?"

"Miss Milsland, you are making fun of me. What could I do with you?" he replied, laughing almost hysterically between each word.

"Fun? fun on the rack,—without you I am turned off to a living death,—in all the fullness of my life, I am set in a silent desert to wither up my blood and swallow my tears. Yet, no—one thing more is left me—to be revenged!"

Laura, in this climax of her speech, had touched the chord in Victor's nature, calculated to harden his heart and restore his self-possession. However frivolous he might seem, he was no coward. As soon as she appealed to the emotion of fear, he was at ease once more. While she addressed herself to his feelings, he trembled and was abashed before her; but an attempt to frighten him, excited his amused contempt. As long as he felt it was left to himself to repair her wrongs, he was annoyed and distressed by them; but the instant she proposed to right them herself, he defied her. Her anger hushed his regrets, and her threats extricated him from his dilemma. Since she chose to put the question on the ground of a contest, let her do her worst; he was free to scorn her.

Now Laura, by the help of that intuition with which she was so largely endowed, though unfortunately without its corresponding quality of tact, saw the change in his mind, and felt she had thrown away all the advantages of her position and taken the vulgar attitude of menace, when it was really foreign to her mind. At this time of her life, her outward manifestation of her feelings often did cruel injustice to them as they really existed. She had the strange habit of assuming what her manner ought to be, and then forcing herself to the adoption of that manner, whether it was in antagonism to the true state of her mind or not. Naturally reserved and sensitive as to her own sensations, she had been compelling herself to an exhibition of indelicacy, almost of immodesty, which it made her dizzy to think of. Allowing her heart to be governed by her strong, crude intellect, she had driven herself to the conclusion, that avowing her love for him arrogantly and without a blush, was the only sincere and lofty ground for her to assume with him. So all the while she waited for this interview with her irresponsive idol, she was fashioning in her mind that long address, which was to subdue him by its very lack of ordinary conventionalities; the gross injustice it did to the real tenderness and unselfishness of her love, she herself did not fully know, and he did not even suspect.

So at its end she sat there bowed down with doubt, shame, self-reproach, and despairing love, while he in his turn sat and looked at her in cold and quiet scorn. Wishing to repair her error, she made a still more fatal one. She went towards him with a pitiful, pleading look in her eyes, and attempted to take his hands in hers. But he shrank from her with an instinctive movement of repugnance, that seemed to amount to physical pain. There was no mistaking this repugnance; even the misguided mind of the miserable girl recognized it and accepted it to its most hurting extent. Under the accumulated weight of fever and recent exhaustion from loss of sleep, abstinence from proper food, and long continued nervous suffering, added to this conviction, her desperate courage gave way, she suddenly relaxed her hold on consciousness, and dropped in a deadly faint. The moment before she fell, Victor saw with horror her face taking on that lividness, so ghastly in dark skins, her eyes growing thick and turgid, and he almost fancied he could see a pale bluish vapor hanging about her pallid lips, as though the vital principle were passing out through them, before she fell in a heap of crushed lace and amber ribbons, senseless to his feet.

Very much alarmed, and yet true to his instincts of repugnance, he fled without touching her, to seek assistance from without. In the hall, to his great relief, he met Agnes, who was hovering about with a distressed anxiousness, and having committed Laura to her care, hurriedly left the house.

## CHAPTER X.

Laura's vigorous constitution soon threw off the weight of her physical illness, and before night she was ready to visit the opera. The only thing noticeable in her was the comparative simplicity of her costume. She wore a black silk dress, a white lace shawl, and pearls and black velvet knots in her hair. But it was not particularly noticed by any but the ever watchful Agnes. Laura meant it as the visible sign of a dead love, the renunciation of her hope, and the registry of a vow to overcome that love, and be brilliant and happy without it. Yet all the while she was flattering herself with her self-conquest, she was busy manufacturing plans to pique him by indifference, to crush him by satire, and arouse his jealousy by preference to others—a state of mind that indicated she was still under the dominion of her love, and moreover of its most objectionable phases.

During the course of the week she met him at an evening party, and immediately attempted to pursue her new line of strategy. He bowed to her with a cold, embarrassed air; she returned it with one of patronizing familiarity. Then she deliberately addressed her conversation to him, talked rapidly, laughed often, and took pains to use scholarly and imposing language. Thence she passed into badinage and irony, attempting by them to display the extent of her scornful indifference to him. But he saw through her motive instantly, recognized it as another method of pursuit, and swept it away like a cobweb. To her badinage he opposed sneers; when she was majestic, he yawned, when she was satirical, he was simply impertinent. He scarcely listened to her; his eyes wandered away from her face, and at last, to her most brilliant remarks, he replied with meagre and listless common-places.

The most desperate flirting with others, in hope to excite his jealousy, succeeded still worse. He took no notice of it unless she forced it upon his attention, and then he resented it, as the most aggravating form of siege.

Before the evening was over, people began to remark the want of respect with which Victor treated her, and did not fail to put an unjust construction on it. Not only did he look at her with undisguised contempt, but he cut her short in the midst of a remark several times, as though nothing she could say was of the slightest consequence.

And yet for one week after another did Laura struggle on to bring herself to his notice, and in some measure recommend herself to his acceptance. Every effort was met by the most determined resistance; for Victor had made up his mind to submit to any misfortune on earth, except to be loved by her. Reticent and sensitive as Laura was by nature, it was a dreadful ordeal through which she dragged herself, but it came to an end finally. Hope, in her vigorous, intense mind, died not without many and desperate struggles, but it did die at last, and left her quite aimless, to drift about on the sea of life. In the midst of these, there seemed to her to be but one straw to clutch at—the possibility of falling in love with another man. Then she determined to love somebody at once, as though it were an effort of the will, and entered into the determination with a species of madness. But there was method in her madness. She carefully elaborated the theory, that she loved Victor not as a man, but as a type of men; and then she proceeded to find one of his type and—love him. It was not long before she discovered an unfortunate gentleman, who resembled Victor as far as his nose went, and on him she pounced like an affectionate bird of prey. He fell a speedy victim to her affability, and was out of his depth in love for her, almost immediately. But when he proposed a union of their hands and fates, she recoiled at once, and of course obtained the reputation of having heartlessly drawn him on for the sake of refusing him. But in spite of this reproach, which she knew was justly merited, she was soon at work again to find an object to fit her love to, and succeeded in finding a man who had no earthly significance to her, expect a trick of the eyes, which was peculiar to Victor. He winked his eyelids, and drooped his eyes straight into her imagination, until she deceived herself into the belief that she really cared for him. She talked with him, danced with him incessantly, laughed at his jokes, listened to his confidences, and distinguished him above all her acquaintances, until he too solicited a conjugal culmination, when all at once she awoke as from a dream.

What made this style of flirtation so dangerous, was the savage earnestness which formed its ground work. Coquetry is not a very dangerous weapon in the hands of triflers; the wounds from these little toy-guns are but flesh wounds at worst, but it is by no means safe to have a heart of the calibre of Laura's deliberately aimed at one. For she went about like a lion, seeking whom she might love. She was so fearfully honest in her determination to love somebody, that she succeeded in deceiving herself, as well as others. Groping out blindly after her ideal, clinging to false resemblances, and determined to carry her own inclinations at the point of the sword, as it were, she did not fail to drag others into the restless and miserable agitations which consumed her.

No wonder she fairly earned the reputation of being a thoroughly heartless and dangerous flirt. Not that such a reputation prevented her from being more admired and followed than ever. Let the moralists say as they will, that the entire charm of women is comprised in their affections; it is not less true, that the common run of men are instantly attracted to a woman, whose conduct argues in herself the absence of all affections.

But if Laura gave trouble to others, it was not the means of lightening her own burden. She had no vent for her restless, seething mind. She was living for the time under an exhausted receiver, a human being devoid of all the privileges of humanity. She was a desolate dove, with the great waste waters of indifference flowing under her, and leaving her no place in which to fold her weary wings. And if sometimes she swooped hawk-like down on some green shadow, mistaking it for the olive-branch, what then?—are the pangs of hunger sharper in the hawk than in the dove?

During these affectional experiments Laura was gradually learning a lesson of despair, that the mere outward seeming of the man was not the object of her love. She found eyes like his, but they said no more to her heart than imitations in glass. She heard voices that resembled his, but to her ear it was a mere empty mockery of sound. Once she met with a face that was very like his, but it only repulsed her like a mask behind which there was no life. True, Victor's personal traits were the realization of her physical ideal, but far behind them all lay the shadowy essence which centred the individuality of the man, and there was seated the malady of her soul. What had she to hope for? What earthly means would aid her to pluck out her love from that mysterious soil where it had taken root? "No," she told herself, "it must continue to grow there, and bring forth for her the perennial fruits of despair."

## CHAPTER XI.

About three months after Victor's return, he was announced to appear for a number of nights at the leading theatre of the city. On the occasion of his first appearance, Laura was fortunate in being enabled to occupy alone with Agnes, the box her father had procured for her, as her elder sisters preferred to fulfill an engagement elsewhere, and her father was only too well pleased at her suggestion, to accompany and leave them there.

The play for the occasion was "Romeo and Juliet," the one in which Victor had made his debût on the English stage. All that part of the play which preceded the entrance of "Romeo," to Laura was but a cloud of "wild and whirling words;" yet impatient as she had been for Victor's coming, at the very first burst of premonitory applause announcing his presence, she closed her eyes, and felt her heart reel as though it staggered on the verge of an abyss, sway, clutch at steadfastness, right itself, and again grow firm in her breast.

When the tumult of applause subsided, out of the dead stillness that indescribably sweet voice rose vibrant on the air, rose and permeated the whole building with its fresh, youthful resonance. Then Laura opened her eyes and gazed on that face, into whose mobile features a nervous intensity of organization was forever pouring its passionate expressiveness—gazed on it through the tears that began to stream down her pale face.

The first scenes which introduce "Romeo" to the public, are not calculated to wring tears from the most susceptible eyes; but even there Laura's tears began to flow, and they did not cease until the curtain fell on the last closing scene of tragic anguish. For the first time in her life, Laura really wept. Silently, without convulsion, as freely as though her very soul were melting away, the tears streamed from her eyes, till she felt as though she were weeping from every pore.

So located in her box, as to see without being seen, she could watch the least movement of that pure and perfect profile,—she could watch, and long, and weep, without fear of being noticed, except by that kind sister, who could scarcely keep her own eyes from filling through sympathy.

In the balcony-scene, where Victor's slender frame, in its suppleness, giving the most perfect idea of strength and grace united, ensured him a certain amount of success, even had not his peculiar face and style of intonation specially fitted him to excel in it, Laura recognized many of the caressive tones in which he had first moved her. This similarity, instead of throwing an artificiality over that past wooing, only invested the present scene with a profound realness. It seemed to her as if every scene and nearly every sentence, in some way pictured her own state of being. The play, like a mirror, pictured to her the absurd futility of her recent efforts to subdue herself and her love.

Victor was not fitted by nature for any great physical effects: he had neither the lungs nor the frame adapted to that school of acting, therefore he was weak, he was actually ridiculous in his only attempt at "Richard." Many of his scenes in "Othello" were tame and lifeless; and if he had never played anything but "Shylock," a just critic would have pronounced him to be a very bad actor. But in parts where tenderness, grief, passionate love, and romantic impulsiveness are required, he had no equal on any stage. All that fitful uneasiness of manner, which in private life amounted to actual fidgeting, upon the stage absolved itself into an impulsiveness, which caused him to speak every line of his part as though he were originating it at the moment. Thus, in his lips, the most insipid words took a color from him, and were uttered with a fresh earnestness that made them seem like an inspiration. Besides, he possessed that rare and mysterious personal magnetism, which above all things else, draws, woos, enchains and ravishes an audience.

When the play came to an end, Laura was forced to wait until the lights were turned down and the theatre in a great measure emptied of its occupants, before she could venture to leave, because her pale cheeks, and torn, sunken eyes, made a very startling change in her appearance. Indeed from that night the abundant bloom of her youth and beauty was touched with a faint, but perceptible change. A worn and wearied look crept into her face, and contrived slowly to grow as the days went on.

Yet Laura's life, during the four weeks of Victor's engagement, was one of celestial enjoyment, compared to the period which preceded and followed it. The days were not so drear, after all, when they preceded an evening spent in legitimate admiration of him,—when it was not a crime against self-respect, modesty, nor womanhood, to gaze on him and listen and adore. For when overflowing audiences culled from the choicest cultivation, experience, refinement and critical acumen of the city, gazed in wrapt and breathless silence on his seductive representations of the youthful heroes of the drama; when indifferent faces grew pale in the passionate cadences of that most pathetic voice,—who could condemn the admiration of a girl of nineteen, from whose thoughts, for four weary years, he had never been absent for a moment?

The time passed swiftly, and Victor's short engagement came to an end, with the prospect of a renewal after the lapse of one or two months. And what did this engagement profit to the two beings most interested in it—Laura and Victor himself? Good heavens! what is the meaning of this partial destiny which shapes our lives, giving to one all the fulfillment of the heart's best longings, and to the other hatred and hunger of despair.

To him it has brought admiration, respect, a gratification both of his pride and vanity, and an assumed position of success in the world's most fascinating art; —for her it had cut away all the moorings to which her soul clung, and sent it to wander adrift on the dull waters of listlessness; it had robbed her of hope, and in its place given her the power to weep, and her tears were very bitter.

## CHAPTER XI.

In the meanwhile, Agnes' husband returned from his fortune-hunting expedition, having got rid, not only of Mr. Milsland's latest donation, but of the greater part of his wardrobe. The money had been expended in testing some absurd piece of mechanism, which would not have been of the slightest use had it succeeded; the clothes were left at his last hotel, in pledge for a long bill. Having learned that Agnes had nearly two hundred dollars in her possession, he opposed impertinences to Mr. Milsland's just reproaches, and the consequence was, the latter ordered him out of the house, and he took his wife and child to a hotel. The next heard of him was his playing a star engagement in a small provincial town, and then they lost all trace of him for a couple of months. At the end of that time, Laura received a note from Agnes, begging her to call on her immediately, as she had something of the utmost importance to communicate. Laura went to the address given, and found it a very cheap, dingy boarding-house. Having rung the bell, the servant girl requested her to walk up into the lady's room, which she found to be a small, back room, in which Agnes was sitting, attired in an old silk dress.

"Oh, Laura!" she cried, throwing herself into her arms, "I am so glad you are come, for I know you will help me."

"How, Agnes—are you penniless again?"

"Yes; but that's not what I want to talk to you about. I didn't think that the American people could be so ungrateful to their own talent. If Joseph had come from London now, he would be on the summit of fame and fortune. Now, Laura, you needn't laugh; I hoped you would be above such prejudice. But that's not what I want to say—Laura, I have made up my mind to go on the stage."

"Look here, Aggy; none of that nonsense, or I shall think you are getting ready for Bedlam. Let me see your face. You have not been reading De Quincy or Ludlow, have you? There is no opium or hacheesh about—is there? Come, Aggy, put on your bonnet, if you have one; I insist on your going out to sign the temperance pledge!"

"I don't see why you should sneer at me, Laura, when I am confiding to you the most fixed and dearest purpose of my life. Why should I not go on the stage?"

"One reason is, the extreme opposition you would meet with from your family. What would papa say?"

"I can't help the disapproval of my family; papa despises my husband; told him to his face he was a low-lived scamp, in their last interview; my sisters live in luxury and splendor, and I live in a boarding-house, where the table-cloths alone are enough to make life a burden. My lot is cast with my husband; he is an actor, why should not I be an actress? I'll tell you a secret: I played once with Joseph, while he was starring in the country."

"Indeed—What did you play?"

"'Pauline,' in the 'Lady of Lyons;' and, oh, Laura, I'm sure I'm fitted for the profession; I do love it so much. It's glorious! Joseph says I'll make a splendid Juliet, and I ought to play it in this city."

"Agnes, let me hear you read some of 'Pauline's' part."

7

"Certainly." She began reading some of the most sentimental love speeches, in a high, excited strain, without firmness, ease, accentuation, or proper tone.

"Why, Aggy, it seems to me that you mistake a fondness for love-scenes, which charm you, from their resemblance to your own state of mind, for a love of the dramatic profession. Then your voice is rather shrill and weak."

"Of course it sounds so in a small room, where I have to restrain it; but on the stage it is very different. Indeed, Laura, nothing on earth can prevent my going on the stage, whether you help me or not; only you can make its hardships less to me. I don't see why you should object to that profession, when the one you—— like best belongs to it. That's as good as saying he's beneath you."

"It is nothing of the kind; I think him above me, and every body else in the world; but I fear you are not fitted to succeed on the stage, and it would make poor papa so angry."

"I don't believe it would. I could make money then, and Joseph wouldn't have to worry him. Don't talk to me against it; you can't dissuade me. I take my oath before heaven that nothing shall move me; but it rests with you, sweetest sister, whether I am to make a debut in tawdry rubbish, from a costumer's, or something delicate and gorgeous from your wardrobe. Will you lend me the dresses, Laura? You have so many of them, and in such heavenly taste. Will you, darling? Won't you help your own poor Agnes, who always loved you so dearly?"

"That you always did, Agnes; I wish I could make you understand it is only out of love to you that I oppose you. You are welcome to any, to all of my dresses; I would like to assist you in every way; but the question is, would it not be a cruel kindness,—if by refusing my dresses I could prevent you "—

"But you can't do that; I shall play any way. It is only a question whether my path shall be smoothed or roughened."

"Agnes, give me time to think about it; I will come to you to-morrow; don't urge me any more to-day. Won't you come home to dinner? Where's your baby?"

"Down stairs in the kitchen, with the chambermaid; I have no nurse now. I should be afraid to go home in my present situation. Papa wounds me with his unkind remarks about my Joseph; and then, I have nothing fit to wear."

"The old story,—I have two rich silk dresses at home with the fronts of the waists spotted and stained; but as you are so much smaller than I, you can have a breadth taken out of the skirt and new waists made of them. I will come in the carriage to-morrow, and bring them."

Laura intended to tell her father and sisters the facts of the conversation which had occurred between Agnes and herself; but self-possessed as she generally was, she shrank from disclosing it, and so determined to take the night to consider it. And she absolutely did give up the night to its consideration, for it kept her awake till daylight. As she tossed about from side to side, the subject kept presenting itself in different phases; one moment she resolved to put every obstacle in Agnes' way, to save her in spite of herself; then the possibility that Agnes might really have dramatic talent, would appear to her. On the one side, she summed up her small figure, delicate features, weak voice, want of early training, timidity, and the anger it would call forth from her family; on the other, she placed the recollection of how Agnes had always been fond of reading plays, and how she was very prominent in school tableaux, and was now married to an actor, which actor had a favorable opinion of her powers, and how desperately in earnest she seemed in her determination, and (far above all other arguments, in importance to Laura), how she had appreciated Victor's declamation of tragic verses, in those child-days, when she herself had found in them only matter to laugh at. Laura had a very strong sense of justice, and she desired to give this quality its fullest weight, in taking her own part as regarded Agnes. Personally, it would be a great pain to her to see her favorite sister come before the public as an actress. The usual prejudices against that life were strong in her; she had an undefined belief that all dramatic associations brought a taint with them; the machinery behind the curtain, the wrong side of the scene, was invested, to her, with a mysterious infamy. Even the fact of Victor's belonging to that profession did not redeem it; for to her he seemed to transcend every art, and to justify every thing he touched. But Agnes must be dealt justly with; if clearly the stage was her vocation, no personal objections of her relatives ought to sacrifice her. Thinking of all these things, and mingling with them feverish, saddening thoughts of him who was all to her, and yet to whom she was less than nothing—dozing and starting up with his vexed face bending darkly over her, and then dozing and starting again, until she at last fell into the troubled sleep, more wearying than wakefulness, which had now become habitual to her.

## CHAPTER XII.

At the breakfast table she told her father and the two elder girls of Agnes' wish and decision. As she expected, they met with a perfect storm of disapprobation. Mr. Milsland said Agnes was a heartless, selfish, ungrateful girl; and, in case she should carry out her ignominious intention, declared he would never speak to her again. Even Miriam, usually so neutral as hardly to remind one of her existence, broke out into bitter invectives; while Charley, who always made every matter infinitely worse that she touched, turned, as she usually did, upon her younger sister, saying, in her most irritating manner (and she had carried the power of producing irritation so far that it assumed the proportions of a fine art), "I believe, Laura; this is more than half your fault; you have encouraged Agnes, the stage is your standard of perfection now, since you threw yourself at the feet of an actor, who won't pick you up, but prefers to walk over you."

Mr. Milsland, like an imprudent papa, overlooking the apparent anger produced in Laura by this speech, added, "Yes, it all comes of encouraging that wretched Doria. But how was I to dream that my most intelligent daughter would throw her heart away on the first itinerant who came along!"

"You do not know what you mean by itinerant; your education has been neglected: and as for Charley, she has neither heart nor brains, so it would be useless to ask her for an explanation. They used to call her a dunce in school."

"No danger, at any rate, Miss, of my being called something worse."

"Who is in danger of it, I should like to know, except that every body is liable to be slandered by such a false tongue as yours? What do you mean by your insinuations?" Saying which, Laura approached her as though threatening a personal assault; at which Charley rose up to defend herself, and there is no knowing how it might have terminated, if Mr. Milsland had not interposed his expansive person between them, almost shaking them both, while he said—

"Charlotte, you are to blame for making such an allusion, false as you know it to be. If there were a doubt of its truth, do you suppose this girl, even though she were my best loved child, would sleep under this roof, and eat at this table? There would be no forgiveness for her, if such a thing were so. I would never relent to her; I would let her starve; I would not even give her a grave; she should be buried like a pauper. Never dare to disgrace yourself by bringing up this story again. You first suggested it, or I may say you first fabricated it, so let me hear no more of it." And ending, he almost forced the two girls back into their seats. Miriam broke the awkward silence with, "What did you say to Agnes, Laura, when she told you of this horrid notion?"

"I begged her not to think of it, and tried my best to discourage her."

"Well, just go back to-day," cried Charley, "and do something more than try to discourage her. Tell her it cannot be thought of; tell her we will all renounce her; tell her what an idiot she is."

"I shall do nothing of the kind; you may convey your own insults."

"Now, papa, didn't I say so? Laura has been encouraging her; she thinks my effort to dissuade an insult."

"There was no dissuasion in your language; it was insulting, and I won't take any message to Agnes at all. I tried to do my best, and you've all turned and abused me; so you can settle it among yourselves. I shall not say one word more to Agnes on the subject."

Having said this, she retired from the breakfast-table, leaving her father and sisters secretly to regret that they had lost her invaluable aid in the troublesome case in question. They were well aware that Laura's influence was great over Agnes, but they also knew, that having said she would have nothing more to do with it, she would firmly cling to her decision. So they went to work like three ineffable geese, and produced the most anserine letter among them it was possible to concoct. They loaded Agnes with reproaches, declared they knew Laura to be on her side (a statement which of course at once strengthened Agnes' decision), called her husband a plebean and a rascal, stated that they knew his acquiescence in her project sprang entirely from a wish to humble her family, who would not stoop to consort with him, and from a hope that money might be realized from a public curiosity to see a lady of her former social position degraded into a player (which was entirely correct, but exasperating). It ended with a proposal to Agnes to abandon that vulgar husband, who was unworthy of notice, and return to her father's roof and protection, where she should receive all the rights and privileges of his other children.

It was just the letter to aggravate the husband, and drive a sentimental, loving little wife like Agnes, to extremes. If she had been determined to attempt the stage through a romantic fancy before, she was resolved to it, as a means of vindicating her conjugal allegiance and affection afterwards.

Not long after receiving this letter, she had one from Laura, detailing to her the manner in which she had been assailed at the breakfast-table, for only mentioning the circumstance, and expressing her determination to have nothing more to say about it.

The next day Victor began another engagement, which at once absorbed all Laura's thoughts and desires. Not long after Laura received a note from Agnes, begging her to call on her, as she had something new to communicate. Laura went and found her sister repeating passages from "Juliet," before a looking-glass, with all her hair over her shoulders, and a long shawl confined at her waist, and training down on the floor.

"Oh, Laura," she said, "I am going to play 'Juliet,' this day week, to Victor's 'Romeo,' think of that!"

Laura did think of it, and her first thought, or rather sensation, was a poignant, suffocating pang of jealousy. Her second thought was one of amazement. "Agnes, Agnes, how is that? how did you contrive such an arrangement?"

"Why, Josey and I went to him, and begged him to let me play it. He couldn't realize it at first, but when I persisted, he consented willingly. Josey knew him well; he assisted him when he made his first appearance, so you see it would have been ungrateful in Victor to refuse to oblige him."

The truth was, Joseph had played the part of "Tybalt," on the occasion of Victor's *debut*. During the rehearsal, never having heard his name, he took him for a novice, and treated him with languid contempt. He listened to him with a manner which indicated disgusted weariness, answered him in a tone that was a combination of a mumble and a sniff, appeared to consider the whole thing a trifle below his dignity to recognize at all; in fact, displayed a vulgar assumption of superiority, nowhere to be found in such perfection as in an ignorant, conceited, brainless actor. Victor was so much amused by it, that he did not resent it at all; but he did resent Willister's sycophancy at the end of the first act; his cringing and fawning on him after the audience had almost risen in tumultuous applause, after popular enthusiasm amounted to delirium, till the house fairly reeled, as though shaken with an earthquake of applause.

Agnes had always been a favorite with Victor, and to please her he complied with her request, though he wondered exceedingly at its nature.

Laura recovered her self-possession after a minute or so, and questioned her sister minutely. Agnes replied to everything; but always ended with an entreaty to lend her the dresses necessary for the performance.

"Dear Laura, think what a difference it will make if I can wear some of your dresses, so rich, and in such superb taste. Victor told me to get you to dress me, for you had the finest taste in the world."

"Did he say that?" cried Laura, her thrilled heart sending up bursts of crimson color to her cheeks; "did he indeed say that?" while an emotion of gratitude stirred within her, gratitude for this poor morsel of praise, flung unthinkingly to her who was laying down her youth, her hopes, and her beauty for him.

"He said so, Laura, and you wouldn't like to shame him, by making me play with him in mean clothes; would you? Do you know, light and trifling as he seems, he is very proud and sensitive, and I don't think him heartless after all; he can be very kind and cherishing when he likes."

"Do you think so? Oh, Aggy, I am so troubled; my heart is strangling. Must I die? Ought I to die? I don't want to go into that black, lonely world where he is not. Let me only live in the same world with him, though he never look at me again! And yet, he ought to love me for one brief moment, to teach me how to die; one moment of love, for I feel that I can neither live nor die without it!"

By this time she was almost lying on the floor, with her head in Agnes' lap, and weeping with deep, shuddering sobs.

"Don't cry so; it distresses me to see you suffer."

"Oh, let me suffer in your presence; let my heart bleed before you; don't drive me back to that dreadful silence of all these months."

"But will you not try to conquer it?"

"I have tried; I have done nothing else but try,—but I cannot. I have such a dull, dreadful, eternal pain—oh, what am I to do?—what can I do?"

"I wish our mother were alive; if you only had a mother."

"What could she do for me, when Christ died to save us all, and yet will not save me. What does it mean? Will He never give me rest? Am I to bear my burden on for ever?"

"Oh, my poor sister!"

"I am growing wicked too; I would like to burn up this world, destroy the immortality of the soul, and throw all back into the black depths of chaos."

"Laura, Laura!"

"What have I done to suffer so? Am I outside of God's mercy? I look into that sweet face, stern and relentless only to me, and I see in it a reflection of God's wrath. I was a child, a poor, fond, foolish child, when he stretched out his tender, cherishing arms and took me in; took me out of the world,—and now I cannot live in it; I have no home there,—I'm in a desert, I'm alone, lost, in terror; I—and yet I have done nothing to deserve all this. How can this be? How! When he hates me, is it possible for me to love him so?"

"Oh, Laura, I'm so sorry for you; if I could help you, even by bearing your burdens myself"——

"Yes, you would; you are my only friend; the only one in the world that loves me. Nobody else cares for me. My father reproaches me, my sisters sneer at me, every body else laughs at me. *He* shivers at my touch,—and yet, oh, in those old days how he took me to his breast,—but that's gone for ever. I have no one in the world but you to love me. You shall have my dresses; take anything—all I have. Let them be angry at home; perhaps papa will never forgive me; but what does it matter? I shall not be more miserable; I cannot be. Take all I have; you are my only comfort; my only friend."

She rose as she said this, and wearily resumed her chair. Agnes began to declare that she would not bring trouble upon Laura by wearing her dresses, but she remarked that the latter's head had drooped on her breast, and her eyes were closing in a sleep of weakness and weariness; so Agnes remained silent and sorrowful.

Laura, on returning home, did not acquaint her father and sisters with Agnes' intention; she retained the sullen silence she had previously adopted, leaving them to learn it from the newspapers, which only announced it three days in advance. When Laura's father questioned her about it, she said she knew it from the first, but had no wish to expose herself to further insult, by volunteering the information. Her cold, sneering manner was well calculated to estrange a father whose love for her had already received a deep wound; for had she not taunted him with inferiority to herself, educationally, a subject on which she had always been so tender and respectful hitherto? He thought of it twenty times a day; it rankled in his mind until it laid the foundation of a gradual alienation from her, which was afterwards worked to the most disastrous consequences.

But it was not only her father whom she was estranging by her coldness and indifference, it was every one. She seemed to think, that, being entirely loyal and devoted to one man, she had a right to treat all the rest of the world with chilling arrogance. A mistake; for it would be far safer for a girl to treat the man she loves with arrogance, and all the rest of the world with affability. But Laura was very unwise, very narrow-minded, very self-conscious. She took no pains to please those around her; seldom listened when they tried to interest her; even her kind father, when dissatisfied and displeased with her, she disdained to conciliate; her elder sisters she barely noticed at all. In fact, she was the most painful picture of a proud, willful, chafing, rebellious, tortured, angry spirit, who wore her sorrows like unsheathed daggers, to pierce every one with whom she came in contact.

On the other hand, her family, inadvertently, did everything they could to irritate her already inflamed state of mind; for, themselves of the most mediocre type, they could not conceive of the amount of suffering her deep, misguided nature could swallow up, nor of the extent of those pangs which wrung her great, fond, agonizing soul.

## CHAPTER XIV.

Laura having decided to furnish Agnes with all the paraphernalia of the toilet, for the part of "Juliet," prepared to array her with a delicate splendor and costliness, not as a usual thing considered necessary for the occasion. For "Juliet's" first scene, in which she is supposed to be attired for a ball, she caused a white silk of her own to be elaborately embroidered almost all over in silver lama, and this covered with the most transparent robe of white crape, which chastened the silvery brilliancy, without obscuring it. A fringe of pearl beads edged the crape, and costly pearls were braided in her golden hair, and wreathed around her soft arms and throat. A girdle of pearl beads, strung loosely on a silver thread, so that its faint shimmer gleamed out among them, completed this delicate and sumptuous toilette. The other dresses were of necessity far simpler, but they were equally tasteful and well chosen.

When the day arrived, she ordered some dinner in the early afternoon, and, not liking to ask for the family carriage, procured one from a livery stable, and before six o'clock was on her way to the theatre, having taken Agnes and Willister from their boarding house.

Willister was in admirable spirits, for Victor had offered him the share of the receipts of the evening accruing to himself, and he had most unhesitatingly accepted them. Joseph was in good spirits, for every seat in the house was taken, and he was to have a chance of howling through the short part of "Tybalt," before a select metropolitan audience.

But Agnes' courage was beginning to fail her; she

told Laura, on the way, she wished the theatre would take fire and burn down, before the curtain rose, or that she herself might be blessed with a stroke of apoplexy. Laura, while carefully dressing and beautifying her, was constrained several times to administer small doses of valerian, to keep up her sinking spirits and nervous system. But, at last, three-quarters of an hour too early, she was all dressed, and begged Laura to try and find her husband.

For a minute, or so, Laura wandered about quite aimlessly, in her ignorance of the wings, corridors, dressing-rooms, etc., of a theatre behind the curtains. The newness of the scene quite pleased and interested her, instead of administering that shock and repulsion it is generally supposed to produce on romantic minds. It is the custom to point a perpetual moral with the difference between the right and wrong side of a theatrical display, and to groan over the bare materialism which is concealed behind "the curtain." But is there no right and wrong side to other phases of existence? How many lives are there which have no "curtain" dropped between their inner and outer selves?

Laura, for one, knew the difference between the right and wrong side of a fashionable young woman's life. She was aware of the contrast between that young lady, glittering in silks, jewels, and laces; smiling, reaching after brilliancy in conversation, while playing at happiness in the parlor—and that same young person, behind the scenes in her bed-chamber, angrily snatching the ornaments out of her hair, tearing off her costly garments, and, with them, the mask of gaiety from her face; so, casting off every restraint, till her stormy heart lies bare, to convulse itself with those longings, furies, despairs, from which all description retires in dismay.

She went from one place to another, and finally thought she saw Willister at the end of a passage. On approaching, it proved to be Victor Doria. She asked him where Agnes' husband could be found; and when Victor had told her Willister was not in the theatre for the moment, he offered to go and cheer Agnes up himself. With a cordiality that was new to him, in his treatment of Laura, he drew her hand through his arm, and guided her cheerfully through the half-set scenes, back to whence she came. Poor Agnes was delighted to see him. He soothed, quieted, and invigorated her spirits so quickly, it seemed like magic, stroking her bright hair with such a pitying, protecting look, as he might have cast upon a guileless child, about to pass through an ordeal of suffering. He seemed to lift her right out of her despondency, and hold her away from fear, with his warm, impulsive hands. And Laura, with a wistful look in her hungry eyes, gazed on, and felt grateful to him; and yet, she was envious; yet, the keen arrow of jealousy whizzed through her breast, leaving in its train a dull, bitter, aching sensation. Only for a moment though, for Laura's faults were mainly at the surface; at heart, she was a good and thoroughly kind girl. So, after the first sharp, jealous pang had passed by, she felt nothing but gratitude for his kindness to her sister.

After a few minutes, Willister came in, dressed for "Tybalt," and, with his lavish use of India ink and vermillion, he had brought his face up to a vulgar showiness, which made Laura shudder, but only elicited the admiration of Agnes, whose vision was so sharpened by her love, that she could find beauty in this face, where her sister could only blush for its vulgarity.

While the husband and wife were talking together,

Laura wandered out into the wings, listening to the orchestra, which was now sending forth its premonitory strains. The employées of the theatre looked curiously upon this very beautiful and elegantly attired lady, but did not disturb her, when she took possession of a battered chair, and settled herself in a corner. As soon as the overture was finished, she ran back to Agnes, and found her in the green-room, where Willister had indiscreetly taken her. There the young ladies of the ballet, supposed to be the august guests of the house of " Capulet," stood, dizzened out in tarleton and much cheap, tarnished finery. There, also, was "Juliet's" lady mother, attired in a rusty cotton-velvet dress, with huge and horrible triangles of coarse crochet sewn up the waist and front of the skirt, and with a miscellaneous jumble of emaciated wax beads, sprinkled all over her. The "nurse," too, loomed up among them, in monstrous cap and pre-Raphaelite gown. They were all staring at the shrinking debutant, with eyes of curious contempt and dismaying pity. It occurred to Laura, as she looked on this scene, that all these people were simply sapping Agnes of the little vitality and courage that remained to her. In her annoyance at this thought, she swept them all over with her proud, steady eyes, till before that high-blooded, aristocratic face and magnificently simple toilette (which was only a grey silk dress, having a deep flounce of chantilly lace festooned about it; a shawl of the latter, and a bonnet of point-lace, with a small cluster of scarlet flowers in front), these bold, dissecting glances fell. The two sisters were standing together in agitated silence, when the call-boy came to warn "Juliet" that her time had come, at which Laura, losing all self-possession, threw her arms wildly about Agnes' neck, almost crushing her with their strength, and would not, would not let her go. But Victor, who had stepped quietly in after Laura, with his keen perception, seeing that nothing would influence her but a stronger feeling, gently, but firmly, unlocked her arms, gave Agnes to her husband, and himself led Laura back to the dressing-room, putting her in a chair, and talking to her on indifferent subjects, in a low, soothing tone, till she was as calm as a baby on its mother's breast. No man could be kinder and more helpful than Victor, when he was in the mood, and at this moment he was putting forth all the tact and delicate discrimination in which he was so rich. It was not long before the exigencies of the drama demanded his services; but when he left Laura, she felt as though all the sedative remedies in nature had been applied to her fevered mind. By the time the balcony scene was set, she felt quite able to go and watch it from the wings. Poor Agnes looked like an angel in her balcony. Judging from her appearance, it ought not to have surprised people if she had spread her wings and soared up to heaven before their eyes. But when she came to speak, her feeble, high-pitched, untutored voice brought her down to earth again. Oh! how her voice contrasted, in Laura's sensitive ear, with Victor's ripe, mellow, dewy tones. Agnes seemed to think that expression was to be conveyed only by protracting her words, and intensity by speaking in as high a key as possible. Besides, she scarcely looked at Victor, while Laura thought, when he stretched up his lithe, supple arms to his "Juliet," and his lingering eyes swam with unspeakable tenderness over her face, and every word he uttered was as round and deep as notes from a skilfully touched organ; had she been there, he would have quite blotted out for her all that sea of blank, meaningless faces beyond.

At the end of this act, Agnes received a recall and quite a profusion of choice bouquets, probably as a compliment from her former friends.

Act by act she weakened and grew shriller, until at last Victor was obliged to cover her palpable defects with all manner of ingenuities.

She had all the intelligence and enthusiasm necessary for the dramatic profession, but she was quite ignorant of the way in which these qualities were translated into visible signs. She was like a person penetrated with natural love for music, suddenly brought before a piano for the first time, and trying to pick out melody from a keyboard, of whose use even, she was ignorant. Of all the fine arts, the drama is the one where improvisation in the first place, is most unlikely. The utmost dramatic talent is at first but a helpless ball, and experience and self-possession together make up the propulsive force which impels it to its aim.

Between the fourth and fifth acts, Victor came up to Laura, drew her hand within his arm, and walking up and down with her, told her Agnes must not dream of attempting to appear in that city again. If she resolved to continue in the theatrical profession, she should be advised to go with her husband to the smallest provincial theatres.

"But I would," he added, "try to persuade her to renounce the idea; she is too delicate, too sensitive, too yielding, for it. She has neither the force of character nor fixedness of purpose necessary for it; her extremely delicate beauty, both of face and disposition, would shut her out from broad comedy, and the same thing, coupled with her petite figure, would close the doors of tragedy upon her. Nothing then would remain to her but sentimental parts, and she has not the necessary individuality to color them and raise them out of insipidity. Now, if you wished to try the stage, it would be very different,—every part you touched would be your own; besides, your appearance would carry everything before it. But your sister Agnes is such a sweet little creature at home, so domestic a woman, so affectionate a wife, and such a cunning little mother, that it makes my heart ache to see her cast herself like a fragile porcelain cup on a stream which is full of vessels of iron and brass. You now would be like a diamond, more brilliant and beautiful than any of them; but still with solid power of resistance that would be far more likely to break other vessels than to be broken by them. Try and convince Agnes, won't you?"

"I will give all my powers to it. How strange it seems to hear you speak of me as being so strong, when I know myself to be so weak!"

"Yes, it is strange, that misdirected strength will often show itself like weakness. Are you not well?—you have looked pale lately," and he dropped his wildering eyes down her face with a curious psychological glance.

"Have I? I have not been ill. I'm always well; but often tired." The perceptibly worn look in all her features proved only too well the truth of her words; but Victor seemed to be considering them, for his eyes, now half extinguished in their drooping lids, still languished up and down her face. They wandered to and fro in silence—he seemed to be dreaming; but he never allowed her long-floating dress to catch in any of the irregular ends and angles by which they were surrounded. He was one of the men who could not be guilty of an awkwardness, even though he were asleep. He never committed a blunder, never trod on a lady's dress, or knocked anything down, or stumbled, or dropped anything. A natural tact took care of him in all these things, almost without his knowledge.

As Laura walked beside him she felt the button of her shoe give way. Afraid of losing it, for it was of pale, costly coral, and loosely put on, she took a seat, and turning her back, prepared to adjust it. But quicker than thought, before she had time to touch it, he was on his knees, had taken the little foot in his hand, clasped the button, and pressed the foot lingeringly to his lips. The next moment he was called to the scene, and still sitting there with that foot throbbing so that her heart seemed to have slipped down into it, she heard his clear, penetrative tones, tincturing the air with sweetness.

When the play was over, she undressed and dressed Agnes, and hurried her into the carriage, like one nearer to death than life. On the way home, Willister was rejoicing over the "high figure" to which the receipts had mounted.

"What is that to you?" said Laura.

"Everything; Doria gave me his 'sharing terms' for the night."

"Surely, you did not accept them?"

"To be sure I did. Wasn't Ag to have anything for her services? She drew the house."

"Mr. Willister, you know that Agnes was only permitted to play as a kindness, and the houses have always been crowded when Mr. Doria played here. I shall be excessively, unspeakably mortified if you take advantage of his generosity and accept his receipts for the night. The dresses and ornaments that my sister wore to-night, belong to me; take them, jewelry and all, and dispose of them; they will certainly bring much more than the sum you would receive from him. Take them, and if you have the least consideration for me, or respect for your wife, refuse to accept Victor's offer."

Willister thanked her, and kept the costumes, but he went next morning and got Victor's money from the theatre, all the same.

After this, neither of them spoke for a moment, and then he began to reproach his wife for not having followed his directions in her playing; reproaching and uselessly arguing with her, while Laura leaned back and closed her eyes, and was silent. Things had gone so softly for her to-night, who will blame her if her heart put forth one slender shoot of hope! But it fell off like a poor little bud withered by untimely frosts,—except on the stage or in the street, she never saw Victor again before his return to Europe, at the close of his engagement. More than a year had elapsed since her first interview with him in the city, but during all the year, that was the only time he ever voluntarily touched her, or gave the slightest recognition to her attractions.

## CHAPTER XV.

Mr. Milsland was more than vexed at the circumstance of his daughter's appearance on the stage; he was hurt, mortified, and permanently depressed by it. Laura's conduct, in providing Agnes with the dresses, and accompanying her to the theatre, he considered as a direct defiance of his will and wishes. He regarded it as a violation of filial respect and obedience, and was convinced that she had encouraged and sustained Agnes in the act, even if she had not suggested it to her.

When he charged her with it, the next day, she listened to him in the kind of scornful indifference which had recently become her habitual manner: "I am not responsible for my sister's actions."

"You are, in a manner; you had such influence over her, you might have prevented her taking the step."

"I could prevent nothing; I have no influence over any one."

"You furnished her with the dresses, and took her there."

"She would have got there without me; and if she was determined to play, I wouldn't see her play in second-handed rags."

"That was just your blind folly. If she insisted upon placing herself in such a position, the more marked the disapproval of her relatives, the better. To go there with her yourself, and array her in finery, which she could not have procured without your assistance, was almost a public way of justifying her act."

"That is where I differ from you in opinion; and, since we do differ, I don't see that there is any more to be said about it."

"But there is more to be said about it; you seem to forget, you are speaking to your father!"

"No; why should I forget it?" in a weary, gloomy tone, looking out of the window, as if it was too much to expect that she should fix her attention upon the subject.

"Because you are an unkind, ungrateful daughter."

"How am I that?"

"You seem to have entirely forgotten, it was I who brought you up from babyhood."

"Then, I wish you hadn't; I wish you had been kind enough to strangle me, before I came out of my cradle."

"What do you complain of—have you not a good father, sisters, a luxurious home, and every conceivable comfort?"

"I suppose so—but it's no matter."

"Exactly so; you make no more matter of us, than if we were so many puppets."

"If you wish me to understand you, you will have to explain yourself; if not, it is of no consequence."

"You may find it to be of some consequence, before it ends. For, I tell you, once for all, I will not tolerate your conduct much longer. I have done for you every thing an affectionate father could do; given you the most thorough education, left my old home, and come to a strange city, at your instance; borne with all your whims and caprices, allowed you to squander money in a way that you will do no more."

"Didn't you say, my uncle's property would come to me?"

"Only if I willed it so. I begin to think I was too hasty in that decision. I doubt whether it would be wise to entrust a large sum into your hands. I am afraid it would be spent in a very unworthy way—buying theatrical gew-gaws and rubbish, for instance."

"That remark is not worth answering."

"To be sure not; nothing that your father says is worth answering. Perhaps you will think it worthy of consideration if I inform you that, should you desire to form any justly grounded expectations of inheriting any undue proportion of your uncle's fortune, your conduct must change, must very materially change for the better, in the future."

"Am I to consider that in the light of a threat?"

"Consider it as you please—sit down, sit down, I say; I have more to say."

"Excuse me; I thought from the tenor of your last remark, this very delectable conversation had come to an end."

"I tell you, I will have your conduct changed. What is the matter with you? Why do you treat me so? You used to be the most affectionate, respectful little girl in the world, and such a precious comfort to me. Now you seem to despise your father. You are ashamed of him in the gay world, to which you have so readily accommodated yourself. I may not be wise; you taunted me the other day with a lack of education, but I know enough to see you no longer love me."

"Oh! yes, I do; yes, I do; try to believe that I do. I don't know myself what has come over me; you cannot conceive how every thing wearies and sickens me. I am not myself now, but the feeling will pass away in time. If you could only wait, and trust me."

"I will. Now you speak like my Laura again. And you don't look well; had you not better see a doctor?"

"Oh, no; no doctor could help me; I must fight my own way through. I shall come out victorious, or I shall die, one or the other; sometimes I don't care which."

"Why, Laura, what have you got to trouble you so? I know of but one thing to produce such a state of mind—secret remorse."

"Remorse for what?"

"I don't know."

"Neither do I, unless it be for having permitted myself to be created. Not being guilty of that unfortunate circumstance, I am not guilty of my own suffering—the one springs immediately from the other."

"I don't understand that."

"Don't try, then; let us be good friends, without entirely understanding one another. I do love you."

"You seem to look upon me as not worthy of an explanation; why cannot I understand my own child?"

"Because your own child does not understand herself."

"I know more than you think I do. Charley tells me every body is talking about your love for Victor Doria, an actor, a painted stroller, and one who will not accept your love."

"Charley is an idiot; besides, she is as mean and treacherous as a monkey."

"A very improper way, it seems to me, to speak of your elder sister. She may not have quite so much useless book-learning, or so many big words at her finger-ends, as you have; but at least she knows how to conduct herself decently, and without shaming her family."

"Which means to say that I don't. Very well, if you are so perfectly satisfied of my iniquities, what's the use of arguing about it? have it as you choose. I shall not take the trouble to defend myself."

"Where do you meet this infernal scoundrel—this actor?"

"In your parlor, and those of my acquaintances."

"Was he not at the theatre the other night?"

"Wonderful, as it may seem, he was; but his appearance was not unconnected with the trifling part of 'Romeo.'"

"Did you not familiarly converse with him?"

"Not more familiarly than at Dorn, under your own eyes."

"Can you deny that you love him?"

"No."

"And are you not ashamed to confess it?"

"More angry than ashamed,—if one of us two has cause to be ashamed of it, it is not I."

"You can't mean that I have been to blame in the matter."

"Yes, I do."

"How am I concerned in it at all?"

"This is how you are concerned. He came to Dorn when I was fifteen years of age; for some reason, noticed me, singled me out for his attentions, flattered, conciliated, followed, wooed, won me. You looked on, and never put forth a hand to help me."

"How could I suppose that my daughter would fall in love with an itinerant player?"

"How could you suppose I could do anything else than worship the gloves he wore out and threw away. What had I seen in the way of a man before? And yet just at the most impressionable time of my life, you saw me thrown into the society of a man of genius, handsome, young, graceful, tender, passionate, and for some inexplicable reason, attracted to me. Did you put out a finger to save me? Did you not see me like a frail, unfinished boat, drift out straight to the great mysterious waters, and not lift a finger to save me?"

"But an actor, a"—

"Yes, one who lived by the cultivation of grace, tact, eloquence, memory, sentiment, and intelligence; one on whose passionate, impressive words thousands had hung enraptured, and who charmed by his delicacy, agitated by his impulse, and drew tears by his pathos, from wise and cultured audiences. How marvellous that he was able to move one poor, witless—I may say friendless girl (for no friend interposed to save me). You saw him take all the fire of that rich, organization, that subtle, delicate genius, and bring it to bear in one intense focus on me, and you wonder that I was scorched by it. The only wonder is that I am here at all; I ought to have crumbled into ashes long ago."

"But what,—I scarcely understand you—what can I do?"

"You can let me alone. I am struggling to save myself from an abyss, and you reproach me because I do not go through all the antics of ceremony on its brink. Don't you see that my soul is vexed almost to death? If you cannot help me, let me alone. If I do not please you in everything, bear with me. If I am peevish, irritable, sullen, bear with me! Let your hands deal tenderly with me, for God's hand bears upon me, heavy with the weight of an eternal no! Let me seem strange, let me be inexplicable, remember it is all comprehended in this—I am working out my own salvation in fear and trembling!"

## CHAPTER XVI.

MR. MILSLAND was very much touched by his daughter's words. Probably they would have returned to their old affectionate relations, if it had not been for Charley's influence. Listening at the door, while the conversation just related was taking place, she heard every word of it, and made a cunning use of it to Laura's disadvantage.

Charley had never loved Laura, and perhaps she was not altogether to blame for it. Though the eldest of the four sisters, she had always seen the youngest of them all preferred above her, consulted before her, quoted to her, and in school, held up as a perpetual example to humble and shame her. Charley was an incredibly dull girl at her books, but her younger sister, instead of assisting and sympathising with her, showed plainly that she looked down upon her. Released from school, it was Laura whom her father idolized, Laura who won her uncle's heart, Laura whom all the gentlemen admired and courted, Laura who was allowed unlimited credit at the milliner's, and finally, Laura was the presumptuous heiress of the bulk of her father's present property. At his death the other girls would have barely an income sufficient to live upon; but Laura would be very rich. As if this was not enough to drive any envious, intriguing mind to madness, it had all culminated in the only man who had ever moved Charley's heart, being at the moment visibly enamored of Laura. This was a lieutenant in the navy, a certain Paul Elphinstone; a man exactly to Charley's taste, and an object of unmitigated contempt to Laura. But like many men from whose composition the perceptive faculties seem to be entirely left out, he went on forcing his attentions upon Laura, never seeming to notice the scorn which she lavished upon him. In one way this was partly Laura's fault; she made herself so repulsive by her manners that nothing remained but her rich, voluptuous beauty, which thus called forth only the lower forms of love. One day the determined lieutenant managed to see her alone, and detain her in spite of herself. With the look of a conquering hero he cried, "No, no, Miss Laura, you can't run away; don't be frightened. I have nothing to say to you that could frighten you."

"Nothing that you could say, could ever do anything but tire me."

"Cruel beauty, you know I love you; don't you?"

"Your question is not worth answering."

"Not if I ask you to marry me, to be my wife?"

"In that case, I regret that our language does not permit me to use more than one negative in the same sentence, for I feel that one is too weak to carry the strength of my refusal."

"I'm not offended with you, poor girl; I know what leads you to refuse me; but be assured I am willing to forgive past mistakes, bury past errors, overlook past attachments. It is only in the future that I shall take the liberty of being jealous of my beautiful Laura. Come, is it all settled?"

"It is quite settled to my mind, that you are neither a man nor a gentleman."

"That's rather strong language, Miss Milsland. I beg to know what it may mean?"

"It means that for the last five weeks you have been forcing attentions upon me that were perceptibly disagreeable, and have now, in spite of my evident wish to the contrary, compelled me to listen to an offer of marriage as offensive in manner as in matter to me. You have used language which no gentleman ever uses to a lady, and not even a creature as contemptible as you, shall use to me. I beg that you will excuse me, sir," and she swept from the room like an Até, leaving Elphinstone almost stupified with mingled surprise and anger. He went from the house registering a vow to have his revenge, to humble her at some time, as she had humbled him.

In the meanwhile, Laura sank lower and lower every day. It was almost insufferable to live in the house of which she tempered the atmosphere. All gaiety, cheerfulness, and content seemed banished from it, and nothing but sullenness, discontent, bitterness, and contention of spirit held possession of it, from morning to night. If Laura had been a little woman, or a less imposingly splendid woman, or one of a feebler character, she might have been neutralized or moderated in some way; but what were a father and two sisters, none of them large in the intellectual regions, nor overfavored in "managing" powers, to do with this Cleopatra turned into a Niobe; this magnificent Nemesis, who turned the whole play of life into a grand, gloomy tragedy; who distributed misery even in the rustle of her flowing robes; who filled up the whole house, and turned it into a "moated grange." Mr. Milsland was weary of it, the girls found it intolerable, and the servants marveled over it in the kitchen. Visitors stood in awe of Laura, and whispered harsh comments behind her back. She was herself alienating all her friends, and sowing the seeds of enmity broadcast. Of these the most cunning and determined was Lieut. Elphinstone, who, for a while, disappeared, and then returned, gradually establishing himself as the admirer of Charley. When proposed to Mr. Milsland, as a son-in-law, the latter gladly accepted him. After Agnes' marriage to Willister, and Laura's unfortunate attachment to Doria, an officer of the navy, who was well born, even though he had nothing but his pay, seemed to him a most desirable party. Charley did not require much pressing to make her name the earliest possible day; so, in the course of less than two months, she went to church, with Laura and Miriam for bridesmaids. Then, the newly-made husband, being on leave of absence, became an inmate of Mr. Milsland's house, and set himself earnestly to work to undermine the intentions of his father-in-law, as to leaving Laura his fortune, impelled to the task both from revenge and self-interest. At first he only determined to induce Mr. Milsland to leave a will equally in favor of the three sisters.

Elphinstone succeeded far more rapidly than he had expected. For a long time deprived of his greatest pleasure, that of being kindly influenced by a will stronger than his, Mr. Milsland seized upon his son-in-law's guidance with delight. If there was one privilege on earth he was desirous of getting rid of, it was the right of private judgment. The Lieutenant, assisted by his wife, soon read his father-in-law's character, and managed him with a shrewd cleverness and cunning. He flattered him, while he saved him the right to think for himself; deferred to him, while he was actually drugging him with ready-made opinions. At the same time, he was always neatly goading Laura on, to make herself intolerable to her father, and then he seemed to step in and interpose himself between them, soothing the father, and still more completely irritating the daughter.

Charley's feelings to Laura would have softened after her marriage, had she not seen her husband still visibly attracted by Laura's charms. Half of the time, he called his wife Laura, and then blushed a dull, dark red when she looked astonished at him. When Laura was in the room, he was never easy; he was always moving about and knitting his brows, and when she was absent, sometimes he used to vow, with an almost fiendish look on his face, that he would "be even with her yet." All this Charley understood, and it only added sharp jealousy to the other unkind feelings with which she regarded her sister. It heightened the feelings with which she desired an alteration in her father's will; for what other hope had she of retaining any place in her husband's thoughts, unless she could acquire a distinct financial value. Elphinstone desired the same thing, partly to reduce Laura's fortune, parlty to increase his own; but the unholy sentiment with which she inspired him, almost to madness, finally suggested a still more comprehensive play. Why not work to make Mr. Milsland exclude Laura entirely from his will, and leave her to the charge of himself? Why could he not persuade the father that this was not only the justest, but the safest way to order things after his death? In this attempt he was most ably seconded by Laura herself. Just at this time, she was approaching the turning point, the darkest period of her life, when either she would sink down raving, despairing, and be swallowed up in the quicksand of utter darkness, or the light would begin to break upon her, and the day-star to tremble up the sky, ushering in a new dawn. At this moment, when she was tossed about in whirlwinds, dragged through storms, immersed in desert seas, brought to that extreme of doubt when nothing seemed to have any reality but evil and pain and malignant exultation in pain; at this moment, when her very soul seemed to be darkened with the passion of death, Elphinstone brought her into direct antagonism with her father.

Her father certainly chafed and wounded her dreadfully; but, on her part, she acted almost like a demon. Her father swore, if this continued, he would place her in a mad-house; and she retorted, before he did that, she would kill him, or herself, and the dangerous gleam in her eye, as she spoke, was actually paracidal. That closed the interview, and was the crisis of Laura's fate; from that hour her state of mind began to change for the better.

As she lay in her bed that night, she remembered her angry threat to her father, and longed to tell him how she regretted it. The wish dwelt with her all night, and it brought softer tears to her eyes than they had wept since the evening when she first saw Victor play.

In the morning, her father did not appear at breakfast, and, as Elphinstone was there, she did not like to show that she was concerned by it. She hardly knew what to do with herself, so she spent the morning writing to Agnes, who, a short time after her appearance on the stage, had received five thousand dollars from her father, in exchange for a solemn oath never to repeat the experiment. Willister had been made to understand it was the last penny they would ever receive from him, and, accordingly, thinking there was nothing more to be gained by remaining, removed with his wife and child to the West. This had happened six months ago, and from the tenor of Agnes' letters to her sister, there seemed to be no appearance of an attempt at entering into any business, on the part of her husband, from which Laura argued that he was again illustrating his own capacity for absorbing money, and having nothing to show for it. Agnes' last letter revealed, moreover, the fact that he was growing less kind to her than formerly, in fact, decidedly indifferent and neglectful; besides, her own health was failing, and her little girl was exhibiting symptoms of morbid delicacy of constitution. This letter Laura had allowed to lie unanswered for two weeks; to-day the sight of it smote her heart with regretful pity. But the whole aspect of life seemed changed from what it was a week, a month ago; she felt as if she had passed through a second birth, and was about to commence life over again. She began it by writing a long, tender, sad, consoling letter to her sister. It gave a passing picture of her life for the last sombre half year; is was tinctured with self-accusations and melancholy regrets, and it entered minutely into her sister's case, both as to sympathy and advice.

After finishing this letter, she busied herself in writing other ones, and in setting her desk and papers in order, which she had neglected for so long a time. Not caring for any luncheon, she had a cup of tea in her own room, and then lay down and fell asleep. When she awoke, it was within a half hour of the dinner-time; so, determined not to be late, as she usually was, she carefully attired herself and went down. In the parlor she found her two sisters, and brother-in-law; to Miriam she spoke.

"Is papa down yet?"

Elphinstone immediately replied: "After the shock he suffered yesterday we do not expect him down for several days. We dread to have him encounter a similar one."

"I did not speak to you, sir."

"I am aware of it; but, under the circumstances, we think it better that you should not communicate with your sisters just at present."

"Whom do you designate by we?"

"Myself, your father, and sisters."

"Is this so?" she said, appealing to the young ladies.

Miriam replied only by a troubled, wistful glance, but Charley answered a scornful "Yes."

The new-born spirit of repentance and gentleness in Laura's breast was quite overpowered for the time with the old evil, so she returned them scorn for scorn, and when the dinner was announced, went in and awed them all by her imperious willfulness and arrogance. Every now and then she caught Miriam stealing a frightened, guilty glance at her, which convinced her there was something to her injury being concealed from her. But, too disdainful to question, and too proud to let them know she was annoyed, she continued to bear herself as though utterly indifferent to what was passing around her. But she could not help feeling that the manner in which Elphinstone regarded her was exceptionably repulsive. And so it was, for this is the way in which his thoughts ran. "What a delicious vixen she is, to be sure! If I only could succeed in making her father disinherit her, will she not be at my mercy? Used to the gratification of every expensive taste, the want of money will bring her to the dust at once. Then, she must look to me for every thing; my hand must dispense to her every luxury. They say women are like spaniels, ready to caress the hand that beats—and feeds them. She is not lost to me yet. If the property all comes into my grasp, why may I not fly with her? the world is wide enough to enjoy oneself in. But when I am tired of her, sated with her proud beauty, then I can have my revenge for her disdain—I can spurn her, as she spurned me."

The next day and the day after, Laura did not once inquire for her father, though she longed to know if he continued ill, and to go to him. But false pride still lingered in her breast, and made her satisfy herself with —"if he wants me he can send for me." The next day, no longer able to restrain herself, she wrote him a note, saying how deeply sorry she was for her unfilial conduct, and asking to be permitted to see him. No answer came, for of course the letter was not permitted to reach him. Next day she wrote a still more humble and affectionate letter, begging him to see her out of pity, for she could never rest until she was forgiven. Again she wrote, making one more appeal, and stating that it would be her last. The foolish girl never seemed to dream that these letters did not get to her father, but concluding that he had hardened his heart against her, resolved to supplicate him no more.

Day followed day, until more than a week had passed since she parted with her father. Laura struggled hard to keep her courage up, and sustain the pretence of indifference, but it was a trying ordeal. The most careless eye would have seen how ill she was looking, for the brightest part of her beauty was quite extinguished in the swarthy pallor of her skin, and the sunken, hollow look of her eyes.

Laura was essentially a very self-conscious mind—she had no ability to throw off her cares in occupation or amusement; every thing that excited her only rendered them more poignant. To analyze her feelings, and in so doing additionally irritate and inflame them, to brood like a great insatiable vulture over her own heart, and forever tear it to pieces, was the unhappy nature which had been given to her. Now she was suffering from the keenest pang, with the exception of passionate jealousy, possible to the human heart—remorse. It may be inferred that all her powers of self-torture were fully brought into play, and that not one phase of anguish her ingenuity could devise, was spared to her.

While she was in this deplorable state, both of body and mind, she one day encountered on the stairway, the family physician. She was about to stand aside and let him pass, when a sudden determination moved her to say, "Oh, doctor, do you come to see my father—is he ill?"

"Quite ill, Miss Laura; and you will pardon me if I use the privilege of old friendship and say, that in my frequent visits here, I have been astonished never to meet you in his room, especially last evening when he was really in a critical state; and though he begged piteously to see you, you refused to come."

All the while he was saying this to Laura, she was looking at him with a confused, stony stare, as if she only half understood him, and wholly disbelieved him.

"Ill, you say, in a critical state, begging for me, and I refusing to come to him! I don't understand one word of it all. Dr. Archer, I know I am a wicked girl, an unnatural daughter, but how dare you think me such an utterly inhuman beast as that?"

"I had no occasion to form any opinion; I heard your brother-in-law tell your father you would not come to him, unless you were perfectly satisfied about the will."

"The will, what will? I know nothing about a will."

"Your father's will, of course; perhaps you think you have a right to the whole property; and yet it seemed cruel to think of that, when your father might die at any moment."

"I think I understand it now. I see why my sister's husband wishes to separate me from my father; it was to get Charley an equal share in the property. And what do I care if he does; there's enough for us both if it is divided, and for Miriam too; money will never be of any great use to me again. It is of no matter to me if he has altered his will. But will you take me to my father this minute, doctor? for I see now, they will try to keep me out."

"To be sure I will; the sight of you will be the best medicine for him. Come."

At the door of her father's room Elphinstone refused to allow her to enter, declaring that her father said it would kill him to see her. The doctor was beginning to remonstrate, but Laura had not lost all the muscular strength of her arms yet, so she simply took suddenly hold of her brother-in-law, dragged him out of the way, and rushed to throw herself by her father's bed-side.

Mr. Milsland was asleep, but the noise awakened him, and the first thing he saw was his daughter on her knees beside him. "So you have come at last," he said with a look in which joy and displeasure were strangely mingled: "to what am I indebted for your late compliance with my wishes? I have not acceded to your demands about the inheritance."

"Why, papa, I wanted to come so much, but they told me you would not see me—could not bear to look at me; and I did not wonder at that. Now, I hope, I think, when you know how bitterly I repent of my wickedness, you will forgive me. But, papa, why did you scorn my poor little letters? They told you how sorry I was."

"Letters! I have seen no letters. Who did you send them by?"

"By Jane, the chambermaid."

"And did you not ask her what I said, and why I didn't answer them?"

"No; I didn't want her to know how anxious I was. I was ashamed to seem anything but perfectly indifferent about them."

Jane was called, and said Miss Laura had certainly given her three letters for Mr. Milsland; but as she seemed nowise particular about them, she thought they were bills, and handed them to Mr. Elphinstone, who said it was all right. Elphinstone was then called, but the servants below said he had gone down town, and would not be at home till dinner time. But Laura having reminded her father that he could not accuse her of ever uttering an untruth, he was soon brought to allow himself the pleasure of believing her.

"And so you were sorry you treated your father unkindly, and wanted to tell him so after all."

"Oh, yes; and wicked as I was, I have been punished for it. You can't think how miserable I have been. I don't know which was the greatest, my wickedness or my misery. But won't you try to forget all about it? I am going to be such a different girl for the future. You know I used to be so selfish. I thought I had a right to extract happiness out of the world, and because I failed in that, I tried to make every body as unhappy as myself. But I am quite changed; I don't feel so bitterly now. And I see that all my troubles sprang from my own faults. A girl must not think she can take life by the throat, and choke her own wishes out of it. Must she, papa?"

"No, my child; I suppose she couldn't exactly manage that."

"But, papa, you'll give me another chance—won't you? and you'll see what a good girl I mean to be; and you know I do love you, dearly love you."

"I always thought so, my daughter, until you said"—

"Don't, papa; don't," she cried, and put her hand up as if to ward off a blow; "never say those words I spoke again, for I don't think I am well, and they make me feel so sick, I don't think I could bear to hear them."

"You don't look well, Laura; indeed you are very pale. Why, what has changed you so in these few days?"

"Nothing but fretting; and you know I deserved to fret."

"And yet you went every evening to parties and places of amusement."

"I? Never; I haven't left the house since you were ill. What made you think that?"

"I was told so."

"By that viper, Paul Elphinstone?"

"Laura, do not speak so of your sister's husband. True, he has persuaded me to make a new will; but I thought him right as long as I believed you perfectly hard and impenitent towards me, and unwilling to approach me in my illness, unless the fullest pecuniary benefits were guaranteed to you. I feared it would be dangerous, wicked, to put such a sum untrammelled into your hands."

"I don't care anything about the property; I want to be on my old terms with you,—and what good friends we used to be! Besides, what does it matter about a will? you are to get well immediately, and very likely live eighty years yet."

"I hope I shall get well; but I am afraid I shall never be so strong again."

"Oh, yes, you shall; we'll go up to Dorn, and drink some of the mineral waters; they ought to cure any thing. They are mixed up enough to meet the requirements of any disorder."

"I would like to go to Dorn; but I won't drink any of that rubbish. But I am afraid you'd find it very dull there; no parties, no opera, no theatre, no matinees, no visitings"—

"What do I care for any of those—what good have they done me? You'll see whether I'll find it dull or not. I'll take up all my old accomplishments. My swimming is very rusty; for what really good practice can you get at Newport and Long Branch? as for rowing, I'm afraid one mile will tire me. Climbing is hopeless—it's a lost art; I'm too big now; I weigh too much—the trees wouldn't stand it. I believe you're laughing at me."

"I'm laughing out of joy, to see you like your old self again."

"Yes, I'm going to be a good girl now, and I'm so happy you've forgiven me, and I needn't feel like a monster any more."

"Laura, I am not sure you were altogether to blame. I know I was unkind of you, and it seemed to be as if some outside influence was working upon me, to make me continually anger you and outrage your feelings."

"Don't say that; it was all, entirely, totally my fault, the fruit of my dense self-love and obstinacy," cried Laura, who, never able to go half-way in any thing, having begun to reproach herself, necessarily went to the utmost limit of self-accusation and self-disgust.

"I'm not so sure of that; and after all, a will made is as easily destroyed as "—

"Pray, let that bugbear of a will alone; let it stay as it is. I'm satisfied."

"Do you mean to say you are satisfied with it—do you know its tenor?"

"Yes; the doctor told me all about it, and I'm quite content with it. For heaven's sake, let us hear no more about it."

"But you have no love for Paul. Can you trust "—

"I can trust him as far as that. Let him have the money he covets."

"We'll talk of this again, dear child; you always did run into extremes. There is such a thing as too great self-sacrifice—and I think this is an instance of it."

"Think what you like, but promise me to say nothing more about it to-day."

"Agreed; but you must try and be on good terms with your sisters, Laura; you know they have your good at heart, even when they seem most harsh."

"I hope so; I will be only too happy to be reconciled to them; and I believe after all, our troubles sprang from my being so proud and conceited. We'll get along far more pleasantly now. See if we don't, for I'm going to treat them like sisters, not like inferiors. I'll go and find them now."

## CHAPTER XVII.

AFTER this, notwithstanding the remonstrances of both Charley and her husband, Laura continued to remain, almost continually, beside her father. But, though they could not succeed in banishing her, they did succeed in arousing her worst feelings in his presence. The transformation of character, after all, is gradual. Whatever may be the real change in the heart, old habits will continue to assert themselves long after they have any vital connection with the feelings. And, therefore, though our poor Laura had actually passed through that mysterious process, fitly described as "second birth," yet much of the leaven of her old nature remained on the surface, and was easily fermented into painful exhibitions. The old habits of bold self-assertion, domineering willfulness, and explosive temper, were easily raised to an ephemeral life by the cunning hands of her brother-in-law. Perfectly cool, phlegmatic, and undisturbed by the possession of an emotional nature, he always had the advantage of Laura in any contest. For, while he remained quiet, calm, and seemingly just and patient, she, with her sensitive, nervous organization, and the fiery blood which rushed to her face and drowned it in a purple suffusion, had the appearance of being ill-tempered, reckless, and even malignant. After such a quarrel, he was always able to tell her he was sorry he had angered her so, would advise her to restrain herself, for the sake of her health, and hoped they would understand one another better, and be truer friends in the future. It did not mend the matter much for Laura to show the reaction of such ebulitions, by throwing herself on her knees and weeping bitter, burning tears. Common-place people are instinctively suspicious of exceptionable dispositions. Used to a straight pathway in life, and never beset by any metaphysical difficulties themselves, they are apt to be impatient of such things in others. They see nothing but one broad turnpike road in the world, and they are indignant when they find other natures dragging themselves on, with torn and bleeding feet and fainting hearts, telling of the rocks, and floods, and quicksands, which have beset their way. So, Mr. Milsland, tired of Laura's impulsiveness, he found it impossible to comprehend her at all; and sometimes in puzzling over the riddle of her life, he found himself gliding from curiosity into annoyance. Even the fact of her changed looks, her worn and wearied face, gradually produced a feeling of irritation in his mind. She was reconciled to him; she had distinctly said she cared nothing about his disposition of the property, and yet she had a settled grief established in her heart. Again and again he came to the shallow conclusion that there must be remorse for a sin, to cause such an effect as that. Not able to rise to the perception of the fact that there are natures so wide in their ambition, so profound in their devotion, so boundless in their desires, so high in their aspirations, that the world has no adequate satisfaction to offer them; he dimly surmised she was sad because she had not been like others, not acted, not felt like them. That sadness which grew out of utter loneliness, and of a heart that would not stoop to anything lower than its highest needs, seemed to him a recantation of her birth-right, an acknowledgment that she had sinned, and that the ways of the material world had justified themselves to her, as above those of the spiritual world.

In Laura's absence, he held long conversations regarding her with his son-in-law.

"Paul," he would say, "I am very anxious about Laura; I do not quite understand her. I wish I knew what my duty was."

"You are certainly very indulgent to her, sir."

"I am afraid you do not like her; I don't know that I ought to trust her welfare to your hands."

"Indeed, sir, it is because I like her so well, and consider her interest so deeply, that I would guard her from herself. You see how unfit she is to be trusted to her own will, and any woman so unfortunately constituted as Laura, needs a man's control."

"Are you sure you could control her?"

"Thus far I have proved it; did not my treatment, which you thought too severe, bring her to penitence and acknowledgment of her fault?"

"I don't quite know whether that was entirely the cause of it; it seems to me something more than that."

"Did you ever see anything like it in her before,

sir?" he replied, consciously taking to himself the credit of her signal change of feeling.

"No, I cannot say that I have. But she does not seem to like you, Paul; she distrusts you; your presence is offensive to her."

"My dear sir, we naturally feel that towards the person who disciplines us. When she sees her conduct in its right light, she cannot fail to give me credit for my honest intentions. I should not be surprised if we ended by being the fastest of friends."

"Yet, it does not seem to me exactly right to put her so entirely in your power. Though I cannot think you would break your solemn promises to me, so often reiterated. You would not prove unfaithful to your trust, and yet"——

"Why, you told me yourself, sir, that she was satisfied with the provisions of your will, and wished it to remain as it was." (He knew that Laura was quite mistaken as to what the conditions were, for he had cunningly questioned the doctor.)

"So she did; but she always goes to extremes. She was so excessive in her humility and penitence that night, that she would have taken pleasure in inflicting the worst punishment on herself. Yet she has told me since, she was quite satisfied with it; but I am not."

"As you please, sir; you know I thought it best for her. You know we came to the conclusion, that with her unaccountable attachment to this actor, there was no telling what she might do, if left perfectly independent. But then he is not here; so, perhaps, we were over cautious."

"He may come back, though; there is no safety in that."

"I am afraid not. Dear sir, sometimes, I am inclined

to think our poor Laura, not entirely accountable for her strange conduct, I fear her mind may be a little affected. For that reason, she needs a firm, though kind, hand to restrain her."

"I don't agree with you. I don't think her mind at fault. You don't know how bright she was at her school. Why, she left all her companions ever and ever so far behind her."

"That is no proof to the contrary; the finest minds are most liable to go astray. Yet, I hope I may be mistaken. Her conduct towards Doria was strange, strange and unaccountable."

"So it was; but I sometimes think, if she really is so much attached to him, I had better not put any obstacles in her way. Perhaps she had better marry him."

"If it is as we have painfully suspected, he would not be willing to marry her."

"I no longer suspect it; if I thought she had disgraced me, I would have no hesitation in discarding her at once. In my family, no woman has ever disgraced her name; and if she had"——

"But consider her youth, her ignorance of the world, her orphanage, her"——

"No excuse at all, in my eyes. She was born of a pure mother, and brought up in the purest associations. Virtue belongs to a woman as essentially as her life; nothing extenuates her departing from it. That is the sin that should never be forgiven, in my opinion."

"But one sin, sir, might be forgiven, if she were thoroughly penitent."

"Any other sin than that. But I don't believe it of my girl; understand, the very way in which she rejected the accusation, proved the pride of her innocence."

"Did she ever deny it?"

"No, for she was too much offended by the mere supposition to stoop to defend herself."

"I am delighted with your confidence, sir; it removes a load from my mind. You see, I thought it a very remarkable circumstance, that a young lady of Miss Laura Milsland's position, fortune, and extraordinary beauty, should be slighted by a man of Doria's profession, so openly, too. I cannot quite understand it; so very elegant a creature as your daughter. Why, I've seen him actually rude to her in the presence of others; not too civil, either, in his way of speaking of her when absent—strange, strange!"

"It is strange; there must be some meaning in it. I will, I will question her again."

"Sir, sir, I beg of you"——

"It is quite useless for you to plead for her; I know my duty to my daughter. And try to satisfy my doubts as you may, I can see you are not satisfied yourself. Why, Paul, I am afraid you'll end by being too indulgent to her, just as we've all been. But I must think about her future more fully; after a day or two, or next week, when I feel a little stronger, I must consider the terms of that will. I will insist on its being read to her, and will see whether she is still determined to abide by it. Next week, Paul, when I feel better, you must remind me of it."

"I will do so. In the meantime, try to think as well of her as you can; for, indeed, I am not so—so doubtful as you think. She is such a fine girl, I hardly think, I "——

"Well, no matter for the present; she is not of your flesh and blood; you cannot be either as tender, or as severe as her father can."

To Laura's surprise, her father still kept his bed, when nearly two weeks had elapsed after their reconciliation. More than that, instead of improving, he seemed to be gradually getting worse. One day, she questioned the doctor closely, and learned from him that he was suffering from an old complaint, which had been, seemingly, mastered years ago, and yet had worked its way to the light again. A horrible fear smote her then, lest her own irritating behavior might have developed this malady; but the doctor told her it must have been gradually ripening, in secret, for more than a year.

"Very likely," he added, "the very fact of his feeling so frequently angry with you, as you tell me he did, may be accredited to the secret irritation of an insiduous disease, rather than to your behavior. I can well understand how easily he would have been provoked under the circumstances, and how ready to take offence at nothing."

"You say that, out of kindness to me, to save me from my own self-reproach. I shall never cease to reproach myself though; if he were ill and easily angered, I ought to have perceived it by instinct, and been doubly tender with him. Besides, I was always the aggressor."

"I fancy not always; your father can be rather aggravating when he is under an evil influence; and my own opinion is, that your brother-in-law is any thing but a friend to you."

"I know that; but I despise him. I am not afraid of any harm that he can do me. He is beneath contempt."

"Yet he is capable of putting you in a very trying position; he is more subtle than you think."

"I know he is, and he has good cause to hate me. I

taught him a lesson he will never forget. But how can he injure me?"

"Don't you know what a tool your father is in the hands of a strong, artful will?"

"Yes; I know he is easily influenced, and I'm satisfied the first trouble between my father and myself came from his interference. As for the money question, if that's what you allude to, I am perfectly willing he should have his wish. I am sick of the whole subject, and a part of the property will be as good for me as the whole."

"You know your own mind best; but if I had a right to interfere."—

"Never mind that. Tell me candidly, do you think my father's illness will be a long one?"

"I can hardly tell; it has proved more serious than I supposed it would. At his time of life, such an illness is very uncertain."

"Why, you don't think him in a dangerous state, do you?"

"Not just now; but it is impossible to foretell the future. Still you have no cause to alarm yourself."

After this conversation, Laura thought it her duty to write to Agnes, knowing how she would feel herself, if her father were seriously ill, and she not warned of it.

Agnes came as quickly as she could, accompanied by her husband, who, concluding that Mr. Milsland was about to die, and would surely leave Agnes something, thought himself justified in setting to work at once, to dissipate the remainder of the sum last received from him. As usual, he selected the most expensive hotel in the city, and there established himself with his wife, child and servant. Mr. Milsland did not seem very glad to see Agnes at first, for she insisted on intruding her husband and his views into almost the first remark that passed between them. To convince Mr. Milsland that her husband had led her to form expectations from his death, did not require the promptings of the ready Elphinstone, though those suggestions were most clearly set forth by him. Mr. Milsland was disgusted with the idea that his daughter could hope to benefit herself by his death, and he determined more than ever, that such expectations should be disappointed.

Agnes came every day; often bringing her delicate little girl, until by degrees a better understanding was brought about between her father and herself. Willister enjoyed himself immensely, strutting about the corridors of the hotel, and indulging in numerous games of poker, at which he invariably lost, being a most insufferably bad player, with the conceit that his skill was unrivalled. But then he argued, what was the loss of twenty or thirty dollars a day, to a man who might soon inherit a fortune? and a gentleman must have his amusements.

Mr. Milsland at one time seemed to be getting quite well. He left his bed one day, even came down into the dining room, and consumed a dinner that aggravated his complaint immediately. From that time he did not attempt to get up. He was better one day and worse the next, until from a habit of seeing him so, his family lost all alarm as to a serious result attending on his illness. In the meanwhile, the question of the will was often agitated. Mr. Milsland frequently declared his intention of altering it; but it was put off from hour to hour, until one day he suddenly changed for the worse. Everything was in confusion; doctors sent for, servants running about in confusion, Agnes and Miriam in hysterics, and Laura pale, and overcome with fear. There was no attempt on the part of the physicians to disguise the fact from his family, that his life was drawing to a close; indeed it was too palpable to bear a disguise. For some time the sufferer lay in a kind of dead stupor, then he gradually shook it off and called for Laura.

"I am here, dear papa;" she cried, "always here."

"They have made me wrong you, my child. I want somebody to draw up a will. Quick! Send at once."

"Never mind that, papa; think of yourself now. What is a little money more or less to me, when you are going from me?"

"But I will not see you sacrificed. I can understand you better now; the clouds are clearing away from my mind. Laura, you once asked me to forgive you, now I ask you to forgive me!"

"My darling, how can you talk so—what could a daughter have to forgive her own father?"

"Having doubted her. I accused you of having disgraced me; I now see you far above even the never having disgraced *me*. I see you as never having done anything unworthy of yourself. But I want you to swear here before two people, one your sister, who has never known how to value you, and who taught me to do you the grossest injustice—that you have never been guilty of one act, you know in relation to what man I speak, of which you have cause for remorse, or for one blush of real shame to color your face. Swear this, if it be true!"

"I do swear it, on my soul and yours."

"Is the man coming to make the will? I haven't much time."

"I did not send for him; let the will remain, I know

what it contains. Instead of giving me a greater part of the property, you divide it equally between myself and my two elder sisters."

"Who told you that was how it stood?"

"My brother-in-law, for one, told me in Charley's presence."

"Then he is a liar; and neither he nor his wife shall inherit one cent. I'll give her share to poor Agnes. I see now why you were satisfied with the terms. Paul Elphinstone deceived you as he has often deceived me."

"Did I understand you to call me a liar, sir?" said Elphinstone, in a loud voice, and advancing rudely to the bed-side.

"Yes, and a scoundrel, and a traitor," and with a great effort he rose in bed, as if to strike him. It was too much for him, he fell back speechless and almost black in the face.

"In the meanwhile, Agnes ran out of the room, and sent for the nearest man who knew how to draw up a will; but when she brought him in, it was only to find Mr. Milsland in this dreadful state. Restoratives were applied, stimulants tried, but though they brought him back the use of his voice, they never restored his reason to him. He wandered on in incoherent ravings, until passion seemed to wear out his strength, and he sank into a troubled sleep. During all this time he kept fast hold of Laura's hand, as though it were the only thing that linked him to hope and safety. After a long, uneasy slumber, he woke, and his face was so changed that he looked like a little child. His eyes wandering at first, gradually fixed themselves on one spot in space, and to it was also extended one trembling hand.

"See," he said, "see what a scholar she is in geometry. Look at the state of that black-board. What kind of thing do you call that—is it not equal to pictures? What a mind Laura has! Always at her books, and always at the head of the school. Her mother had a great mind too. Just look at the way those angles come out—how the chalk shines, it looks as though she were writing with a star. Squares, and triangles, and straight lines; and see the circles how they grow; they grow till they take in the world, and carry me away. Oh, how fast—how light!"——

His eyes remained fixed upon the same spot; but his weak hand gradually ceased its trembling and dropped down. The one which was clasped in Laura's had such an irresponsive contact to her own tender clasp, that she gazed in alarm into his face, and saw the vacant, meaningless look in his eyes, and knew he was quite dead.

## CHAPTER XVIII.

Days swelled into weeks, and still Laura remained in her father's house, wrapped up in her grief, which, in itself, was grievously heavy, and more heavy still, for other griefs which it made still more vivid to her. During this time, not one thought of any monetary trouble invaded her mind. Judging others by her own pride and justice, she never imagined for a moment her brother-in-law would fail to restore her at least an equal share in her father's property, after the determination the latter had expressed in the presence of witnesses. In pursuance with this belief, she had ordered the necessary mourning for herself and for Agnes, leaving the bills to be paid from the estate. A month after her father's death, Elphinstone informed her he desired to have some particular conversation with her. She assented, of course, supposing it referred to the proper division of the property. What, then, was her surprise when he opened the conversation, by saying: "Well, Laura, what do you intend to do—how do you propose to settle yourself?"

"I don't at all understand you!"

"After the manner in which you have treated your sisters, you will hardly expect them to support you, and, indeed, you will pardon me for saying that I would hardly like my wife to be associated with you. I don't say I have any well-grounded reasons to suspect you; but you know appearances must decide the value of a woman, actual facts have little weight. For all I know, you may have been as innocent as an angel, but you have not been above suspicion, and therefore, according to all social laws, you are guilty."

"Mr. Elphinstone, I see you are trying, by again bringing forward that absurd question, to move me to anger and the loss of self-possession. But you have succeeded in that for the last time. I have never been suspected by any one but your wife and yourself, for my father's doubts of me were only parasites, borrowed from you."

"Well, have it so, if it pleases you; but how do you propose to live? you are aware that you are disinherited."

"I heard what my father said on his death-bed; he had been deceived by you into making that will, and intended to substitute for it the original one. But I don't care for that; I am willing to share with my sisters."

"Upon my word you are very generous, considering you have not one penny of your own."

"Do you intend, then, to disregard my father's last wish?"

"The expression of a wandering reason; almost the ravings of a maniac. In his hours of cool and healthy deliberation, he made that will, and allowed it to remain unaltered for months. Do you suppose the last incoherent death words are to undermine that? Ask the law, and see what it will answer."

"I have not the least doubt, that when you laid your plans to rob me, you made perfectly sure of having the law on your side. But as for stating that my father's last words, with regard to me, were not those of reason, you lie when you say so, and you know it. They were the sanest words he had spoken since he first knew you; for approaching death made him wise enough to see you in your true colors, and he spoke like a man, in individual dignity, not infected by evil influence, and accountable only to God."

"All that may be very fine, but I don't see what it will contribute to your support. The will, will remain as it is. I promised your father to assist you, if you deserved it, to keep you from want, at least"——

"There again you are slandering the dead. I know that my father expected you only to hold my property in trust for me, blindly believing that your sex and shrewdness would enable you to prevent me from making an ill-judged use of it."

"Then, why did he not so register it?"

"I don't know. I suppose because you persuaded him, it would be better to leave it to your honor. He was weak-minded, but his heart was strong; he never knew what it was to be untrue himself, and he could not realize its possibility in others. Heaven only knows what arts and devices you used to work upon him. I can only be certain they were the worst and meanest possible to the human mind."

"You are severe, Miss; but I must remind you again, that abuse of me will not put bread in your mouth, or a roof over your head. I ask you again what you mean to do?"

"To leave this house to-morrow; the rest does not concern you."

Having said this, she rose, with a perfectly cool and quiet dignity, and was about to leave the room; but Elphinstone, who was terribly dissatisfied by the turn affairs was taking, called her back, with a tone almost of alarm. He had expected to see her bowed down with dismay and distress, appealing to his generosity, wooing him with prayers and tears. He did not know that poverty seems a very light burden to those who have never borne it, and that a person weighed down with mental grief, is sometimes really relieved by the addition of a material one, which acts like a counter-irritation on internal inflammation, its sharpest sting having actually a soothing quality.

"Don't go yet, Miss Laura. I only wanted to show you, you were now subject to a man of resolution, and not to a vascillating father. I do not intend that my wife's sister shall be a pauper."

"Indeed! Well, what are your views?"

"A modest little income, enough to keep you out of harm's way, and yet not enough to lead you into temptation. When that is settled, I want you to sign a paper, stating that you are perfectly satisfied with my actions, and think they have justified your father's generosity to me."

"I will do nothing of the kind. I would starve first."

"Don't go, Laura, why are you in such a hurry? I want to talk to you."

"I am in a hurry to get out of your presence, and I will sign nothing, and I will not accept a pitiful stipend from you."

"You are right, dear Laura, and you haven't the slightest idea of how beautiful you look when you show such spirit. You are right, a modest income would be an absurdity for you. Your charms would be obscured in poverty. You need all the splendors and luxuries of wealth. They suit you and you suit them. Nature intended them for you, and it would be wrong for you to be deprived of them. Your father's wealth has not vanished, it has only changed hands, and these hands are as able to dispense it to you as his were. Yes, and as willing—it only depends on yourself——"

He stopped, hesitating, as if he expected some reply from her, but the interruption which he thought essential to a woman's manner, did not come: he had only to meet the clear, steady glance of her searching eyes, and feel that he must make himself thoroughly understood, before he could expect an answer. He went on in an uneasy, almost abashed way to say—

"You see I have all the power and you all the needs. Now, if you make a friend of me, you shall want for nothing. I may have seemed inimical to you, but it is not so. I desire nothing but to make you happy, to gratify your every desire. Laura, I always loved you; you have more influence over me now than anybody in the world. You can lead me where you will, if you will only be kind to me."

Again he paused as if he expected an answer, but her stern silence caused him to continue, "I married your sister, but on my soul, it was only as a means of keeping near to you. You don't know me, Laura; I have been acting a part; you think me harsh and severe, but one of your smiles would bring me to your feet—I would be your slave. I would fly with you to the ends of the earth; but if you are afraid to brave public opinion, the world need not be the wiser for your kindness to me. I am not hurrying you; take a month, take a year to consider it. In the meanwhile, my purse is yours, just as my heart is—use them as you like; all I desire in return is the hope, that some day you may respond to my love."

The last words of this speech were spoken on his knees, in which position he tried to seize Laura's hands and carry them to his lips. But she rose with such an amount of scorn and loathing in her face, that he remained almost petrified under their influence.

"Mr. Elphinstone, words would not express the horror with which I have listened to you, and as being a woman, I have no other weapon but words, I will not try to express it. I will not refer to the outrage you have offered to all my womanly instincts, nor the insult to all that is worthy of the name of honor, for I feel you would not understand that; but I will tell you one thing you can understand, and that is the utter and awful loathing with which you inspire me, personally. If I were the worst woman in the world, I would be willing to fly to the North Pole, only to escape the touch of your hand. As it is, in comparison to what you offer me, I would go through the eternal depths of darkness, and find it full of peace. I will not remain another night under the same roof with you; and I command you never while you live, to speak another word to me."

She went out of the room without his attempting to

detain her. Indeed he was so crushed by her scorn, he had only strength to mutter, when she was out of hearing, "Go and be starved, you haughty devil. I wouldn't give you a penny to save you from dying in a gutter."

Before night Laura had packed up all her things, and gone to her sister Agnes, who was still residing at the hotel. Before leaving, she made an effort to say "good-by" to her sisters. She first sought Miriam, whose neutral friendliness encouraged her to hope for some kindly feeling; but the dry, cool manner in which the latter received her, was proof to Laura that Elphinstone had been successfully at work in disparaging her. So she went out of the house, in which she had reigned like a queen, without one kind look or wish—went forth penniless, homeless, almost friendless, and quite hopeless, to face the bleak, bitter world from which she expected nothing but disappointment, contempt and forgetfulness. She went forth alone, stripped of all that made life bright to her, and without a shred of quiet, homely happiness to lean upon instead. All her youth, beauty, talent, education, fascination, perseverance had brought her nothing but this; everything had failed her; her spirit was cast forth naked to the tempests of life. And yet she was richer as she stood there denuded of all the world holds precious, than she had ever been in her proudest days of wealth and beauty; as much richer as the angel is above the beast, for who shall say, it does not all profit a woman, to lose the whole world, and gain her own soul!

# PART, THIRD.

## CHAPTER I.

Six months after that moment when Laura left her father's house, for the last time, Victor Doria was perseveringly groping his way through the unpleasing east end of the city, in a search after her home. The night had fairly fallen, but the scanty array of lamps were just lighted, and as he went hurriedly on through the long, dull, old and mean streets, he contrasted the present hour with the one in which he had unexpectedly come upon her in a dwelling that was almost a palace. He did not fail to deduce from it a philosophical reflection on the vicissitudes of life, which was all the more impressive, because its changes had brought only an increase of good to himself. Victor was in rather an ill humor as regards this visit, he was giving himself so much trouble to accomplish. A few days before, when he arrived from Europe, he learned for the first time of Laura's affliction and trials, in consequence of which he felt it to be his duty as a gentleman, to seek her out in her poverty and distress, as he had been always a welcomed visitor in the days of her ease and comfort. But the idea was not a pleasant one; for frivolous and heartless as Victor seemed, he was capable of very manly delicacy, under circumstances qualified to call it out He felt assured that Laura would persecute him with exhibitions of attachment to him, and he feared his patience would give way before her accustomed violent, uncongenial professions of love. To repulse her, to be even rude to her, seemed easy enough, in the days when she was in social position unmistakably above himself, and was surrounded by friends, family, and every thing that enriched life. Her own advantages, even when added to her womanhood, made her stand on equal terms with him in contest; but now that she was poor, friendless and destitute, he was ready to bear every annoyance from her without complaint. It would have been inconsistent with his own self-respect and good breeding to slight, rebuke, or wound her feelings in any way.

So he groped his way through those unenticing streets, with the feeling of a victim going voluntarily to the sacrifice. Finally he reached the address that had been furnished him, and touched the bell of the narrow, grimy door. It sounded with a harsh, discordant jangle that made him start impatiently, and feel like running away before the summons was answered from within. But he controlled himself, and soon slip-shod steps approached the door, and awkward hands opened it. Of a slatternly, tired-looked servant girl, he inquired whether Miss Laura Milsland was at home. Having received an unqualified affirmative, he was at once ushered up one pair of stairs, and unceremoniously into a front room. His heart throbbed with the most unpleasant anticipations as he entered, indeed he lingered on the threshold, till a figure rose from a chair in which it had been reclining, and came forward to meet him.

Was that Laura Milsland, from whom he had parted

scarcely fifteen months ago? He could not believe his eyes, when he saw how changed and faded her face was. Pity led him to meet her with a show of warmth and pleasure, but when he had taken her hands and looked into her eyes, it was no longer a show. He knew now that he should never again be forced to defend himself against her. With all that tact and quickness of perception which were characteristic of him, he instantly sounded the depths of the change that had taken place in her, and in consequence laid down his arms and stood off his guard at once. He no longer feared to look into her eyes, for they were bright with a gaze only of unutterable kindliness. They were bright, and yet with a brightness far other than that of the old days; they were like stars that had not lost their lustre, but were drowned beneath clear waters, and were sending up their lights, softened by the liquid depths through which they had come.

"I am so glad to see you," she said in a voice whose tone consorted with the change in her face, "and you must have had so much trouble in finding me!"

"Oh, no; none in the world," replied Victor, forgetting the amount of grumbling he had indulged in on his way thither, and almost persuading himself he had come with enthusiasm."

Victor and Laura seated themselves side by side on the sofa; but after a moment, as if seeming suddenly to recollect herself, she rose and took a chair at some distance from him. It was an exact copy of the way in which he used to take refuge from a seat beside her, into the one which was at the greatest distance possible for conversation. And yet there was not the least touch of pique or coquetry in the movement; it was so simple and so earnest, that its humility partook of the highest kind of pride. What a dignity that humility had to Victor's eye, as compared to the former obstinate arrogance, with which she had forced herself and her emotions upon him.

"Have you been happy, fortunate in your visit to Europe—what have you been doing?"

"Oh, a little of everything; pursued the life of an actor in England, of course; one that I'm heartily tired of, and was rewarded with praise and money for being disgusted with it. In Italy I tried working in marble for a while, but all to no purpose. I love the art, but I have no real talent as a sculptor; I can only model indifferently well in clay.'

His brows clouded up with a trace of anger and bitterness, but her "Indeed, can that be so?" expressed such an unlimited amount of faith in his powers to do anything, that his face smoothed itself out into good humor again.

"Now, Laura, tell me something about yourself; tell me about your life since I left you."

"I have little to tell, though the time has brought signal changes. I miss my father very much."

"Go on; tell me more about yourself."

"I have nothing to say; nothing in the world that could interest you."

"Why, anything you could say would interest me. Why, Laura, you did not use to need so much urging, you were so much more confiding."

"Was I?" she said, with a smile, compared with which, common tears would have seemed joyful.

"Of course you were; but I see you no longer regard me as a friend. You forget how long and well we have known each other."

"Ah, no, I don't forget it; why should I?" she answered, looking at him, and through and beyond him, till the liquid lights in these soft eyes seemed to be fixed on some point to which he could not follow her.

He had no fancy for sitting opposite to her, and being looked at in a way that seemed to set her at indefinite heights above him; so he stole over to where she was sitting, approaching her in his gentlest and most soothing manner. She looked slightly puzzled when he came so near her, and seemed to be about to draw her chair away, but as there was no possibility of doing that, without putting it out of the window, she was obliged to remain where she was. Noting, with surprise, the contrast between this utter lack of self-consciousness, and her former nursing of her own sensations, and perpetual bringing them into prominence, he hardly knew how to arrange his conversation so as to amuse her. Under the influence of this doubt, he exerted himself to entertain her, as though he were seeing her for the first time, and his future happiness depended on his power to make a good impression. He had the satisfaction of seeing her listen with the most vivid interest, and that he contributed to her amusement, was certain, by the soft, merry way in which she laughed. She seemed to him, so much more human, now that she could laugh, like others; now, that she had left that grand, gloomy pedestal of woe, on which she had posed herself like a double-dyed Niobe, and had come down to the natural interests of humanity. Finally, however, he brought back the subject of which she seemed least conscious, herself, by saying—

"But, tell me, Laura, have you been ill? you look so changed, so different, I should hardly have known you."

"Am I so changed?" with a pang in her voice she could not suppress; for however entirely a woman may have abdicated her own hopes, and laid them down submissive before an all-wise but mysterious Providence, she cannot, for the first time realize that the spring-tide of her beauty is gone; that henceforth it must glide backwards with the inexorable ebb of years, and learn it, moreover, from the one for whose eyes, above all others, she would be beautiful, without feeling a sharp and awful pain. Hitherto, she had been so entirely occupied with other things beside herself, in fact had revolted so wearily from all self-consideration, that she had never given a thought to her gradually changing face. She put up her hands to it now, and her trembling fingers seemed to feel the cruel changes that had been worked in it. At twenty-two a woman is not old, she is scarcely come to her fullest development, she thought; but then, with a moment of lingering self-tenderness, she remembered what years of sensation she had crowded into the last fifteen months; she remembered the parched and arid deserts of despair, in which that beauty had withered; she remembered the mountains of doubt, of fear, of remorse, of penitence, which had crushed her down; the weary wringing out of every hope, of every interest, from her life, drop by drop; and the hands that had gone up to her face, deprecating and almost angry, spread themselves over it with a tenderness and consolation in every trembling pulse.

Victor took the slender fingers in his, and pulled them away from her face, gazing into it, with a disturbed, reproachful look, which Laura entirely misinterpreted. He, in gazing on those fine, pure features, sharpened by over-thought and much grieving, and on the eyes, burnt larger and softer under the prominent brows, and the skin grown darker and yet paler, like transparent white muslin stretched over dark purple, was smitten with a pang of self-reproach. The lost beauty seemed to him like an etherial spirit, which he had killed. But, while he was looking upon himself as a species of murderer, Laura mistook his look for one of criticism, dissatisfaction, almost of disgust. He always acknowledged her beauty hitherto, but even that was changed now; even that small morsel of comfort, her ever-hungering spirit had left to feed upon, was taken from her. For a moment, her heart turned upon fate, like a soul that has gone through every earthly ordeal and torment, only to find, at last, the great dead wall of annihilation, against which to dash itself, and be lost to all existence. Only for a moment, then, she accepted this view of the case, accepted it with a tender, soft resignation, and answered his deprecating look with another of those smiles, which had tears in it, and something far deeper than tears.

Fortunately, just at this moment, Agnes came in, from a visit which she had been making with her husband, and welcomed Victor with every expression of delight. Indeed she threw her arms around him, and gave him a hearty embrace, and Victor returned it with all the more warmth, for not having dared to touch more than the tips of Laura's fingers.

"I am so glad to see you, Victor. You must come to see us often; you will always be welcome here."

Victor looked into Laura's eyes, to see whether this invitation was echoed there, but he only saw them glance wearily around the dull, faded appointments of the room, and then down the gaunt, ungenial street. They said, as plainly as words could have spoken, "I have not the courage to invite him to this poor, unpleasing place."

This look at once appealed to Victor's generosity

and made him secretly determine to prove to her, how little her unattractive surroundings could influence his attention and deference to her. The usual questions, as to health, etc., having passed between Agnes and Victor, the former drew his attention to her sister.

"I suppose you were surprised to hear how Laura was treated? isn't it dreadful? did you ever hear of such a wretch as that Paul Elphinstone? Do you know, he made love to Laura at the last and "——

"Agnes, I entreat you to drop the subject. It only concerns me, and cannot possibly interest Mr. Doria."

"Oh, yes, it does interest him—it must—you know, you were quite sweethearts once."

"Agnes, you are unkind. I insist on your dropping the subject."

Victor noted the blush that came up in her cheeks, as she spoke. He could see no tenderness, no consciousness, but only mortification for a feeling past and scorned. He was not pleased, but he came to her rescue, by drawing Agnes' attention from the subject, in questioning her about her little girl.

"Oh, she is well; that is well for her, for she was never strong. She is very fond of Laura—strange, for all children used to be afraid of her. I think she has been better since Laura has been with me."

"I am not surprised, but you are looking stronger yourself, Mrs. Willister."

"Indeed, it is from the same cause. You don't know how much happier I have been with Laura here. I know, Victor, you don't think so, but she is the best and truest girl in the world. I am sorry you are prejudiced. I find her such a comfort, and I like you." This said, after Laura's retirement to the other side of the room, where she seemed to be in earnest conversation with her brother-in-law.

"I prejudiced, Mrs. Willister? I esteem, I respect Miss Milsland beyond all computation."

"I am delighted to hear you say so. Come here, Laura—Victor and you can be quite friendly. He isn't in the least prejudiced against you."

"How came such a question to be raised?" she answered, with that quiet dignity, that quite awed Victor, and fluttered Agnes.

"Well, I spoke about it, Laura, but I will not again, if it displeases you. You see, Victor, Laura has only to frown on me, to quell me instantly. In the days of her splendor, proud and arbitrary as she was, she used to come to me for sympathy. But now she gives sympathy, kindness, everything, but asks nothing. I don't know what I should do without my Laura."

Laura lost her annoyed expression, at this encomium from her simple-minded sister, and looked as pleased and as innocent as a child, as though it were something extraordinary, that brilliant understanding, rich and varied information, refinement, and sisterly tenderness, could be supposed to lighten up a mean dwelling, cheered otherwise only by the billious eccentricities of a Willister.

"Yes," continued Agnes, "you may be surprised, Victor, but she has not a dreadful temper; no, not even a hateful one, for she has just the sweetest temper in the world."

Victor resented being cast in the character of Laura's detractor, and gave Agnes to understand he would not serve in that capacity, at which Laura dropped upon his face another of those mournful smiles, at which the tears, that seemed denied to her eyes, almost came to his, and he hurried away, to hide his confusion and surprise.

In returning home, he forgot the length and dreariness of the streets, in continually going over and over the details of his interview. Every word of Laura's, every look, every tone, dwelt in his mind, and puzzled and baffled it.

"It is plain," he said to himself, "she no longer loves me, and I am heartily glad of it; it was so painful, so hard to repulse a young lady of her merits," forgetting how easy it had been for him, in the past, to trample upon her like a weed. "No, she no longer loves me, but she is a good girl, without any malice in her; if she had, she would try to show me how well she is cured; but I see nothing in her but kindness and friendly feeling. Yet, after all, she may not have the feelings of a friend to me. She has a strange character, having once openly acknowledged her love for me, she is too proud not to seem to like me now. Her kindness, her approbation are only the way in which she justifies herself in her former passion. Pride makes her blush to own that the man who was once the object of her wildest love, is, in reality, unworthy to be her friend."

In the meanwhile, Laura sat at the window, looking quietly into the street, down which the now risen moon rolled its long flood of vague, soft light. Lonely and silent, she sat fighting down the "climbing" sorrow in her breast, and wondering, with a weary helplessness, whether the work of all these long, dreadful months was to be undermined by the one hour's presence of a man whom she had every reason to forget.

Agnes came to her, folding her soft arms about her, begging her to come to bed.

"No, Aggy, let me sit here awhile; I want to think. Leave me to myself."

"But you won't fret, darling. Do you know, Laura, I think Victor likes you better than he did. I shouldn't be surprised, if, if"——

"Agnes, be silent! do you take me for a fool? What kind of an idiot do you mean to make me seem?"

"But, Laura, you don't know"——

"Oh, Aggy, I know more than you could ever dream of! what it would wound your tender heart to hear, but never speak to me of this again."

"But you once told him you loved him."

"Ah, me! ah, poor, pitiful me, I did; it makes me so sorry for myself, when I think of it. And yet, Agnes, do you know that in those dreadful moments, when I did force a confession of my love on his indignant hearing, I never did it with a hope to move him, still less to win a return. I don't know what impelled me, but I couldn't help it. It seemed as if my heart was filled with something bigger than itself, which burst its way through. My heart has grown wider and deeper now, and can hold more. Only, Aggy, if you love me, don't insult me with the suggestion of a hope, or even an interest in that direction. What I have to bear, I will bear cheerfully, if you will only seem not to mind me."

So, Agnes left her, and all night she sat battling with herself, fighting down the bitter murmurs and wild longings of her heart; that heart which, in the brief happiness of the past evening, had already rebelled against the desolate void of its life, and which clamored for the old stormy rage against God's decree, rather than the new submission to it.

But, by the time the slow morning broke, she had again

accomplished her own conquest, and brought forth from the battle a new resignation, which was full of strength and sweetness.

## CHAPTER II.

When Laura left her father's house, after her interview with her brother-in-law, she at once went to the hotel at which Agnes and her husband were residing. Having related the story of her misfortunes, Agnes was overcome with sisterly sympathy and indignation, while Willister was still more grieved, for in the hope of Laura's inheriting a fortune, lay his own expectations as to future maintenance. But as he was loud in his denunciation of Paul Elphinstone, his demonstration passed current for sympathy. With the exception of an insignificant sum, Laura had no money. She had always been in the habit of keeping very little about her, and sending her bills to her father. Her wardrobe and jewelry were her own, and the latter might realize several thousand dollars, but that was nothing in the way of a future outlook. Agnes declared that it was utterly impossible to suppose that nothing should accrue to Laura, out of her father's estate. But Laura assured her, nothing on earth would induce her to accept anything, that should come to her through Paul, "And I know, Agnes, he would never allow me to have anything, except as a charity from himself."

"But, Laura, surely you might sue to have the will broken."

"On what grounds?"

"Undue influence, not being in his right mind, an

openly expressed wish to make different provisions before dying."

"Ah, but, Agnes, papa let that will remain months after he was reconciled to me, and had, in a measure, found out Paul's treachery."

"That was because he was afraid of Paul."

"Perhaps; but how am I to prove it? You know before the servants and visitors, papa always seemed to control him,—he seemed more afraid of papa than papa of him."

"So he did; oh, what a sly villain! But then, papa's intention just before dying, to make a new will in your favor."

"Who is to prove it? You left the room as soon as he expressed the wish, without intimating what the change was. Charley was there, but we know whose case her testimony would help, whether true or false; and as for me, what could I do?"

"I think you could do much; you used to be bright enough to help yourself."

"Not much, indeed, Aggy; the law wouldn't help me. I feel that by instinct. The law is just a miniature of the world; its leanings are always on the man's side. The odds are always against a woman. I sometimes fancy every force in this world prefers helping a man to helping a woman. I don't see why, either; we are not to blame for being women; we couldn't help it—could we?"

"I don't see what that has to do with it, if you have a clear case."

"But I haven't a clear case; I have a very doubtful one. Why, Aggy, don't you see what weapons Paul would use against me, if I tried legal contest? All my unkindness, wickedness to my father; all my faults, all his own suspicions, all my pitiful sufferings,—alas! do but think of it! What mere slender chance of success could be set against such an ordeal as that?"

"That would be hard. But do they bring everything that happens before the public so?"

"Yes, and a great deal more. No, Aggy; it seems to be the will of God, I should be bereft of every thing, of money with it all. Perhaps I need it—who knows? Oh, Aggy, you don't know how disgusted I am with myself. I think, taking everything into consideration, I must be the worst girl in the world."

"I think you considerably nearer to being the best. But, dear Laura, what do you mean to do?"

"I am young and strong; I mean to support myself. Why shouldn't I? Other women do."

"Oh, Laura, how could you, you have been so expensive?"

"I must change that. I'll find some way of living; or indeed, Agnes, it makes little matter to me, if instead, I only find some way of dying."

"Don't talk so, Laura."

"Well, the question now is, what we are to do to-morrow. In the first place, we must leave this hotel, and find humble lodgings somewhere. Do you know how your husband's bank account stands?"

"He has more than money enough to pay his bill here, and next week, he has reason to expect—but it's a secret; I mustn't tell you."

"Never mind his expectations; if he has money enough to pay his bill here, it is more than I hoped. I must sell all my jewelry; I shall have no more need of it. That will give us a start at any rate."

The next morning Laura was up almost before daylight, with a view to commencing her search for lodg-

10

ings at the earliest possible hour. Strange as it may seem, there was something in her unexpected position that she secretly enjoyed. The idea of poverty, drawn entirely from novels, was flattering to her imaginative and romantic tendency of mind. Little dreaming of the utter monotony of poverty, she looked to it for a certain measure of excitement and adventure. Besides, being at the height of her self-depreciation and accusation, it gave her pleasure to materially punish herself.

In pursuance of this feeling, she at once turned into the eastern quarter of the city, pushing her way through narrow, homely streets, of whose existence she was not previously aware. The idea of procuring a comparatively inexpensive lodging in an agreeable part of the city, never occurred to her. She must have not only poverty, but the confession of it, and the humility of it, and the separation of it. So when she had traveled very far away from all familiar neighborhoods, she began to inquire in every house that advertised apartments to let. Finally she fixed on one, in a very dull, dark street, in rather an old house, with a dingy door; in fact, if there had been an atom more of paint on it, Laura would have passed it by. She rented the second floor and a part of the basement, furnished in a grim, worn, old-fashioned way.

She went home to find her sister, feeling confident she had been very fortunate in her undertaking. Agnes, however, seemed very far from pleased with the home provided for her.

"I don't see at all, Laura, why you should come over to this horrid neighborhood. Why, it's a cemetery for dead houses. If we want to go to the theatre or anywhere, I don't see how we are ever to get there. I had as leave be out of the world at once. It's not so cheap, either. We could have done as well in some of the nice new streets. I shall never see any body I know pass here, there'll be no use sitting at the windows."

"Why, Aggy, that's just the reason I came here, that we might not have to come in contact with the people we used to know."

"Used to know! Do you expect to drop all your acquaintances? Do you never mean to go into society?"

"What should I go into society for—without money, spirits, or anything else? No, indeed. I sought this place especially, to learn how to be poor, and to work. I couldn't do that in any neighborhood where I should have to keep up old acquaintances, and live in a kind of semi-genteel, lacquered poverty."

"But, wouldn't you like to live in a street where you could see fine horses pass sometimes?"

"What, when I had no chance of riding on them myself? That's not my style."

"Well, I suppose I'll have to try and like it; at any rate, there's a nice bit of garden at the back, where baby can play," said Agnes, brightening up; and with her sanguine character always ready to seize on the slightest morsel of consolation.

In a few days they were well established in their unappetizing dwelling, and Laura had procured a rough, good-natured maid of all work, to wait upon them. Her jewelry was disposed of and brought nearly a quarter of its original cost; but even with that great deterioration of value, the proceeds filled her purse for the present, and prevented pecuniary anxiety for some little time to come. Laura's friends called on her kindly and attentively enough after her father's death; but when she left her home, she determined to receive no more of their sympathetic visits. Partly out of pride, partly out of an exaggerated sense of duty, she determined to put an end to all intercourse between herself and her former acquaintances. She need not, however, have troubled herself to pile up such barriers between herself and her past world. It had not the insurmountable desire to keep her of itself, that she fancied. To speak truly, Laura had never been the girl to make friends. Among the many and wonderful gifts the fairies had bestowed on her at her birth, the very necessary one of tact, had been wanting. Laura, therefore, as a member of society, though she bore a great many guns, never knew how to manage them, so that it often happened that at very inopportune moments she fired promiscuously upon her friends as well as her foes. She was invited everywhere, because she was fashionable, and elegant, and a splendid figure-head for a festal occasion. But she was much more feared than loved, and admired than esteemed. Her beauty was worn with such an arrogance, and her wit with such abandonment, that simpler, and sometimes worthier women were driven to the wall before her least effort. People treated her with great deference, because it was not convenient to do otherwise; besides, what was the use of trying to "put down" a girl who was sure to get the best of you in any warfare you could possibly invent! Great beauty as she was, of course she excited a vast amount of interest in the male world. Many men had even loved her, but it was not the right kind of love; it was that feeling falsely called love, that serves to lower rather than to elevate it's object. She had used men like tailors' blocks, to try experiments on; she had endeavored to fit her affections to them, and failing, had thrown them by, like stocks. Wounded desperately in her own pride as well as her love, chafing under it, and desiring to do all manner of distracted acts in order to heal her wounds, she never seemed to remember that others might possibly experience the same sentiments. When she seized hold of a gentleman and tried to love him, and changed all her arrogant ways into caressing tones, and unspeakably fascinating treatment, and strove to force him to call out her love to himself; when she made such experiments and utterly failed, and then threw them aside, like vessels of clay that had broken in the shaping, and were only good to be tossed by as rubbish, she never seemed to imagine that there could be any sentiment of revenge and malice on the part of her failures. But poor as her imagination was, such was the case, so that before her father died, she had got the reputation among men of being a perfectly heartless, hardened and dangerous flirt, who would take any natural or supernatural way of winning a man's love, and then getting rid of him afterwards. Of course they couldn't know that this apparent heartlessness was the result of an undue excess of heart; external coldness, selfishness and subtlety, could not seem to them what it really was, the distorted, distraught reflection of a morbid, monstrous, and self-consuming internal passion.

Thus, when the clouds rolled over and swept this great, fiery star out of the social firmament, almost no one felt anything but relief at the circumstance. Even some very kind, considerate women believed it to be a just retribution for her conduct. The most lenient judges condemned Laura and forgot her, not knowing how all her faults lay on the surface, and what ceaseless travail of spirit and unutterable yearnings after better things were beneath it.

As for the shallow, and not over-amiable members of society, the women who were hard and spiteful, with that fathomless littleness of mind peculiar to a certain female type, they offered up their hallelujahs at being rid of her, and joyed over her eclipse with exceeding great joy.

It would be idle to say that Laura felt no soreness of mind when she found that her retreat was never invaded. She was thoroughly in earnest when she determined to sever herself from the world; but she had secretly contemplated the pleasure of being wooed to its allurements and turning a deaf ear to it. That she should fall out of the ranks and never be missed, after all, was mortifying to her. But when, day after day, she sat in her dull room, and cheated herself with the belief that she dreaded visitors, and nobody came, she made an effort and thoroughly took in the idea that she was completely forgotten, and set her mind at rest on the subject, permanently.

By degrees the exceeding monotony of poverty broke in upon her, its dull routine, its fixed paucity of events. She had looked to it at least as giving her some excitement, even if it was of a painful kind; it was pledged to agitate her; to give her occasion for heroism, to bring out that element of life which all imaginative people long for, the dramatic element. It had held out to her a false hope of a plentiful cup of scenes. But here it was giving her a decent subsistence, an insufferable regularity, an intolerable freedom from agitation, and a life so drearily dull that Bridget's occasional wailings over "a lovely ash-barrel" ravished from the area, by juvenile vagrants, was actually a source of interest and excitement.

Agnes and Willister spent the most of their days in long, verbose, ridiculous bickerings, ending in reconstruction through conciliatory efforts on the part of the wife. At first Laura essayed to enter in and adjust all these quarrels, but her patience soon gave out. A girl may have vowed herself to poverty, and be capable of self-sacrifice, of working in a factory, or anything of that sort, but when it comes to listening to a three hours' dispute, as to whether he did or did not entrust to his wife's keeping the black button that dropped off of his second best trowsers, human nature gave way and rebelled.

She tried her best, however, to amuse and interest her little niece, who soon became excessively fond of her.

Laura was not fond of reading; even that last resource of the lonely was denied her, so she determined at once to make an effort to obtain a means of livelihood. True, there was no immediate need of it, for even with the Willisters to be taken care of, she had enough for two years at least. But that did not take from her the unresting desire to have a means of living for the future. When she talked it over with Agnes, she could suggest nothing as a genteel occupation but the marrying of a rich man, at which Laura was very angry. But Agnes clung to the point that she didn't see the use of her sister's working for her living, while there were so many rich men to be had by a little "management," with a pertinacity so unusual to her, that Laura finally traced it to the suggestion of Willister, and laughed at it.

"Oh, Aggy, if I were only a young man, now," she cried, " I could be a soldier, I could go before the mast, I could be a peddler, a highwayman, or some one of those dashing professions. But a woman, and especially a woman like me, is more useless and more helpless than a weed. I could work, but not in the way women work. I could be a light porter, for my arms are as strong as steel; I could carry up trunks in a hotel, or roll barrels in a store, all day, but who would let me do it? I could drive an omnibus very well, and make the change quick as lightning, for you know what I am at arithmetic; but then that's out of the question, so we won't talk about it."

"Couldn't you teach school?"

"Well, if there is one power above all others lacking in me, it is the one of imparting knowledge to others. I don't know what is the matter with me, but I sometimes think it's because I'm an intellectual vampyre. If there is a morsel of knowledge in question between me and anybody else, I'm sure to absorb the whole of it, and leave the other party more ignorant than before."

"Why, Laura, it's only because you're so quick yourself, anybody else gets discouraged and looses self-possession in learning with you. I used to feel so in school."

"When I try to teach any one, I almost always find out I don't know anything about the subject, and have to study out a profounder view of it on the spot. Oh, no, I'd make an intolerable teacher, but I might get copying to do—I write pretty fast."

"So you might. You'll have to get it of lawyers, and I'll tell you one that likes you, and will be sure to be pleasant—that Mr. Middleton you hated to dance with so, the one that used to bounce like a ball every step he took."

"I remember, and I used to do a thing I didn't often do—that is, dance with such a horrid partner, because I thought him such a good, manly fellow. I always liked him."

"Well, he's just the man to give you papers to copy."

"Exactly. I'll find out where his office is, and call on him to-morrow."

## CHAPTER III.

On the whole, though Victor's tour was an incredibly successful one, in every dramatic way, he was not satisfied with it. Like many men of genius, his mind wanted that happy narrowness and unity of purpose, so conducive to content in this world. He was scarcely satisfied with himself as an actor, for his ideal was very high, and the dramatic art has its limits. With one exception, he loved all the fine arts, and longed to work out that love in acts. He loved the art of sculpture; but his executive faculty for it was feeble. He modeled in clay with great dexterity, so that a few touches of his nervous fingers put much sentiment and expression in that base substance; but when it came to marble, he never did anything of any consequence. But he brought his swift facility in modeling upon the stage— a play having been adopted for him with that express view—and the public heart responded to it enthusiastically. But, on the whole, his brilliant European visit was not a happy one. In the first place, he was attacked by his old enemy—dyspepsia—and this time it was of the type which suggest a general downfall of that shadowy but potent department of human life, entitled the nervous system, and is called, by compliment, nervous dyspepsia. Then, the plaudits of the multitude did not move him so much as they formerly did; and in the midst of glory and distinction he became subject to attacks of depression, he would have considered ridiculous, had he noted them in a woman. A third trouble lay in the conviction, which was stealing insidiously over him, that the first flush of his youth was passing by—a conviction he had quite too much of the feminine in his nature, not to chafe under. True, he had not yet arrived at his prime, and was daily advancing to that manly maturity that promised better things than his youth; yet, that did not console him for the loss of that indefinable freshness of face and feeling, that belongs to the threshold of life only. He had no reason to complain of any diminution of the personal interest he was accustomed to create in the breasts of both sexes, but he was secretly dissatisfied with himself, and could find no consolation in the satisfying of others. Before he returned to America, he grew so moody and listless, his best friends began to fear he would lose that hold he had obtained on the public by his unfailing vivacity, and what almost might be called, tenderness of manner. He began by avoiding the companionship of others; he ended by abhorring that of himself. The satiety of an entirely successful life was upon him. Cherished, admired, courted, flattered, caressed, loved, enriched by the world, what more could he ask? and, yet, a sudden distaste, disgust for everything, suddenly fell upon him, and smote him like one of the seven plagues of Egypt. He asked himself, continually, what was it all worth, and where would it lead? or rather that still, small voice, so long silent in his breast, asked him these questions. A new faculty seemed to gradually quicken in his spirit, and demand something more than his present life could give him. It was then that he essayed the sculptor's art, imagining it might be only the yearnings after high art that moved him. But the still, small voice would not receive sculpture as a response to its demands.

About this time, his mind awakened to a feeling for that art, the highest, grandest, and truest of all arts.

which hitherto he had failed to sensate—music. For a time, he was unable to listen to orchestral music without weeping; but the doctors said it was caused by a general feebleness of the nervous system, and advised a change of scene, rest, freedom from care, and all those indefinite mental prescriptions which physicians delight in giving. In order to get that change, accompanied by the benefit of a sea-voyage, he suddenly concluded to return to America.

When, on arriving there, he learned, for the first time, of the heavy troubles which had fallen upon Laura, he felt ashamed of himself, for having indulged in nervous melancholy, because, to him, fate was too tediously kind.

In setting out to make his first call on her, he hopefully looked forward to the vexation which her manner to him, generally, produced on his mind, believing that it would serve as a counter-irritant, and rouse him out of the weary, bitter languor into which he had fallen. The first sight of his former adorer and enemy shattered that hope, but a better one sprang from its ruins.

Generally speaking, a man sets down the freshness of a woman's first youth to her credit, as though it were a deliberate virtue; the loss of it he equally condemns, like guilt, instead of nature. Victor's judgment accorded with that of his sex; consequently, it amazed him to find in Laura certain qualities of candor, gentleness, and simplicity, taking possession of her after the departure of the bloom of girlhood, when, by all the laws of poetry and sentiment, these qualities should have accompanied rather than succeeded it. Here was the old image of the rose, loveliest at budding time, with the other floral and vegetable figures which metaphorically represent the gentler half of humanity, all of them no better than false witnesses. Instead of being like the rose, which, when it ceases to be incomplete, hastens to lose its charms, Laura's life was like the expressed juice of the grape, which begins with a sickly insipidity, ferments through all manner of harsh, violent crudities, till, with its own tumults, it casts away its impurities, and mellows itself into the rich ambrosial wine.

It was nothing more than his duty, he persuaded himself, to call on her very frequently; it was clearly the part of an old friend like himself to endeavor to enliven the solitude in which she lived. So it fell out, that scarcely a day elapsed without his calling some time during the twenty-four hours. Laura was always at home, interesting, cheerful, gentle, and pleased to see him. He pulled her work about, learned of her a crochet stitch, read her favorite poets to her, brought her flowers, instructed her in miscellaneous matters of general information, and acted altogether as though he considered himself the specially appointed agent of fate for amusing her. The only thing which marred these pleasant interviews was the misguided efforts of kind but blundering Agnes, to establish an understanding between them stronger than mere friendship. Such efforts always disturbed Victor, and brought on Laura those attacks of dignity, marked by unusually low, quiet tones, and by the deepening in of dark tints around her mouth and glooming eyes — a look which fairly awed Victor, because it seemed to lift a veil from her face and reveal glimpses of the desert agonies, over which she had staggered, despairing, and just failing to perish in its withering sands.

But as soon as the pressure was removed, he did not fail to mark how that vigilant soul struggled with itself in mingled strength and tenderness, till the darkness was driven out, and the lights of peace and patience illumined it again.

One evening, he asked Laura where her jewelry was, observing that, contrary to her former custom, she wore almost no ornaments. She replied—

"I have sold it all. It would have been useless to me here, and I wanted the money."

"Pardon me, Laura, if I take the liberty of asking you a question: did you inherit nothing from your father? Did he not even leave you a mere competence?"

"Not even that. I came from my own home with nothing but my personal wardrobe."

"I am very sorry to hear it, my dear, dear girl. I can scarcely credit it; it seems too bad to be true. And do you owe it entirely to the interposition of your brother-in-law?"

"And to my own pride and obstinacy."

"I can't believe that. But had you no friends to force him to right you?"

"I don't know whether any one could do that. Besides, Victor, I have never acted so as to win friends. I am about friendless, and have no one but myself to blame for it."

"I shall be obliged to differ from you again. But could nothing be done in the courts? What reason could Elphinstone assign as causing your father to disinherit you, who were so evidently his favorite child?"

"A reason which it would take something more than a problematic success to make me sit before a jury and the newspapers, and hear discussed. I don't know— perhaps certainty of success, would have persuaded me to try the ordeal."

"But if it were a false reason?"

"Not much difference—alas!—an open, though unproved accusation against a woman, especially in matters scarcely susceptible of proof, is almost equally injurious to her, whether true or false; you know it is."

"I am not so sure. But don't be angry with me, if I speak to you freely; what do you intend to do—what are your plans? Could I aid you?"

"Oh, dear, no! Well, I'll tell you; my plan is to work for my living."

"How?"

"Well, I can scarcely speak for the future. I am copying law papers now."

"But you can't pursue that permanently. The remuneration is so contemptible!"

"Not so poor as you think. I am very well satisfied."

"I wish it were in my power to be of some use."

"But it isn't; so, let's talk of something else. Have you seen your former friend, Mrs. Middleton, since you returned?"

"Oh, yes; I think highly of her."

"So do I. I want to show you a letter I had from her yesterday. She is so kind!"

Laura rose and went to seek it in an inner room. In a moment she returned, with a jeweled casket in her hand, from which she took the letter. It only urged upon Laura a kind invitation to make the writer a long visit, because she really needed a change of scene for a time. It also stated that the writer needed and supplicated just such companionship as Laura was able, above all others, to give her. Altogether, it was a very genial letter, and far too charming to merit the interruption of Bridget's bursting into the room, almost in tears, from the agitation caused by a scene with the milkman. Laura couldn't help blushing with mortification over the girl's frowsiness and tearful bluster, so she drew her out of the room, as quickly as possible, and descended with her to settle the quarrel in the kitchen.

Left alone, Victor began abstractedly to examine the few simple ornaments which, spared from the sacrifice, were yet left to inhabit the casket. Toying idly with them, his finger chanced to strike on a concealed spring; forthwith a secret drawer was suddenly revealed to him. It contained more than one thing, yet a single object enchained and bewildered his sight—a miniature picture of himself set round with the finest diamonds. In the surprise of the discovery, they seemed almost to burn his eyes with their radiance. Yes, all of her jewels were gone, none of those brilliant ornaments left, that so enhanced and exalted her beauty. No ear-rings for those shapely ears, no necklace for the graceful throat, no bracelets for the supple arms, nor rings for the taper fingers; and yet that senseless, greedy, cruel image of himself seemed to flaunt its wildering glances out of a wreath of adamantine flame.

He felt as though he had personally robbed her of just the value of those great, pure, flawless brilliants; he experienced all the consciousness of such guilt, without the power to acknowledge or repair it.

He took the simple little gold chain to which it was attached, in his hand, looked at it intently, as though for the first time he were making acquaintance with himself. What a warm, rich light seemed trickling out from beneath the drooping lids, and inundating the whole subtle, softly-vivid face. In looking on it he began to exonerate Laura Milsland from the burden of her past obstinacy of feeling; he began to pity her, to sympathise with her, to comprehend her. Artist as he was, he understood in all its bearings the power of that ardent, glorious face, over an imaginative girl; its power, not only from its perfect outlines, but from the vague, melancholy depths of its expression. Then the conviction smote upon him with a hurting thrill, that the face before him belonged to the past, and would never be his again; the pursuit of ephemeral pleasure for one thing, had blown out the light of youthful enthusiasm, and merely vacancy and fretfulness, usurped its place. Yes, the young, earnest, rapt beauty of that mocking image was never to be his again, and doubtless, Laura in seeing it, awoke from her dream of devotion, and no longer loving him, had come to treat him like a common-place mortal. No wonder she was so much at her ease with him now; it was not self-control, but the absence of feeling, that made her so calm. He told himself he was very much pleased with the conviction, and very much relieved; but one way or another, this peculiar item of self-communication ended in making him just a little peevish.

A moment after, when Laura returned to the room, giving him scarcely time to replace the necklace and close the spring, she found him looking abstracted and decidedly cross. Not knowing what she had done to offend him, she did not notice it, even when a short time afterwards he took leave of her, without being restored to tranquillity; two years before, such a circumstance would have left her in a state of dreadful suspense and anxiety; but now, it no longer moved her. Ah, me, what a useless strength the absence of hope brings! Nothing Victor could do could have any sensible effect on Laura; having resigned him out of her thoughts and her hopes, she suffered no more by him. What could it matter to her, whether he were kind, or cross, or cruel, or generous, when God had plainly answered her prayers of unspeakable anguish and supplication with an unswerving—no! Had she not given her heart to idolatry in the wilderness of her passionate love! and now the promised land of happiness was forever denied her. No, she understood and accepted with dreadfully patient resignation, God's dark decree that she and Victor were two parallel lines in His universe, and though they might be produced to all eternity, they could never meet and be tranfused into one another. No, her approach to him was forbidden in all the long, calm, unanswering cycles of the ages. She felt like one lying drowned in a fathomless sea, and staring up through the interminable waters with dead, unsentient eyes, at the shining of the summer moon.

## CHAPTER IV.

"LAURA, I wish you would let him have it, it would be the best for us all."

"Why, Aggy, I wish I could think with you; I hate to contend over it. But it seems to me to be simply a trick to defraud both me and you."

"But, dear, you don't understand how necessary it is for him to secure the situation."

"Why, Agnes, do you mean to tell me that in our informal country, a man cannot get into a mercantile situation without previously spending three hundred dollars on his clothes?"

"Well, but you know how necessary it is to make a

good impression, and Josey has such a commanding figure when he's dressed up."

"I fancy it doesn't command any body but you, Aggy. Your husband isn't fit for any mercantile position. He might play the walking villians at some theatre."

"What do you mean by the walking villians?"

"Why, the counterpart to the walking gentleman; the villian that walks in to fill up crevices, not the one that sits and plots and helps to carry the play on his shoulders. The villian that comes on only to scowl and grimace, and mutter preposterous menaces, and is always the same whether he comes in, in tarnished finery of scraggy gilt lace, or in a slouched hat and cut away. The one whose chief business it is to roll his eyes, and grind his teeth, and look very terrible and ridiculous."

"The worst trait in your character, Laura, is the persistent prejudice with which you always judge my husband. Of course, he is not perfect; but he has in him all the elements of greatness, crushed by adverse circumstances, and an unsympathetic world. I see you are laughing at me. I know you never understood my love for him."

"I ought not to say that to his wife."

"Still it is true."

"Yes, if you will have it."

"I should think, considering the kind of man you loved yourself, you might understand any kind of a wretch getting love."

"I beg your pardon, Agnes, Victor Doria never was a bad man in any sense of the word. Indeed, if you will excuse my saying so, I never could have loved a man who was not in himself worthy of it."

"And do you mean to say he was that?"

"Yes, I do. I never did and never expect to see the man so rich in all the qualities fitted to call out and retain a woman's love."

"He did not always show them."

"No, but I was so fortunate, or rather so unfortunate, as to see below the surface. A vast deal of trash and drift-wood he has gathered in flowing through the world, but he's a deep stream underneath, for all that."

"Oh, Laura, when you begin to talk sentiment, I don't understand you."

"Don't you, Aggy? Well, then, I'll speak plainly. Tell me where you ever saw so much strength, tenderness, grace, impulsiveness, kindliness, generosity, tact, warmth, chivalric feeling, personal beauty and genius combined, as in him?"

"Well, I cannot say, there's a great deal that is delightful about him. I'm very fond of him too; but then, Laura, don't you think he was at fault in his treatment of you?"

"In a measure, yes; but I didn't say he had no faults, did I? for he has many."

"But how could you love a man who so evidently hated you? explain me that."

"That was because mine was an ill-balanced character. If I had been a truly self-respecting girl, I could not have done it. It was a blind and rapacious selfishness that made me love him under such circumstances. I was always a quick judge of character, you know. I saw what qualities made up his nature, and greedily clutching at them, strove to make them mine, without waiting to see whether I had any right to think of him or not."

"What does a right to think of him mean?"

"Why, the power in myself to inspire a feeling, before I asked for it. Not having that power to inspire it, I was simply acting the part of a marauder and desperado, when I tried to extort a feeling, I had no right to demand."

"You are cured now, quite changed, are you not?"

"Changed? Yes, I am changed. You don't see me fretting and pining now."

"No, but you always were such a strange girl. You look so wearied at times."

"And so I am; life seems a long, dull road to me, down which I am to travel, without looking forward to any pleasant stopping-places."

"Well, however that may be, I am always happy with you. I don't feel in the least angry with you for not letting me have the money I wanted. I've no doubt you are right, you always are; but Josey will give me a terrible scolding; he said I *must* get the money; he would not take no for an answer."

"Let him come to me, and I'll settle that matter."

"He would not come; he's dreadfully afraid of you. All his anger will be visited on me."

Several hours later, when they were all three dining together, Agnes' words were proved true, by her husband's almost savage treatment of her. Laura endured it as long as she could, but at last she turned to him with, "Mr. Willister, let your wife alone; don't attack her because you know she can't defend herself. If you wish to quarrel, be man enough to face me."

"I have no quarrel with you—but you don't know what a nuisance Agnes is."

"Let your wife alone, I tell you, and address what you have to say to me."

"Oh, my darling Josey," interrupted Agnes, "I

hope you don't think I'm to blame; you know how much I love you."

"Your love be hanged; of what use is it to me?"

"Oh, my dear," and she began to press some caresses upon him, which he brushed off as though they had been flies.

"And now, Mr. Willister, I don't intend to bear your treatment of your wife much longer; it has become intolerable."

"If you've been complaining of me, you beastly, deceitful little fool, I'll settle it by boxing your ears for you," finishing this speech with a brutal push, that sent her crying on the floor.

"Mr. Willister," cried Laura, rising and drawing her tall figure up to its proudest height, "it would be a compliment to call you a coward. I will not endure the contamination of your presence a moment longer. Leave the room, leave the house, leave the world! if you have the courage!"

Under this address, he dropped his bold eyes, stole out of the room like a beaten dog, and Laura and Agnes were alone together.

"Oh, Laura, call him back," cried Agnes, through her tears; "how could you? What if he never came home?"

"That would be too blessed a consummation, to be expected."

"Do you think, he will ever forgive me?"

"I don't know whether he will give you his forgiveness. I am sure he will sell it to you for fifty cents."

"Laura, how cruel you are!"

"No, I'm not; I'm only kind. See if you are not better treated after this. Beside, don't you see it was an indirect insult to me, to abuse you in my presence?"

"Why?"

"Any man who scolds, censures or rudely criticises his wife in the presence of others, offers a gross insult to every one who witnesses it. It is laying down life's best covenances, and intimating to the company that they are not worthy, even of a pretense to decency."

"But I suppose I am to blame sometimes."

"You are very much to blame, and I will tell you how,—by forcing upon him attentions and caresses, he gives you to understand are disagreeable."

"But how else am I to prove I love him?"

"By showing a little consistent dignity and good sense. He is the best judge whether your kisses are acceptable, and since he strongly intimates they are not, don't fortify yourself with your marriage certificate, and force them on him like a punishment."

"But I've always thought continual demonstrations of affection, the way to win a return from a husband."

"But your experience has proved it is not."

"Yes, but I always thought——"

"Never mind what you always thought; common sense and discretion were given to us as guides in the marriage state, as well as in anything else. Be a kind and loyal wife, and let your husband understand that you love him, but show some self-respect, dignity and reticence, and don't wrangle half the time he is at home, and whine the other half. Depend upon it, even Willister will respect you more if you show yourself to be a reasonable woman and a lady, rather than a mere crawling, kissing, quarreling creature."

"I will try, dear sister; I wish I had the courage and strength you have."

"I have neither, Agnes. This scene is far more trying to me than to you. Contention is very hurtful to me, because I have no courage left but moral courage; and as I use that on occasions when the cheapest physical courage would serve me as well, you can imagine how very expensive I find it. You think because I am cool and self-commanding at such moments, that I have no agitations to conquer, but it is the very excess of agitation which renders me calm. I feel now as if I had dispensed my vital fluid most wastefully, by some harsh physical fatigue—sawing a cord of wood, for instance."

## CHAPTER V.

Notwithstanding the disagreeable way in which Victor took his leave of Laura, after his discovery in her jewel casket, his almost daily visits were not sensibly interrupted. It was plain to him that Laura was not flattered by these attentions, nor even seemed to consider them as anything but accidents. Indeed, such was her evident lack of self-consciousness at this time, it was difficult to make her trace any occurrence to a personal cause. At this stage of her life, the absence of self-consciousness was even more excessive, than its presence had been at an earlier date. This circumstance made it difficult for Victor to quite understand her. If he put a direct question to her, regarding herself, she always answered it simply and frankly, but then the subject was immediately a closed book; nothing seemed to tempt her into revelation regarding her own inner life. This perfect artlessness of Laura's character puzzled him more than any other quality; for, to a man of the world, nothing is more impenetrable and more mysterious than entire simplicity in a woman. Sometimes, he satisfied himself in his impulsive way that she was acting a part, which explained it all. But sober second thought caused him to ask, " but acting it, why, for what end? what can she have to gain by it?" Because as he had convinced himself she no longer entertained a sentiment for him, he could not respond to the question of sober thought, and so grew more puzzled than ever.

One evening he called, as usual, and, being invited by the servant-girl to walk up, suddenly entered the drawing-room, and found a gentleman, who, just at the moment of his appearance, was handing to Laura two perfectly new crisp bills, for some manuscript, she had laid before him. The stranger, at his entrance, seemed very much confused, so that Laura was obliged to assure him he need not mind the new comer, as he was an old friend of hers, accompanying the words with so sweet a smile, that neither of the gentlemen could help being softened by it.

Laura introduced the stranger to Victor as Mr. Middleton; the gentleman who was kind enough to give her legal papers to copy, and then Victor saw, by the guilty look which stole over his rival's face, that the legal copying was all a mockery, on his own part, copying got up for the occasion, and overpaid at the most enormous rate. Victor would have been delighted to find traces of a treacherous design in this act, but he was obliged to acknowledge to himself it was only the deceit of kindness; a well-intentioned, if not discreet way of aiding a woman whom he had admired in prosperity, and now respected in adversity.

And how tempting the opportunity, to one who wished to befriend her, had been; for what could be easier than to deceive Laura—she who had stepped straight from the pedantry of her school life, into the whirl of fashion and amusement? What could she know of the value of money, and the rates of remuneration in the outer world of labor?

For an instant, Victor suspected Laura of being a party in the deception; but he rejected his own suspicion with scorn the next moment, when he saw her turn her face—that pale, lovely, tender, faded, almost heavenly face—to Mr. Middleton, and ask whether he had any more work for her to do? Victor looked at him like a bird of prey, while he hesitated for a moment, but he returned the former a look of determined defiance, and replied that he had, and always would have as much for her to do as she desired. Laura looked as pleased as a child who has been paid in silver by its mother for gathering peach-stones or flower-seeds. Indeed, as she sat there, with her little hands folded in her lap, and the tender, trustful smile on her lips, in despite of the marked traces of care and sorrow which dimmed her face, she seemed like a little child. Both of the men marked and wondered at this, and it only increased the resolution of the one, and the angry disgust of the other. Laura glanced from one to the other, in the same gentle, childish way, with a half deprecating look, as though she feared if there was anything wrong she was at fault. As soon as Mr. Middleton saw this troubled look, being far the more generous of the two, he at once rose to go, that she might not be annoyed by the evident ill-feeling between them. Before he went he took Laura's hand, with a quiet deference, which shamed Victor's fitful kindness.

Mr. Middleton was precisely the type of man to excite Victor's envy and indignation. He was quite above the medium height, and framed in proportion; his features were large, fine, and fair; his manner a mixture of perfect equanimity, self-control, and a subdued sense of power; which qualities, taken all together, were calculated to set Victor's fickle character, man of genius though he was, at a painful disadvantage. It was easy to see that he knew his own wishes, and intended to pursue them by all the honorable means in his power, which—as Victor was conscious that out of the realms of art he never knew his own mind for two consecutive hours—made him feel, in comparison, like a feather blown about in the wind.

Well, after all, however fascinating he may be to his objects of pursuit, the male flirt, when compared with the man of determined honor and dignity, is, in the abstract, but a pitiful spectacle.

To tell the truth, this was the reflection that passed through Laura's mind, as she saw them together; but, even as she entertained it, it brought, instead of contempt for the man she loved, an infinite pity and tenderness.

It was plain to her that Victor was annoyed and angry, but difficult for her to find any reason for it. It never occurred to her that any act or relation of hers could arouse him, so she quietly came to the conclusion, his annoyance ante-dated his visit. Suddenly, he asked her—

"Who was that fellow who has just gone—where did you know him?"

"He is a gentleman, I knew in my father's house," spoken with an intonation which signalled a determination not to allow his name to be slighted, a determination Victor at once perceived was not to be trifled with.

As he said nothing more, she asked, "When do you expect to play again?"

"Soon. I don't know; I'm not quite certain. I don't care to play at all. I'm sick of it."

"That's astonishing! But, tell me truly, isn't it a real personal pleasure to do anything one can do so incomparably well?"

"No. How many people in the audience are capable of judging whether I play well or ill? It's all a mere question of happy accident."

"Oh, no; I'm sure I could never feel as I do, when I see you on the stage, just from an accidental combination of circumstances."

"Do you mean to class yourself with the common, gaping herd who fill theatres? Why, of course you are one of the few, whom I look to as the final judges."

"How strange! why, I never thought I had any judgment about the drama."

"That shows how little you know yourself, or how much you have taught me."

"Now, Victor, that's too bad; I see you are laughing at me, and I don't think you are fair to me."

"I believe you are right there. But, tell me, how long have you been copying for Mr. Middleton?"

"About six weeks. I think him very kind to serve me. Most men would have hated to give regular paid work to one who was so lately in such different circumstances; but his kindness, really, is genuine."

"Upon my life, I never would have imagined you so easy to deceive. I've remarked always, that when a woman is above the usual size, larger both as to mind and body, than the average of her sex, her capacity for being deceived is proportionably wide."

"Victor, I don't understand you."

"I mean to say, Laura, you are ridiculously fooled by that man. He is paying you at least ten times as much as it is worth for the copying you do; besides, he makes no use of what you copy, unless it be to light the office fires."

"You frighten me. Why, then, does he let me do it?"

"Only as a means of rendering you assistance; he is taking advantage of your innocence and trustfulness."

"I am troubled, truly troubled; but I see you are right. It must be so. It was rather questionable kindness, after all. I am sorry—so sorry!"

Her mobile lips trembled so as she said this, and she looked so much as if she were going to weep, that he replied—

"Don't be angry with me for telling you so, my dear little girl; I thought you ought to know it."

"I'm not angry; I'm only discouraged. I shall try no more copying."

"I'm sure I've offended you, I'm so abrupt. I don't know exactly how to deal with women; you see, I never had any sisters."

Laura was obliged to smile at this sudden assumption of ignorance, on the part of a man of his experience of the female world, simply because he had no sisters,—indeed it was the first time he had failed to let an opportunity slip of informing her he knew women better than they knew themselves; a boast which, foolish as it appeared, was true in the main, and Laura knew it.

"How hard it is, Victor, for a woman to find a friend; I thought I could rely on Mr. Middleton's honor, if on any man's."

"But if you want a friend, cannot I be that friend?

surely our long acquaintance entitles me to your confidence."

"No, it doesn't. I could never expect you to be a strong friend to me, or to place much reliance in me."

"Why?"

"Because I have shown you my worst faults; and however much I may have conquered them, you would never believe it. First impressions are always the strongest. You would always be measuring me by the standard of the worst acts of my life. I could never expect you would believe me to be actuated by any better motive than selfishness."

"How could I think so—how could I dare to think so? But tell me, what will you say to your friend Mr. Middleton?"

"I think I shall contrive to be truthful, without offending him. It may be conceit; but I really think he likes me."

"Likes you? he venerates you."

"Venerates!—what a word to use regarding a weak, wayward creature like me. But I shall not accept any more *work* from him."

"Laura," he commenced, then stopped, for his voice seemed to choke in his throat, till overmastering himself with an effort, he went on, "Laura, I want to ask a favor of you."

"Ask—but a favor from one so helpless as I! it seems strange."

"Laura, you recollect your father was trustee for a piece of property left to me in Dorn?"

"I recollect it, of course."

He continued in a hurried, almost breathless manner, "you know I thought it worth nothing; even wished to give it away, if I could find any body to accept it. Your father kept it, and when circumstances vastly enhanced its value, he took the trouble, gratuitously, to sell it and invest the money for me. When he made it over to me it amounted to nearly ten thousand dollars. I let it accumulate with its own interest—I never needed it, so I fancied to let it lie by and nurse itself. I hardly feel as though it were mine; I shall never use it. I have nobody on earth dependent on me, and the drama's so profitable when one is lucky,—Laura, Laura, will you take it—will you be generous enough to accept it?"

He saw her features quiver and shrink as though she had received a blow, and he saw also how hard the struggle was to keep back the heavy water drops, till her eyes were full of that wide, wistful look that tells of swallowed tears. By degrees she recovered the command of herself, and answered gently, but firmly, "No, Victor. I thank you deeply; but no, no, I cannot touch it."

"Oh, Laura, why not?"

"Because if I did, it would crush me right down into the dust; I would never dare to respect myself again. And you wouldn't ask me to lay down my self-respect. Think how little I have left on earth; I have lain down all, let all go, but I cherish that; it's all I have left to me. You wouldn't ask me to lay down that?"

"You don't understand me; you won't understand the spirit in which I make the offer."

"Oh, yes, I do; do I not answer you gently and humbly, and would I do that if your offer were anything but the most delicate and disinterested?"

"Then why will you not trust me? Why will you not allow me the inconceivable happiness of serving you?"

"You do serve me—you do serve me by your kind

feeling; it takes away from the bitterness of my regrets; I couldn't have been such an obstinate, silly, wicked girl, after all. If you don't—don't quite think ill of me. But don't talk to me of money—spare me that."

"Because you have no confidence in me, because you despise me, because you look down on me, because an act of kindness coming through me, would be tainted from my hands."

"No, no; I would sooner receive a kindness from you than any one in the world, or out of it; but you can't think how little terror the future has for me. Do you know, I sometimes think I would like to endure keen poverty, live in a real garret, and live on bread, and go hungry some days, and all those things one reads of! I don't fear them."

"Well, if you don't fear for yourself, I do for you. If you were to come to any such trouble as that, I should never have another moment free from remorse."

"But why so? You are not to blame, if any harm comes to me."

"I am to blame for every thing. I have caused you more trouble than I am worth. I almost wish somebody had shot me, before I ever met you."

"But I don't; and I am glad of this chance to tell you something; it has been on my mind for a long, long time. I recollect accusing and abusing you dreadfully one day—indeed many days tacitly, by manner, if not by speech; but I was very unfair, very unjust to you. Now, I know that I have no one but myself to blame for any thing that has happened to me; all my troubles arose from the signal defects of my own character. I won't say you were quite blameless; but your faults were against yourself, not against me. If I loved you,—forgive me for saying so now—it was because I needed to love you. You never could have won me against my own wishes; it was my own sophistries that entangled me, not yours. I was perfectly able to defend myself from you, but I did not. When I struggled, it was against the giant-tempter, myself—not against you. Child as I was, I saw through your pretty arts from the first; I could have laughed at them, had it not been that my own impatient, self-confident soul, of its own free will, deliberately elected to love you. Do you think I considered you, or took any thought of your good?—no; the whole absorbing question to me then was myself, myself, myself."

"You say so because you are, you always were too generous to me, and it—it is so easy to speak magnanimously of a feeling entirely past."

"So it is."

"But even if you don't like me, you might be generous enough to accept the offer I make."

"No, no, why will you speak of it, when it is so plainly painful to me?"

"Yet you have been receiving a kindness from another man, and you are not angry with him."

"I thought you quite understood how ignorantly I have received it."

"I do understand, but whether willingly or not, he has been able to prove himself your friend, and not I. It isn't fair. Won't you yield, Laura? will you accept my offer?"

"Victor Doria, I have tried in all humility to show you how impossible it would be for me to act as you propose. I tell you now, I owe you enough already. I owe you this youth, poured out on the desert sands of infruition,—I owe you this heart, that having wept away its blood like tears, will be dry evermore,—I owe you this pale face, with its wasted beauties and its pitiful lines, every one of which marks the grave of a hope,—I owe you the resurrection of all those hopes, that their mortality has put on immortality,—I owe you a lost world, and I owe you the gain of my own soul. I will not owe you any more; my debt to you is too heavy to bear now; I will owe you nothing more."

Long before she concluded, she had risen from her chair, and stood towering over him with her tall, supple figure erect, and her face all ablaze with dark tints of fiery color, while he sat quite crushed and cowed with his head bowed in his hands.

Neither of them broke the silence for a few moments, then he rose and said he hoped she would pardon anything he had said to offend her, and was about to take leave of her. But she seeing him so overcome, held out her hand to him with a wistful, caressive smile. Hitherto he had hardly dared to touch more than the tips of her fingers, but now he grasped her whole hand impulsively, and he felt her nervous fingers quiver and press his own as in a spasm.

He went from her presence touched with a giddy lightness of head, feeling as though the general material world were rocking like a great drowsy cradle. It was not a warm evening, but heavy drops of moisture stood on his face, which he brushed away with an unsteady hand. The air felt oppressive; all the world seemed like a slow furnace, with the fires raked out, but the doors tightly shut, steeping all things in a dull, sickening, insipid heat. Every now and then his imagination reproduced the quivering clasp of those delicate fingers, and each time a subtle thrill slid through all his pulses, leaving a feverish restlessness as it passed. How many times memory re-created this insidious moment, and his heart swam in his breast at the thought it was hard to say, but often enough to make him unable to do anything but wander about the streets, for the rest of the evening, lost in wonder at himself.

Was it possible, he asked himself, that in the old days he had held that form in his arms, kissed those lips, gathered that head to his breast? He answered no; it might be true, but it was impossible, or else how could the light clasp of that hand so upheave his whole mental and physical nature!

He went to sleep with the feeling still at work in his breast, and he dreamed that he walked in a strange field by night, and tripping caught at nothing, and so plucked up her hand, and it did not stir his with its tremor, only because she was asleep in her grave.

## CHAPTER VI.

"You cannot imagine, Laura, how much I am obliged to you. Why, Josey is quite another man; and just to think that one good scolding had such an effect! It quite bewilders me. Why, I've been trying to scold him for two years, and he grew only worse for it."

"I am glad it has been beneficial, my dear, though it has since seemed to me rather a presumption on my part to attempt to reprove another woman's husband. It was unmannerly, but I really think for this once, the end must be allowed to justify the means."

"He never says a sharp word to me now; why, he's as civil to me as though I were not his wife; he couldn't speak more properly if I were an indifferent stranger. Isn't it wonderful!"

"An amazing phenomenon indeed."

"Laura, he brought me three pounds of candies and confectionery the other night; did you ever know any nicer treatment than that?"

"Scarcely—but I remember they made you distressingly sick the next day."

"Of course they did; but you know in the married state one must be prepared to endure trouble for the other party. Why, I'd be willing to live entirely on sugar-plums to please Josey; I should consider it my duty."

"Even though it completely prostrated your digestion. Well, I trust you are learning how to live with him without teasing him, and that I shall never again have to interfere between you."

"O, yes, indeed—but, Laura, don't call it interference; you haven't an idea of how much Josey thinks of your judgment. I believe he would rather please you than anybody. Do you know he almost blushes when you come in the room, and if he seems to be about to get a little cross, I have only to threaten him with telling you, and he becomes as sweet as a daisy at once. Oh! you have a wonderful influence over him, and I am so glad of it."

"Why, Agnes, I am not; I think it very ill-advised of you to use me as an implement of domestic discipline. I don't wish to have your husband governed by the wish to please me; I wish you could employ some better motive."

"What better could I employ, as long as he thinks the world of you?"

"Oh, Agnes, will you always be a child? But no

matter, since you are so happy; I must try to battle with my annoyances alone."

"Since you talk of that, I have some bad news for you, my dearest Laura," said Agnes, with a suddenly rueful countenance.

"Bad news for me! how can that be? I have no hopes abloom to be blighted. I am not expecting my ship from sea, you know, for she was wrecked some time ago—passengers, crew and cargo all a total loss. I am impregnably intrenched in the fortress of no expectations; how can your news be anything but neutral to me?"

"It is something about Victor." In spite of herself, the muscles of Laura's mouth gave a sudden spring. "Laura, he is engaged; he is going to be married."

"Well, Agnes, what is that to me; what possible claim have I to be interested in his movements?"

"Ah, but dear Laura, you feel it, I know you do, and that's why I told you, for fear you might hear it from some one else."

"Who is the lady, Agnes?"

"That is the greatest surprise of all; it is your old classmate, Julia Sydney."

"Is it so? She has a fine head. Oh, how many times I have knocked it against the pump! I always ill-treated her. I had no mercy on her. She was a dreadful coward in water, and I used to duck her gloriously in the bay. I came near drowning her once— I wish I had, now."

"There, Laura, I knew you would be distressed by the news."

"No, I'm not; why should I feel it at all? Agnes, it would be indelicate, it would be impertinent for me to feel anything about it."

"That doesn't make any difference; you can't help your feelings."

"O yes, I can; or at least I can help expressing them, even to my inmost self."

"But, dear Laura, his visits have been such a comfort to you; you were so lonely before; now he can't come any more, for she has arrived."

"Where has she been?"

"At the Springs. They got engaged on the steamer coming over. They say she's a complete beauty; fair as a white rose. I don't mean any offence to your style, Laura, for I think a brunette can be as handsome as a blonde; but Victor doesn't think so; he loves a fair beauty."

"So do I; when I die and wake in a new world, I shall be fair, too, I know I shall. Dark faces, like mine, belong to this evil—cruel earth." Then Laura's tears began to flow, as though her only grief were the brunette nature of her complexion.

"Laura, don't you love Victor still?"

"Not for this world—not for this world."

"What kind of a world do you love him for, then? I think you love him for a talking, dancing, eating, dressing, going-to-theatre world."

"Don't talk so."

"I say so, because I know your fidelity of heart."

"Fidelity!—fidelity to a man who feels as Victor Doria does to me, is simply an impertinence, and I have no desire to offer him one."

"But you know the loving heart remembers even——"

"Don't talk to me about a loving heart; you might just as well hope to entertain one who has been overrun by a train of cars, by talking of the beauty of the locomotive power."

"I am sorry if I've offended you."

"You haven't offended me. I am in a bad humor; I slept too late this morning. I feel a little bitter. I think I will take a long, long walk, to try and sweeten my temper."

"Yes, that you may be alone to suffer; you wish to hide yourself from me. Laura, I fear this is too heavy for you; you will never be able to bear it."

"O, yes, I shall; I can bear anything. You don't know my capacity for existing without living. You were talking about the fine way in which the turnips you planted were growing—think of me, and don't give them all the credit. When you praise them next, I intend to have my share; just be pleased to say 'my turnips and my Laura are thriving so nicely.'"

"You laugh, Laura, but your laugh makes me long to cry."

"Joking apart, Aggy, don't fear for me. I am blessed with great powers of endurance; whatever happens, I shall wear through it some way. One way or another, I shall bear it, and bear it patiently."

Agnes having nothing more to say, quietly cried over the little dress she was making, while Laura set lost in painful thought. Agnes supposed she was thinking of the unpleasant tidings she had communicated; but in fact Laura had a more immediate source of annoyance, which pressed for her weary attention. Agnes had remarked the influence Laura had acquired over her husband; but the fact that he was actually become enamored of her sister, naturally escaped her superficial notice. But Laura had marked it with an inexpressible dissatisfaction. Under the influence of this sentiment, he began to act quite like a gentleman. He followed Laura with his eyes, blushed when she entered the room, sprang up to do her lightest wish, and what to Laura was the strongest confirmation of her fears, he became suddenly timid and self-doubting. Agnes, instead of extinguishing, was continually fanning the flame, with her unceasing eulogies of her sister. All Laura's sweetest traits of character were presented to the contemplation of the man, who was falling in love with her in spite of himself, and they helped materially to accelerate his pace. On Laura the main trouble of course accumulated, for she felt how impossible it would be for her to remain in the same house with him, while this state of feeling continued. How it was to be improved, she could not see, for to a man of Willister's disposition, repulsion was the highest attraction. She foresaw that the more she humbled and conquered him, the more he would love her. He could bully and bluster, and be very savage to a clinging, all-yielding little creature like Agnes; but the moment a woman like Laura took the trouble to punish him for his conduct, his power of resistance was gone; he crumbled away, and out of the ruins of his self-sufficiency, was created a servile affection for her who had mastered him.

There are male as well as female spaniels in the world, and their bark is apt to have been notoriously loud, before the foot comes to spurn them.

Such a reflection passed through Laura's mind, but it suggested nothing on the troublesome question of what to do with Willister. Seductive visions of having him impressed by a master of a vessel, and shipped before the mast for a voyage to Mozambique, floated through her fancy; but delightful as they were, she was obliged to dismiss them as impracticable. Besides, such an expedient would destroy the happiness of Agnes, which after all was before her own, in Laura's estimation.

Turn and turn the subject as she might, it led but to one way of extrication ; her own departure from the roof which sheltered, the always abominable Willister, now insufferably smitten with her own charms.

It was useless to evade that conclusion; so she said, trying to appear unconcerned, " Agnes, isn't it strange, how entirely useless I am in the world? I used to be considered a wonderful scholar at school and very remarkable at home, did I not? I believe you all thought I could do anything."

" So you can—nearly everything."

" I can do just nothing. Think how many young women earn their own living, make their way in the world, take professions—the stage and such things—make fortunes, and are all together grand and independent. Look at me !"

" What for ?"

" Just to notice how incapable I am of doing any of these things. I can't teach anything you know ; I can criticise other people's sewing, and show them how it ought to be done, but I can't sew myself. I am afraid I should boggle considerably in most any occupation."

" Couldn't you write for the newspapers ?"

" Oh, Aggy, really that is too much. Don't you know how I hate to write even letters, and when I do write them, whether they be of friendship or ceremony, they finish before I get to the end of one page of notepaper, and leave me room for a voluminous flourish under my name! When I take a pen in my hand, my whole being seems to concentrate itself in one faculty— that of condensation. Even in my best days, if I wanted to order the whole of a new bonnet, I was as laconic over it as a Cæsar would be over the trifle of a conquered nation. If I wanted a dress trimmed with buttons, I was not sufficiently skillful to skirmish over the whole field of trimmings, with their objections—I just said buttons, and was done with it. Now, you know that kind of style would be entirely fatal for newspapers."

"Well, I believe you have no turn for writing. Would you like to go on the stage?"

"My dear, no; I haven't the courage for it. You can scarcely believe, remembering me as I formerly was, how unfitted I am for contention. Going from private life on the stage, until one has fairly succeeded, is just one long spasm of contention; contention with your friends, who imagine themselves disgraced by your attempt; contention with the already members of the dramatic profession, because they are resolved to keep all its honors to themselves if possible; contention with the public, who, holding the opinion that to act is to be outside of Nature, (I confess they have not been without reason for thinking so,) cannot admit that any one so lately of themselves, could properly undertake anything so monstrous."

"But other people take to the stage and succeed there, in spite of all these objections you have alleged."

"So they do; but I am sure they are less dependent on surroundings than I am. When I am opposed, I simply sink into less than nothingness. If any one disputes my theories, I am paralyzed into having none for the time. If I am to be anything more in the future than the mere suggestion of a woman, I must have sympathy. You know how little of that I could expect in the dramatic profession. But indeed I don't think of it—never did."

"Have you other ideas?"

"Nothing to speak of. I am afraid I am about good for nothing under the sun."

"I'll tell you what you are good for, Laura; good to make those happy with whom you are in daily intercourse. See how happy you make me, my little girl, and Joe! Why, even Bridget feels your influence, and rejoices in it. You say you know how to do nothing; why, just looking at you teaches her more than all my scolding. If you call her, she drops whatever she is doing, and runs as though her life depended on it. I may see her guilty of every carelessness in the world, but she is as anxious to appear well before you, as a young lady before her first admirer. For a smile from you, she will scrub from morning to night; but she wouldn't wash a plate decently for me, though I should get black in the face through ordering it. There's the landlady—I can get nothing from her but frowns, and objections, and rudeness, even when I talk to her by the hour, while you have only to come down and smile and intimate your wishes, she is subdued at once, hastens to do your bidding, and seems to get actual joy out of pleasing you. How on earth do you manage it?"

"I think it is only in your imagination, it exists at all."

"Not at all. Why, even the ice-man told Bridget he considered Miss Milsland to be completely lovely."

"I suppose, then, if I can thaw the heart of the ice-man, it must not be disputed there is some sunshine in me?"

"Exactly so. Everybody likes to be with you; I believe you could almost manage anybody, whether they were in their senses or not."

"I take your idea now. You think me quite capable of conducting a lunatic asylum, of managing maniacs. Doubtless, you are right; I have managed the greatest of them all—myself. You are convinced I would be perfectly adjusted as an organizing frontispiece to Bedlam?"

"I don't mean anything like that; but I can't say the simplest word to you, without your running off into such queer ideas, that I don't even try to understand them."

"For all that, you have given me an idea. I am just fitted to be a companion to somebody, to make life less dull to such an one, and more so to myself. Mrs. Middleton is urging me to pay her a long visit; I think I could make myself agreeable to her, as a companion. I shall go."

"You must consider that you are likely to meet Victor there."

"What of that? Is it also one of my duties to retire from all the earth he walks on?"

"No. But, do you think you would be equal to it?"

"I should hope I might be something more than equal to—that I might exceed that small ordeal."

"Oh, but, Laura, you can't deceive me; I know you still love him."

"Then, why are you not charitable enough to hide my turpitude, instead of forcing me to confess it? Don't you see me trying, like a properly conducted young lady, to be an imposition on my acquaintances—to make them believe I am heartless, when I am not? Do let me be decently hypocritical, nor force me to the degradation of candor."

"Then, you still love him," cried Agnes, with all the eagerness of a childish curiosity.

"If the information is of any use to you—yes. If I didn't love him, what, in heaven's name, would give me the impulse to go on breathing so regularly? I should just gradually evaporate, that's all."

"Then, darling, it seems to me imprudent to go to a house where you are in danger of seeing him; you will be jealous."

"Oh, no; jealousy belongs to a happier love than mine. I am far outside of jealousy. There is always some little hope and claim, however futile, to build jealousy on. I have not enough of these to bear the weight of a cobweb. I have no sentiment, but the one that he exists, and draws me towards himself."

"What do you mean by that?"

"I mean, there is only one drop of comfort for me in the whole cup of life—to see him sometimes, to listen to his voice."

"What sort of pleasure can that be, when he is nothing to you, and you know he belongs to another? I thought when a woman loved a man, it made her wretched to know she was indifferent to him, and his feelings were absorbed by some one else."

"So it does; but a chain of sequences is a wonderful thing, Aggy. I began bravely enough. I clamored for all, or nothing. At first, if he did not seem entirely to return my sentiment; if he noticed another, or was impatient with my follies, I took the privilege of being outraged, angry, and miserable. Then, I dropped my pretentions down to having a part of my feeling reciprocated, to his noticing me a little more than others. By easy steps, it came to hoping he would accept my affection, and be pleased at my noticing him. Thence, it rolled rapidly into a sworn resolution to kill any lady he might fancy, kill him, kill myself; do everything that was dreadful, enormous and useless. You see where it has settled at last, into the habitual suppression of myself, as a daily life, and the wish to see him by chance for a festive occasion. In the eyes of utter privation, small comforts are greatly enhanced as to value; after a few days of wholesale starvation, it is impossible to know what might not be considered in the light of a banquet."

"I don't understand how you can make fun of yourself so."

"You will allow me, I trust, a privilege enjoyed by all those who know me—that of looking upon myself with a just ridicule and reasonable contempt. It would be hard if, after taking so much trouble to wear the garments of my dignity into rags, I cannot have the privilege of enjoying myself in the light of a scarecrow."

"I do hope you will never say these things to Victor."

"Oh, Agnes, that is too much; you know I never speak of anything but what he introduces. I feel as if the whole of my salvation lies between him and the slightest revelation of my love."

## CHAPTER VII.

Not many days after the conversation just related, Mrs. Middleton received Laura into her house, much to the satisfaction of that brother-in-law, who, having now lost Laura's services as a scribe, sturdily resolved to win her in another capacity.

To Laura, the return to an elegant house, whose luxurious appointments were equally consonant with her tastes and habits, was a pleasure greater than she liked to acknowledge to herself. For the first time, she really realized what a daily torment she had been undergoing in the shabby, mean lodgings, which had commended themselves to her as the necessary home of resolute and unmitigated poverty. She was now able to recall how, without the ill-favored street, with all its accompaniments of mean houses, vulgar people, and cheap stores; and within, the unrelaxing order of fried dinners of the present, and boiled dinners of the past, had kept all her senses in perennial punishment.

Mrs. Middleton was unfeignedly glad to see her. Even in Laura's most glowing days, she sincerely liked and admired her. From her age and uncommonly good sense, she never had any occasion to be offended by the girl's arrogance, or rendered envious by her great beauty. Besides, Laura's innate sense of justice, from the first, recognized Mrs. Middleton's superiority, and caused her to bear herself in her presence like a girl of sense and discretion. So, when she fell into the ways of misfortune, Mrs. Middleton was, of all her acquaintances, the one most prepared to offer her a generous and sympathetic friendship. Nor was Laura's heart tardy in responding to it, whatever her outward manner might be. Mrs. Middleton, though a woman of fifty, had always been the cherished friend of Victor. It was in her house he had first become familiarized with that sub-section of society which so greatly conduced to his success on the stage. It is not, then, to be wondered at, that Laura regarded her as a pattern of good taste, discretion, and noble feeling.

Laura had scarcely been there a day, before Victor called. As he did not seem in the least surprised to see her, it might have occurred to any girl with the least penetration, that he had been consulted on the score of the invitation; but of course, no such idea occurred to a mind warped by general intelligence, as Laura's was.

Laura's manner to him, did not in the least indicate the having heard any tidings relating to him, which had in any way excited or astonished her. In the course of the conversation, Mrs. Middleton remarked to Victor—

"You cannot think what a comfort it is to me, to have Laura with me."

"You are not at all complimentary to the force of my imagination."

"I know very well that young men, especially general favorites like you, have no conception of the delight to be procured from the companionship of an intelligent, cultivated, and affectionate girl like my Laura, for I intend her to be mine; I shall keep her as long as I live, if she will let me. Yet I know it would be unfair to expect her to be continually entertained with the society of an old woman like me, so I have invited a certain mutual friend of ours, Victor, to give me the pleasure of her company also, for a few weeks. Don't be too much overjoyed, when I say it is Julia Sydney."

The expression of Victor's countenance indicated any thing but the superabundance of joy, against which Mrs. Middleton cautioned him. A general discontent spread itself all over his features, which, when he recovered himself sufficiently to be able to look at Laura's face, and saw no change in its usual sweet gravity and invincible kindness to himself, deepened into mortification. If he could have seen in that mobile countenance the slightest trace of anguish, he felt certain that every pang of hers would have cancelled, at least, an equal amount of irritation on his own.

Mrs. Middleton, with the best intentions, not being able to mistake the expression of Victor's face for one of pleasure, was making up her mind to be puzzled over it, when the bell rang, and her brother-in-law was ushered into the room where they were sitting. She was delighted to see him, feeling as strong an attachment to him as though she were his own sister, and Laura's face also brightened at his appearance. Of course, Victor looked as disagreeable as possible, and Mr. Middleton's perfect indifference to his looks, intensified his animosity towards him.

Mrs. Middleton regretted that her brother had seen so little of her young friend Victor, one of them having been almost always unfortunately in Europe when the other was in America. Neither of the gentlemen seemed to echo her regrets, and then an alarming silence fell upon the four. It was broken by a well-timed application from Laura to Mr. Middleton, for a piece of information, which it seemed to raise his spirts to give her. Indeed, if it had not been for a vigorous ignorance on the part of the young lady, with an equally persistent resolve for its amelioration, the whole visit might have proved a disastrous failure. Mr. Middleton had studied human nature sufficiently to perceive the amiable motive from which her questions proceeded; nor was he without gratitude for the compliment paid to him, in singling him out as her instructor.

The elder gentleman took leave of them after a moderately short visit, and the younger one finally summoned the courage to tear himself away after an immoderately long one, the greater part of which was passed by him in remarks on the infamous unfitness of this world to serve as a temporary residence even for superior spirits, succeeded by lapses of moody and fidgety silence.

Before he came again, Julia Sydney was installed in

the house. Laura was not displeased to meet her again. In school, they had been, by turns, friends and foes; though the moments in which they had been opposed, exceeded in number those of amicable intimacy. Laura longed, with a certain measure of curiosity, to look on her who had played against her for all the stakes in life (to her mind), worth having, and won them. She was surprised to find no remarkable change in Julia; nothing that indicated that wonderful election to happiness, by whose means Laura expected her to be raised above human nature and its foibles. She was the Julia Sydney of old, who was affectionate and obstinate by turns, who was not much more selfish than young women generally are, but whose face and form were wonderfully beautified and developed by the lapse of time, and the refinements of superior cultivation and associations. It was impossible to deny her the merit of beauty, and of that most pleasing type, the thoroughly blonde beauty. Her eyes were of the most immaculate blue, without a tint of grey or violet in the shade; her hair was of the finest gold, with a natural wave in it; her features were all soft and shapely; her skin was of the most healthy, but dainty whiteness, and her figure was round, full, and well proportioned. The charming beauty of her former friend, scarcely six months younger than herself, although it made Laura, in thinking of her own altered face, feel very sorry for herself, only served to attract her towards Julia. For twenty-four hours they agreed like two twin turtle doves; but at the end of that time, a visit from Victor lessened the regard of Julia for her former friend. Julia was far shrewder and more sharp-sighted than Laura, and so Victor's peculiar manner did not escape her. There was an utter absence of that excessive devotion, and tender, flattering gallantry which had won her hand and heart on the trans-Atlantic steamer. He seemed to be absent-minded; looked rather to be dreaming than listening when she was talking to him, and worse than all, when Laura was in a distant part of the room, she caught his eye wandering towards her, with a vague, melancholy tenderness, which Julia resented by a freezing dignity in her own manner. To sum up his disgraceful conduct, no sooner had Laura made an excuse for leaving them alone together, than he suddenly remembered a most pressing engagement, and was off in less than two minutes.

Laura noticed for the rest of the day, that Julia was rather peevish; she simply let her alone, and amusing herself with other duties and occupations, soon forgot it entirely.

On several occasions after this, Victor called and behaved in so similar a manner, that even Mrs. Middleton censured him, and declared she never would have dreamed such a course of conduct possible to one of his temperament.

"Why, my dear Julia," she exclaimed, "I should have supposed he would be all vows, and sighs, and raptures in your presence; I thought he never could have shown enough gallantry to the chosen object of his heart. Should you not have thought so, Laura?"

"Your application to Laura is unfortunate, Mrs. Middleton, if you desire to have your opinion of Victor's ardent temperament certified. Miss Milsland's experience, we are forced to believe, will only go to show how perfectly indifferent and irresponsive he can be, to a young lady, even when her own attentions leave him no room to doubt of the state of her heart."

Mrs. Middleton, who, of course, had been aware of

Laura's partiality for Victor, and believed it to be now thoroughly eradicated, was amazed at the unkindness of Julia's speech. But her amazement was really superfluous, for there is no unkindness which may not be reasonably expected in the gladiatorial arena of female rivalry, and no barbarities which the successful woman will not consider it a virtue to practice on her conquered sister.

Laura was about to answer that she was not in the habit of parading before the public eye her intimate experiences, but remembering that in former days she had been in that habit, and being overrun by a most inconvenient integrity of mind, was obliged to sit silent and convicted—

Mrs. Middleton, however, in defence of her favorite, responded in rather dry tones—

"I am sure Miss Milsland's experiences, if she would condescend to give them, would be a pleasure and a benefit for us both. As for Mr. Doria, I am almost as fond of him as though he were my own son; but I am not blind to his failings; I know very well that his character is not one to inspire any lasting sentiment in a woman of Laura's superiority."

Laura could only give her defender an affectionate smile in response to this, for her mind was equally divided between gratitude for her tenderness, and surprise for her want of penetration.

## CHAPTER VIII.

AFTER a little hesitation, Victor was induced to accept another metropolitan engagement, to the secret delight of Laura, and the more open mortification of his betrothed. The latter did not scruple to remonstrate with him on his intention, to which he replied—

"I have no desire to renounce my profession, neither could I live without it. I am not accustomed to economy, and I believe you are equally wedded to a life of ease and luxury."

"You needn't exhibit yourself on the stage for that reason; my father is able to give me enough for both of us."

"That may suit your views, it does not suit mine. I never had any intention of entering your family as a dependant."

"You told me at sea you were sick of the stage, and meant to leave it."

"When I spoke of a sickness for anything, you should have taken into consideration my natural antagonism to the sea and its convulsions, and given me a wide margin for exaggeration."

"I don't want to joke on such a subject. You can never be entirely respectable, and act at the same time; the stage is disreputable—you know it is—everybody thinks so."

"Make one exception, just to please me; make one exception out of the solar system—Miss Milsland admires the profession, and honors me with her approbation in it."

"Very well; if Miss Milsland's opinion has more

weight with you than mine, I have nothing more to say."

Laura was busily engaged in some light piece of needle-work, which entirely absorbed her eyes; but Victor felt certain that, could he but see them, he would read the expression of some marked feeling, judging by the slightly compressed look of her mouth, and the general seriousness of her whole face.

"Miss Milsland's opinion," he replied, "must be of importance to every one who desires the best judgment on any subject."

"Indeed! how recently did you discover that? Her opinions were not used to be so weighty with you."

"I trust you will credit me with the power of getting rid of my ignorance as I grow older. I hope, because I was an idiot once, I am not to be held to the consistency of idiocy."

"It is a pity your wisdom had not come a little earlier; it might have saved Miss Milsland the trouble of losing her complexion."

"I should never presume to connect anything in Miss Milsland's appearance with myself."

"I congratulate you on your sudden acquisition of modesty. You used to tell a different story once."

By this time, Laura's tremulous fingers were tracing promiscuous errors all over her embroidery, and feeling unable to bear any more such allusions, she sprang hurriedly up, saying, as she left the room, "I am grieved to be the cause of this contention between you; but I ought not to listen to it, and I entreat you both to spare me as much as you can."

"Laura, Laura!" cried Victor, intercepting her at the door with outstretched hands, as though to hold her back; but she looked him full in the face, with her soft, sad eyes brimming over with a feeling he could not understand, so he let her pass without another word.

"If you are paying your court to Miss Milsland, Mr. Doria, I wonder you presume to continue your attentions to me, at the same time."

"It would be a useless court, any that I could pay to Miss Milsland."

"That's the most sensible word you have said this morning; for she looks upon you with contempt; and, besides, she is going to marry a rich man, and one who holds the position of a gentleman."

"By which, you mean to say that I do not. I suppose you mean Mr. Middleton by that? I don't believe she is going to marry him."

"Why, do you imagine because she was once fool enough to run mad after you, she is never to fancy another man? I can tell you she likes Mr. Middleton beyond all things, and he loves her and treats her like a queen. I see his conduct to her, every day almost, and nothing could be more thoroughly that of a gentleman."

"Another way of saying mine was not—I cannot say no. I believe you are right;" he ended with something that sounded like a groan.

"You are just like the rest of your sex; the way to win you is to despise you. When Laura behaved like a driveling fool about you, and made herself the laughing-stock of the community, with her passion for you, then you hated her. Now, when she has got back her senses, and despises you, you slink after her, like a poodle-dog. And you'll only get spurned for your pains; that I can inform you. I know her opinions of you: she doesn't think you worthy of a thought."

"She is right. I am not worthy of such thoughts as

her's. But Laura is too generous, too much above me to feel any ill will to me. She forgives me, and is only too kind to me."

"Just the very reason why she could never love you again."

"I know it. I don't presume on her kindness."

"And do you dare to intimate, in my presence, you would like to presume, like to sue for a warmer regard from her?"

"I intimate nothing; and since I see it is impossible for me to make myself agreeable to you, I will intrude no longer. Good morning."

For at least three minutes after his departure, Julia remained quiet and lost in thought. She had expected the interview to end with submission, protestations, pleadings, and all the insanities which belong to love-making; and here he had taken his leave as coolly as possible, without seeming to care in the least whether she were offended or pleased. It did not even seem a matter of the least moment to him whether the engagement came to an abrupt termination or not. Julia was decidedly hurt by this conviction, but her pride was more wounded than her love. Victor, as a gallant, tender, flattering lover, was a creature full of charms to her; but moody, troubled, and fretful, he excited nothing but vexation. She decided, at once, she would never marry him, but he was not to have the credit of breaking out of her chains, at his own will. She vowed to bring him to her feet again, and then to have the pleasure of refusing to listen to him. But although she was satisfied of her own power to part from him, it did not make her the less angry with Laura, for having won him from her allegiance. She went over to the mirror, gazed at her lovely face, pictured so softly in it, and then smiled at the idea of the wearied beauties of her rival being set against her. "No, I will win him back, only to scorn him;" and she swept disdainfully out of the room, to work off her ill humor by contending with Laura, which was not an easy task, as her earliest experience taught her. But, then, Julia was not lacking in pluck.

## CHAPTER IX.

MRS. MIDDLETON, with her two young guests, occupied a procenium box on the occasion of Victor's reappearance on the stage. Julia, since the last conversation with Victor, had been unusually kind and pleasant to him. This was in accordance with her plan of action, and a ready acquiescence to witness his first appearance, even after her bitter condemnation of it, was also a part of its policy. Victor was pleased and gratified with her amiable conduct, and treated her with corresponding kindness. Judging from it, he came to believe she might really love him after all, and at this time in his life he was far more easily touched by love to himself, than in his earlier youth.

It was really a beautiful audience which assembled at the theatre to witness Victor's reappearance; beautiful as to array, numbers, and kindly demonstrations of friendliness. He came before them in a new part, or at least, a part new to that stage. In the character of "Benvenuto Cellini," he was made to model a figure in clay, before the eyes of the audience. His skill and celerity in such modelling were very remarkable, so the part offered him a field of success in which he could know no rivalry. In the modelling scene, the whole audience seemed to have resolved themselves into eyes, so intense was the visual attention. Victor on a stepladder, even though his vivid fingers had not been giving life to a mass of clay, would have been a charming sight to see, for it brought out to the full the subtle, elegant graces of his supple figure. He had that beauty of form, which is not only perfect as to flesh, but bears with it a certain delicacy and sentiment that almost sublimates the flesh, up to the standard of the spirit. He ran up and down his step-ladder without seeming to touch it. Yet in these movements he did not resemble an acrobat, but rather a creature of higher faculties than the every-day world, to whom such lightness, elasticity and flexibility were only the normal conditions. Then the sculptor's technical coat of black velvet, brought into pleasing contrast the vague, dreamy glimmer of his soft eyes, as well as the natural charm of his pure and perfect profile. The whole audience felt the influence of these delicate, though manly beauties, and gazed at him with looks of tenderness, as though they all loved him. He marked this, and it shot like a thrill through his heart. But it did not prevent him from yearning to see what look was on the face of that strange girl, who now held the prominent place in his thoughts. The scaffolding upon which the figure was placed, and the step-ladder by which he reached it, were located rather nearer to that side of the stage on which Mrs. Middleton's box was, than the other, so it gave him a favorable opportunity to discover with what look, Laura gazed upon him. He cast his eyes rapidly up towards the box, and saw two faces bending over him, and oh, what a mighty contrast was in those two! In the face of Julia, his betrothed, was an expression of poignant curiosity, well mingled with conceit and arrogance, as if she were pleased in spite of herself, and by that supercillious film of disdain, desired to show that she repudiated it. In the other dark face now tinted with thrills of evanescent color, he could see nothing but the noblest pride in him, floating on the deeps of a pure and heavenly joy. He tried to catch her eyes, but their expression was too wide for that; his own gaze swam for a moment on them, and then sank and were lost in their infinite depths.

He turned back to his part with a new fire in his veins, and throughout the whole play, acted with all his old passion, but with a new fibre of pathos added to it. The audience went home enraptured, the management was overcome with delight, and the prospect of an unprecedented run seemed to set in for the new play.

## CHAPTER X.

The spring was fast verging into summer; in fact, according to the calendar, it was summer, for the month of June had opened upon them. The weather was warm and genial, so Mrs. Middleton proposed to her two guests, a temporary exodus into the country. As she had a beautiful place of her own, very convenient of access from the city, and replete with every luxury and mode of enjoyment, they both acceded to the proposition with delight.

Fortunately, the house was very large, for Mrs. Middleton's chief idea of a residence in the country, was a place to invite people to visit her in. In view of this,

Victor seriously thought of bringing his engagement to an immediate termination. He would have brought it to an untimely end indeed, had he not been afraid of Laura, but he happened to suggest it to her in the most shadowy way, when she said so quietly, " It would be pleasant for us ; but it would not be strictly honorable, and therefore it would be impossible for you to do." He was obliged to accept this high guage of his own principles, and act up to it, much as it secretly chagrined him. However, he managed easily to get two nights of release each week, on the plea of fatigue, heat, etc., as the practice of " off-nights " was not just then unusual in the dramatic profession. This gave him the opportunity of running up to Mrs. Middleton's Saturday morning and remaining until Monday. At this period of the week the house was always crowded to its utmost capacity, a circumstance much to Victor's satisfaction, because it gave Julia a field for general display and quiet flirting, and him greater opportunity for conversation with Laura.

Laura seemed rather to avoid company than seek it. Not because she did not love it, but from that sensitive pride, which will not give others an opportunity to slight it. She felt satisfied people would be inclined to slight her; for she had been haughty and overbearing in her most fortunate days, and it seemed to her but a just retribution now, she had lost all her claims to distinction, that others should return her old scorn with interest. But the world was better natured than she gave it credit for; her record, while under Mrs. Middleton's roof, was an unbroken line of respect, consideration, and deference.

Victor was extremely light of heart, in seeing Julia Sydney's attention absorbed in other channels than himself. He felt as if a great weight of responsibility were lifted from his shoulders. For the prize he had won in the lottery of life was becoming a matter of ineffable distress to him. He had sought and won her hand openly, and now he was too much of a gentleman to fling it by of his own accord; but he fervently hoped she would, herself, annul the engagement. However, it must not be supposed he confessed to himself, during all this time, that he loved Laura. He called his sentiment respect, friendship, admiration, sympathy for misfortunes, remorse for the wrong which had fallen to her through him—in fact, any thing but the only name which could adequately denote it.

Mrs. Middleton was as blind as most sensible women are; but even she was forced to remark the restless, poignant interest with which Victor followed every word, look, motion of Laura's. She said to him, bluntly, one day—" Victor, what is the reason you follow Miss Milsland continually with your eyes?"

" Because I like to look at her."

" But don't you think it a little imprudent to be so constantly interested in her movements?"

" Do you mean imprudent in the sense of disagreeable to her?"

" No; I mean liable to endanger your own cause."

" My cause? I don't suppose Miss Milsland condescends to care whether I notice her or not."

" I don't mean your cause with her; I mean with your future wife, Julia Sydney. Believe me, she's a girl of great spirit."

" Is she so?" mechanically playing with his fingers, and dropping his eyelids in a sleepy, good-natured way.

" Of course she is. You will go on flirting, until you

lose her. You think you have secured her now, and can afford to relax your attentions; but, when you least expect it, you will find yourself discarded, and, of course, your happiness for life wrecked."

"Wrecked, or sunk by leaks, or simply crumbled from decay; what does it matter?"

"You talk in riddles. I don't understand the young people of to-day. My dear Victor, there is another side to the question; have you no regard for the feelings of my poor Laura? What has she done, that you should so persistently deprive her of all chances of happiness?"

"I deprive her of the chances of happiness?" cried Victor, with the sleepy look all gone from his eyes. "In heaven's name, what do you mean?"

"She used to love you once; and after suffering so much to conquer the feeling, it would be cruel to throw her back into a state of relapse. You know she loved you once."

Victor acknowledged it only with a blush; and, after a moment of hesitation, said—"You do Miss Laura great injustice if you think her capable of troubling herself on my account."

"I don't mean to say she is, but I want to guard her from all disagreeable possibilities."

"You define me, then, as a disagreeable possibility?"

"No, no; you understand me well enough. Besides, Victor, I think she is either affianced, or about to be, to my brother."

"Why do you think that? I believe you to be entirely, utterly mistaken."

"I differ with you. I know my brother's attentions are significant, and she certainly accepts them. Indeed, he told me he intended to marry her, if he could. At first I opposed it, for I thought him worthier of a fresher heart than Laura's. I did not like the idea of his bride's having had another image in her heart before his came to occupy it. And what was the use of selecting a girl whose budding feelings had been fiercely developed and blighted; who had known disappointment, and all that kind of thing, when there were so many young natures, free of all impress, and ready to be moulded entirely to his image? and so I told him; but what do you think he told me?"

"How can I know?"

"He said he didn't choose to judge of a woman by accidents That the other girls I spoke of might be perfectly neutral now, free from all impressions, fresh as the dew before the sun rises, but the moment they were impressed by himself, that advantage would be lost to them, they would stand on the same ground as Laura.

"I asked him if he did not wish to be the first one to move his wife's heart?

"He said it was of more consequence whether the heart was worth moving, or not, than who first moved it. That it was all very well to talk of fresh material, but it mattered something whether it was wax, that would melt and blur, and run into insignificance at the first exposure to the fires of feeling, or whether it was gold, that would come out firmer and more refined from it.

"I urged her sentiment for you—pardon me for mentioning it—and how utterly you scouted it.

"He said he was sorry for you and your blindness; but if you chose to pass by a pearl, it was no reason why he should adorn himself with a pebble, because he unearthed it himself. That he thought too much of the dignity of human nature, to rank its characteristics below the mere level of chances. And that Laura Milsland was worth more at any moment of her life, than all the other women he knew put together.

"When a man like my brother-in-law talks like that, of course it would be useless to argue with him, so I only asked him whether he thought she would make him a good wife, whether he could depend upon her?

"He said he could depend upon her to make his home more interesting than any other place. That she might not bustle and fidget with her housekeeping all the time, nor fret over little things, nor grow dowdy and careless in her dress, nor permit him to insult her, as some wives who were considered models, did; but that everything would slip into order in her house, without any fussing; she would be always equal to emergencies, ready to make the best of everything, always coquettish about her dress, and that she would have the most valuable of influences in a wife, that of making her husband act like a gentleman at home. That she would be animated, sympathetic, genial, faithful, dignified, ideal, delicate, and brim-full of good sense; and if a man wanted a better wife than that, he'd better go to heaven to get her.

"When I saw him so determined, of course I made up my mind to acquiesce in his views, and help them as much as I could. Besides, I always liked Laura, only it did trouble me to think she had made her fancy for you so public. But what do you think of it, Victor?"

"I don't think she will make him a good wife, by any means; she can't love him."

"I am sorry to see you so prejudiced. You have no right to persecute her; however much she might have harmed herself, she never harmed you. The attention you pay her, too—upon my soul, I can't understand you. If I thought you were only watching and following her out of hatred, with a view to securing her unhappiness, I would—I would quarrel with you, my dear."

"Her unhappiness? Believe me, I shall never know a moment's peace until her unhappiness is at end. I regret my own share in her troubles, with a regret so strong that it might as well be remorse."

"You talk in riddles, as usual; you are never easy out of her presence, and behind her back you are against her."

"I beg your pardon, you mistake me; I said she would not make a good wife for your brother, because I felt certain she did not love him. She is too much at ease in his presence; she never seems agitated nor frightened when he is with her."

"Neither does she with you."

"Of course not now, but she used to be. Laura is not a girl to take love calmly."

"Oh! she has improved since your day, and I trust you will not be putting any foolish notions in her head. She is only too fortunate to have won the regard of a man like my brother, and you know it."

"Excuse me, I know nothing of him, and do not wish to increase my knowledge. I don't like him; I never shall like him. He is a man whom I would constitutionally avoid, and I cannot wish him success in his suit."

"If it were any other man than you, or if you were speaking of another woman besides Laura, I should say you were jealous—angrily jealous. But you, you are —no, no, it is impossible."

"Certainly. I think I will wander awhile in the garden now, I have something to think of."

And so he had, to think over his own feeling toward Laura, for to own he loved her seemed to him a breach of manly importance and dignity. Years back, when she had every charm that youth, beauty, position could give, he had found nothing to love in her. A confession of love towards himself from her, maintained for years, had won nothing but repugnance from him; so how, he asked himself, could he possibly love her now? It would be wasting his opportunities, throwing himself away, giving her the chance to disdain him, in her turn, and, worse than all, exposing himself to ridicule; and so he told himself it was impossible; and even while he said so, he caught sight of a fluttering, white dress, of a dark, sweet face; and at that sight his blood, which had been falling about his heart with dull, uneasy thuds, leaped up and bounded vividly through his veins, at once solving the problem of possibilities.

## CHAPTER XI.

LAURA looked up at his approach, and welcomed him with her usual quiet smile. "What is the matter, Victor?" she asked, when she had fully measured his face with her kind eyes, "I see you are annoyed."

"Yes, I am; I want you to look at this. I haven't spoken of it to any one else, for you are the only one here on whose sympathies I can really depend. I know *you* sympathise with me."

"I'm so glad you think so."

"Well, just listen to this; it is from a leading journal, which hitherto has been most favorably disposed to me."

"They have taken a new critic on to the staff, I suppose."

"Probably; but see what it says; I am much overrated. It is doing an injustice to native actors, to eulogize a foreigner so beyond his deserts. I lack dignity; I am not large enough; my voice is sickeningly sweet; I am effeminate, presumptuous, overborne with conceit. I look supercilliously on the public; I have grown careless; and finally, worst of all, a suspicion that I buy over other critics to my interest. Now, what do you think of that? Ought I to pull the critic's nose or answer it?"

"Neither, you foolish fellow. Don't you know you cannot fight a pressman unless you are a pressman yourself? I mean, you cannot fight him with answering him, because it would be taking him on his own ground, where he knows all the shifts and turnings, and you know nothing. You would come with your earnestness, and indignation, and sensitiveness, and he would just trip you up, with one flippant carcasm or impertinence. It is just like any other art—strength and right go for nothing when an opponent is thoroughly master of the 'knack' of the thing. As for personal assault, which you technically term pulling of the nose, I think it would be very undignified under the slight provocation."

"Slight provocation!—how would you feel if you were in my place?"

"Upon my soul, it would not hurt me in the least. If I had been sugared over with compliments as you have for the last three years, a little bit of opposition would feel like a tonic to me; a wholesome, delicious bitter, after being smothered in eternal treacle. It makes you of more importance than ever; you are not only worth praising, but worth abusing. You ought to have more of it; a man isn't worth anything until he has been abused, and has not flinched before it."

"That's true; I never thought of it before."

"Besides, what is a critic put upon a newspaper for? Is it to be a chorus to sing the monotonous praises of public people; or is it to speak the truth, and separate the chaff from the grain? Why, if you've only two grains of chaff in you to the hundred weight of wheat, you ought to be glad to have it winnowed out."

"Oh, how different you are from other people—and, Laura, so much better! But how ought one to answer an insult?"

"A great many times (of course there are exceptions), simply by not deserving it. Aim to be genuine in your profession rather than to be simply a reputation. Don't scoff at spiritual integrity—for without it, life on or off the stage, has no meaning. Give all your energies to your art; love it, honor it; and then depend upon it, you can act yourself up, faster than a wilderness of critics can write you down. Set your standard up in the clouds, and climb towards it forever; but above all, always be a gentleman and a man of honor, and you will not have the press long against you."

"I am so very, very glad now, that I consulted you before acting upon it. I had so many schemes of vengeance in my mind, and now they seem so ridiculous! It seems incredible to me that any other opinion than yours could have weighed with me. Do you think the stage a useful art—does it seem to you to have any true aim?"

"I know nothing of the aim of anything in life, but it seems to me that an art that draws, or ought to draw its sources of inspiration from the intellect and the higher passions, is useful—unless it is all to end here in the grave and utter blackness; and if that be so, what does it matter? Nothing is worth thinking about; everything is choas—but I must go now."

"Don't go, you put me in such a good humor with myself."

"I am glad, if it will prove you above the wreaking of a puny spite. But I can't stay here and talk any longer; there's a party, a rural ball, to take place here next Tuesday, and Julia and I are to make some ornamental frost-work on the cakes. We all thought, as it was a country festivity, most of the things should be made at home."

"Can I go and help you?"

"If you are permitted; you can help us, I am sure. You might model dragons and gorgons and harpies out of sugar for us."

"And why not angels and cupids? Is my hand only fitted for evolving distortion; to give ugliness a form and feature?"

"No; but I thought you might like to do something dreadful; to knead off your wrath and vengeance."

"Oh, dear, that's all gone; when I heard your voice speaking of a better way of righting myself, it just vanished like a stage-ghost."

"Still, you don't look quite satisfied. There's something on your mind still."

"But not in relation to that affair. Other things trouble me. I'm not happy; I'm the most dissatisfied man alive."

Laura looked at him with eyes full of incredulity and astonishment. How can any woman understand the man who in himself makes to her the whole sum of desirable things, when he talks about unhappiness? If to her, enjoyment means the moments flavored by his presence, and all content means a hope of some contiguity to him, however remote in the future, how can she conceive of his dissatisfaction, who has himself complete, and for all time? Why, to her, he *is* happiness; and in having himself he has the perfect fruition of joy. No wonder then, Laura looked at him like one hardened in unbelief.

"You don't believe me to be unhappy, then?"

"No."

"Why not?"

"Because you are yourself; and lest you should provoke me to explain myself, I shall make my best speed to the cakes."

When they arrived in the dining-room, the festive preparations had already begun. Julia had the sleeves of her muslin dress looped up so as to leave her lovely arms free for labor. She looked very haughty and much displeased when Laura came in late; and besides that, accompanied by Victor.

"How do you progress, Julia? You must excuse me for being late."

"We progress favorably; and indeed, I didn't notice your absence."

"I'm glad of that. What can I do now?"

"Oh, you can bring the sentiment to our circle; we were getting too full of common sense here; we were wanting something high-flown, and now you are come to bring us the Platonic element."

"I should like to know what obtains me the honor of being draped in Plato's garments at the moment."

"Oh, when people of opposite sexes play at friendship, and brother and sister, and all that, we know what a run there always is on Plato. For my part, I don't pretend to be a sage, neither do I believe in playing a filial relations."

"I do; I believe in anything sooner than playing at

vapid antagonisms and lifeless enmities. Dull friendliness is better than dull malice, any day in life."

"Now, Julia," interposed Mrs. Middleton, "you see what you've brought on yourself; you have nothing to answer to that. Why will you attack Laura, when you know you always get the worst of it?"

"I don't see any trouble about it, Mrs. Middleton; I have no wish to answer her. I never set up for a scholar and a pedant, you know. I haven't the least desire to frighten the other sex, nor to die an old maid. I suppose maidenhood is your chosen aim, Laura."

At this, Victor visibly blushed; but Laura replied as quietly as before, "I am certainly not laboring to put myself in the other state."

Again, Julia had nothing to reply, so she was obliged to keep silence, until another spiteful vein should suggest itself for working.

"Why, Laura, I believe you are getting to be lazy; you don't seem to soar at cake-making."

"No; but I shall help you more at cake-eating, Mrs. Middleton."

"Yes," said Julia, "you were always an adept at eating."

"So I was; but you remember, I never fed behind the curtain. I was a Goth and Vandal at the dinner-table, but no smuggling in of pies and pancakes for me, and hiding them in bed, to be consumed surreptitiously by midnight."

"I don't deny it. I was like girls of my age, not ashamed of a little fun. I was not always hardening my heart over algebra."

"No one knows that better than I do, Julia; your algebra has assisted in my heart-hardening though."

"Laura, you are always so ready to rake over these foolish school reminiscences."

"Am I? but don't you really love to talk of your school-days?"

"No, I despise them; when I think of what years I wasted mumbling over books, I am inconsolable."

"Not so with me; I think of them as my best days."

"You may so. What are you designing there, Laura? For heaven's sake, don't let us go to demonstrating geometrical problems here! Don't let the ruling idea carry you away."

"No fear of that; for if it comes to geometrical designs, I shall have your work and my own to do, as it used to fall out in school-days."

"What an ill-tempered memory you have! Mrs. Middleton, is there any coloring for this icing?"

"We can have rose-colored only. Laura, will you get it ready?"

"Oh, be sure you don't make it blue, Laura; that's not a popular color, you know."

"No, we won't have anything blue, my color here; we will have it green, in consonance with you."

"If you mean jealousy by that color, let me assure you there is nobody I would condescend to be jealous of;" and she turned her dimpled elbows about to give, if not point, at least solidity to the sentiment.

For a time, there was a hollow truce between the two girls; but Julia, who was continually preserving a position of armed neutrality, soon sallied out against her rival. Laura happened to propose lifting a large cake, when Julia stopped her, saying, "Don't attempt it, you will let it fall, and strain yourself. You look thin and weak now-a-days."

"Quite a change from the old days, then, when I used to whip you occasionally."

"By no means. I always whipped you."

"Why, how many black eyes did I give you a month?"

"Not so many as I gave you; only your skin was so dark already, they didn't show on it."

"A good thing for me, Julia, that my skin was so dark; it made the task of beautifying it hopeless. I never was reduced into eating slate-pencils and chalk to whiten it. And they are horrid things to eat; are they not, Julia?"

"You had better talk about what we are doing, and let me take that cake."

"So you think I am too feeble to take it?"

"Judging from your changed appearance, I do."

"Well, take it, Julia; hold it tight now, and start."

Julia seized it with a little toss of her golden head; but before she had made three steps, Laura seized her firmly round the waist and carried both her and it easily out of the room.

When they came back, Victor was modeling a group in sugar, which, happily, occupied all the attention of the combatants for the moment. Still, from time to time, Julia would send a little arrow of speech in the direction of Laura, who never seemed for a moment angered, however sarcastic she might be. Finally, a certain pic-nic of their school-days was advanced by Julia, as a conversation missile for aggravating Laura; but the latter chanced upon one of its incidents, which appealed to the sympathies of her persecutor, and in a minute they were rejuvenating old reminiscences, in a spirit of friendship instead of malice. Julia came down from her pedestal of scorn, and after a few moments it was, "My dear Laura, don't you remember?" and "Oh,

Julia, wasn't it delightful?" until the conversation got so close and confidential, they were constrained to leave the room, and were seen to wander down the garden walk, with their arms interlaced about each other's waists.

Victor, who had secretly enjoyed their open rupture, looked with disgust upon this amicable reconstruction, thinking, scornfully, it was like a pair of girls, to drop the important subject of a man's divided attentions, and throw their whole souls into a discussion of juvenile pic-nics, with the attendant absurdities of broken bottles, puddings drowned in vinegar, and indigestible dough.

## CHAPTER XII.

VICTOR arrived early on the evening of Mrs. Middleton's festive occasion. He found his hostess arranging some flowers in her drawing-rooms. She met him with a profusion of thanks and congratulations, for that morning had arrived to her a piece of sculpture, Victor's work, and a gift to her from him.

"Oh, Victor! how shall I thank you enough for your generosity? Such a compliment, too, to bestow a work of art like that on me! Where was it made?"

"In Italy, but it has only lately arrived here."

"Why did you have it brought out here? it must be returned to my house in the city."

"It's only fit for the country; to adorn a garden, or something like that."

"Oh, the modesty of genius! But your friends know

how to value you, if you are unable to appreciate yourself. In the garden indeed—I would not exchange it for this whole place!"

"Indeed, Mrs. Middleton, it has no value whatever, as a work of art; its only claim to consideration, as a gift, is the feeling of gratitude which prompted it."

"I would not allow any one else to say so; but, my dear boy, what gratitude do you owe me?"

"Were you not my first friend in this country? You believed in me, before I believed in myself. I owe you the success of my dramatic career, for you gave me the courage and the hope to undertake it. Lately, I have had another source of gratitude to you. But we will not speak of that."

"Why not? There is too much mystery about you now; you do not confide in me as you used to."

"I don't ask you to listen to quite so much nonsense as I used to; it should be a relief. Has—has Laura looked at that piece of marble yet? She laughed at it, of course?"

"She has not seen it. I am keeping it as a surprise for this evening. Julia saw it, for she happened to be here when it came."

"Laura will laugh at it, I am sure."

"Why should she? Julia thought it lovely."

"Oh, Laura has such severe taste! Where is she?"

"Up stairs, putting her trunks and drawers in order; though why there should be a necessity for it, I cannot see, for she never seems to disorder anything."

"No, for she touches all things so lightly and gracefully, the mere contact of her hand should organize them into the most harmonious form. Doubtless she is moving about the room now as smoothly as water flows. She overturns nothing; her dress sweeps evenly through all obstruction, for her eye is so true, it measures spaces to the fraction of a hair. She does not tire herself, because she makes no mistakes. Everything she touches takes its right fold, and nestles away by apt articles. There is no confusion, no incongruity, no impatience, no fretfulness where she works; she is full of a sweet, quiet strength, and her face has no part in her labor, but is soft with the spirituality of a busy and always ascending imagination."

"Why, Victor, what is the matter with you? have you become clairvoyant?"

"No, no; I was only dreaming. But I think this twilight has put an end to her labors."

"Very likely. She thought of gathering flowers to trim her dress with this afternoon. Are you going?"

"I thought I would take the air for a while."

"No, you did not; you are going in search of Laura. May I tell you what I think, without annoying you?"

"Yes, you may."

"Well, then, Victor, I firmly believe that—you love Laura Milsland."

"Do you, indeed, believe it—is it true?"

"Yes; and you need not look for a return. How could she love you again?"

"Alas! how could she?"

"Nobody ever loves the same man twice. Unless—but surely that's impossible—unless she has been loving you all this time. But that cannot be."

"Oh, no!"

"You love her, and will break Julia's heart."

"Break her heart! I am neither so fine nor so sharp as to cut a feather in two. May I go now? I feel as though I were buried alive—I want the air."

"Go, my dear, and do not be foolish; never withdraw from an honorable engagement. For such a doubtful hope, too; it would be more than dishonest; it would be ridiculous. Did you know Laura was about to leave us?"

"No. What do you mean?"

"She is going to Europe with my sister-in-law."

"Your husband's sister?"

"Yes; she goes simply as a companion to her. You know she is left without means and wishes to be independent; so she goes in capacity of companion."

"Indeed! That is quite a contrast to the way in which she went before."

"Ah, truly! I always thought her father's will very extraordinary."

"I think it was abominable."

"It looked very bad for Laura."

"It looked as if she were too true herself to suspect the hideous deceit of others."

"Elphinstone and his wife and Miriam Milsland went to France, almost immediately after the father's death."

"I should think he would have been ashamed to look any of his fellow-beings in the face."

"Oh, my dear, the parties that get the money need never fear but what the majority will be on their side."

"And Laura Milsland, once the most thoroughly beautiful, proud and brilliant woman I ever saw, now plays the rôle of a companion."

"Julia Sydney says she would be afraid to have her for a companion."

"I should think she would."

"Julia says, that in her own room, when she thinks

no one is observing her, she sits and looks as if she saw things a thousand miles away, and then she sighs as though her heart were breaking. But the moment one notices her, that strange look changes into a smile, and she seems to be keenly interested in every thing one says. Julia calls that soft, smiling face she carries in company, nothing better than a mask to hide her deep disquiet."

"The mask of an angel then, whose unveiled face we are not worthy to see."

"Victor, I think so too; the more I know Laura, the more respect I have for her. One must have a strong prejudice not to like her. My brother—Laura's suitor, you know—will follow them to Europe. My sister's health is delicate, so she is advised to try a sea-voyage of greater length than a simple traverse of the Atlantic. They are going to take a ship here to St. Thomas, and from thence the colonial steamer to England. Queer idea, is it not?"

"I suppose so. When do they go?"

"On Saturday."

"And to-day is Tuesday—three days more."

"I wish it were not quite so long, for Julia's sake."

"I thought you loved Laura?"

"So I do; but she would be the last person to wish to breed disunion between a betrothed pair."

"Yes, you are right. May I go now?"

"Go; but be wise."

"I shall be, by way of a contrast to my past."

Lest Mrs. Middleton should further detain him, he hurried into the garden, where the light of the early rising moon was mingling itself with the grey twilight. He wandered about from walk to walk, but no Laura was gathering flowers in its mazes. Then, by accident he looked through the windows of the conservatory, and just caught a glimpse through the flowers of a massive braid of ebony hair, which could be nourished by no other head than hers. He opened the door and stepped in towards where she sat on a low chair, weaving and grouping together clusters of heliotrope, with an occasional tube-rose breathing out its ambient odors amidst them.

She looked up as he approached, and said, "You have detected me in my guilt, robbing the conservatory of flowers. Come, be an accomplice; share in the crime and conceal it."

"Let me see them then; let me judge whether they are worthy to buy silence." He knelt gently before her as he spoke, lifting the flowers in her lap, and tossing them about from side to side, without really seeming to notice them, till finally he rested one arm on her knee, and dropped his always wildering eyes, now swimming with liquid lustre, full upon her face. Beneath that gaze, her own quivered and trembled, till it slid down and rested on her throbbing cheek. Not a word was spoken; the silence was so perfect, she seemed to hear her own heart beat, like uneasy water plashing against a stranded boat.

Much as she had organized the forces of her being into self-control, fully as she had resigned herself to the inevitable, ready as she was to accept her unwelcome destiny, patiently, even cheerfully; she had always felt there was danger to her whole philosophy and self-discipline, in the loveliness of sweet summer nights, when the fragrance of flowers was stealing about the earth, and the moon rolling its long waves of splendor down the quiet skies. In such moments, might not her forced content shrivel and fall away from her, and she once more plunging towards her heart's vain desire, dash against that adamantine wall, from whence she had so often been cast back, torn and broken?

If these things were dangerous in their soulless silence, how could she measure the peril of them when made all radiant with life, by this man now kneeling at her feet?

To crush the dangerous spell of silence she said, "Take care not to hurt my beautiful flowers."

"Am I only fitted to hurt what is beautiful?"

"I did not say that. But I must not stay here longer—I have my dress to loop with flowers. My sister Agnes is coming to-night; I have not seen her for two weeks."

"Do not go yet; stay a little while—one minute longer. You intend to leave America in three days,—for how long?"

"I am not quite sure; five years, perhaps."

"Five years! Good heavens! Why not say fifty? Why did you not tell me, Laura?"

"Why should I?"

"You knew it would concern me."

"I had no reason to think so—judging from the past. Besides, had I spoken of it, I should have been foolish enough to show I was sorry to go."

"The more reason why it should interest me. I don't think it was quite generous to be troubled about it, and not confide it to me. You have scarcely treated me fairly."

"Fairly? Why, Victor, when was it that my sorrow ever moved you? Do you forget that the sight of me in the blackest misery never drew from you more than a yawn, or a mocking laugh, or at best a spasm of anger?"

"Yes, I forget it. If another beside yourself said it

—but it must be true since you say so. Is it written down in your journal?"

"It is written in fire on my soul."

"But you forgive me?"

"What does it matter if I do—why should I?"

"Because you are more merciful than I. Where I wounded, you would heal; where I crushed, you would lift up; where I destroyed, you would create. I would not so far wrong you as to expect any similarity between your actions and mine. You can afford to forgive me, because you are so far above me."

He ended by drawing a low footstool to her feet, and placing himself upon it, dropped his head among the flowers in her lap. He accomplished this daring act with an air of perfect ease and grace, but it was not without much inward agitation; for a moment afterwards all his senses seemed to be grouped together in his throat, and to be strangling him.

Laura looked dreamily at that perfect head, as it lay tossed carelessly among the flowers, itself the fairest flower of all; and as she gazed, a tremulous hope crept softly into her heart. But she only said, "Victor, we will both be late; please let me go. What will Julia think of you?"

"Laura, she knows *I love you, she knows I love you.*"

"The words were not spoken passionately, nor pleadingly, they fell slowly from his lips, in a tone more like resignation than expectation. So low was their tone, that they scarcely trembled through the silence, to fade away among the breath of the flowers; but to Laura, they had all the sonority of the final trumpet-tongue of doom. At their sound, the great gates of Hope, which she had hitherto stormed in vain, rolled back on their pliant hinges, and she passed in to join the children of God's Promise.

In all Victor's previous intercourse with Laura, he had never said, "I love you;" it was always, "Do you love me?" or "You do love me;" but never "I love you."

Laura answered nothing; but she recognized the reality of the feeling which prompted those heavenly words, and she was thinking it mattered little whether that feeling bore no fruit, and fell off like an untimely bud, blighted ere it had bloomed.

Laura believed that he did not mean to cherish his own sentiment, because in the mysterious code of masculine self-value, it would feed his pride more not to love than to love her;—for in that strange, weird code, it was more manly to love indifference, and interested motives in a woman, than such a love as would suffer long and be kind, as could bear all things, believe all things, endure all things.

But she would not complain, though he should do his best for worldliness and his sex. Let him sacrifice her to consistency, pass her by and forget her evermore; for one brief moment he had loved her, and that alone emancipated her from the bondage of Despair.

The minutes flew by freighted with perfect silence; the climbing pulses in his throat gradually subsided, and a quiet languor stole over him. A furtive glance at her, revealed to him only a vague look in the eyes, and a rapt expression of the whole face, which was the fittest emblem of prayer. It seemed as though she had swept him out of her horizon, and were wandering in another world. He did not even try to understand her, but yielded up himself body and soul to the happiness of the moment.

When Laura's reverent eyes fell from the Heaven

which had sealed her with its blessing to-night, she scarcely saw Victor's face at all, it was so buried in her lap; but his cheek and one drooping eyelid rested on her hand, and from time to time, she could feel his long lashes quiver across her palm. She felt as though she would like to remain there forever; but the noise of the first arriving carriage startled and aroused her.

She raised his head gently from her lap, and still holding the flowers up to her in her little apron, sprang up and advanced to the door. But he intercepted her and clasped her in his arms. The tube-roses were bruised on her bosom, till they sent up a keen, reproachful odor, and a deep, deep sigh that was almost a sob, was crushed out of her lips by that convulsive embrace. At the sound he loosened his arms, and she sprang out of them, and was lost to sight in a minute.

When Victor came into the room where the guests were beginning to assemble, he found Mrs. Middleton there with Julia beside her. The latter glanced at him astutely, for he was perceptibly flushed, and Laura— the soul of punctuality—was still absent.

He made an effort to be attentive to Julia, for his mood was a tender one, and his heart was softened to the whole world. But Julia repelled him with proper dignity. She felt her beauty and estimated it wisely. Her dress was of pale blue, a color which gave full value to her golden hair, and lent a still more delicate tint to her pearly cheeks. Nothing could be more perfect in flesh (the loveliest of all materials), than the soft, curve lines of her swelling neck and dimpled arms; and Victor as an artist, fully realized it. It gave a more impressive tone to his attentions, and outwardly demanded his fullest admiration. But oh! the difference of his sensations, when the soft rustle of a filmy robe, wafting in the breath of heliotropes and tube-roses, swept by him, and smote like the touch on a stringed instrument, of a skillful hand. Not so perfect in outline, as that of his affianced bride, was that supple figure, clad in natural flowers and white crape, through which the silken underrobe, just glinted like a pearl under water. Neither was this face so free from lines, so fresh as Julia's; indeed it showed a deep pallor under its swarthy tints, and a fixed sadness was sealed into the mouth, yet as his eyes clung to that face, a poignant thrill ran along his veins, filling every vessel with warm blood, tingling to his fingers' tips, and kindling through all his life that ecstatic animation which no other power in the world can produce, but the electric current which flows to and fro from answered to answering love.

As usual, Laura had no glance adrift for him; she would not, unbidden, recognize his existence, and gave all her brightness, tact, and plasticity of conversation to the group which at once surrounded her. As a member of society, her popularity was increasing, on a fast ascending ratio. Her energies being no longer given to the contemplation of her own superiority and the necessity for displaying it, advanced into the happier field of developing the merits of others. Her forte, now, lay not so much in talking, as in making others talk.— Thus the humblest conversationists found themselves growing brilliant when they communed with her. She had a way (metaphorically), of shaking a man about, till his best faculties were afloat on the surface, and then leading him into clear waters, in order that he might drift safely on in the sea of social converse. In all cases, such men went away delighted with their new-found powers, and ready in the good humor of self-satisfaction, to find her the most sensible and agreeable girl in the world.

Indeed, her perceptive faculties, were so quick, her indulgence so large, and her sense of humor so keen, that her mission in society seemed for the moment to make every man witty, if not wise.

Victor soon lost sight of her in the crowd, but he continued to look after her, until Mrs. Middleton touched him on the shoulder and asked "Where is Laura? I have such a rigid set of young men over there, I am afraid they will all petrify before the dancing begins, unless I can get Laura to knead their minds up a little. She is such a beautiful manager."

"If she can brighten stupid men, let her try her powers on me; I feel dull enough."

"She couldn't give her attention to you, of course."

"And why, I beg to know, am I considered outside of grace?"

"Certainly, Laura would not like to appear partial to you."

"You seem to think 'twould be an act of prodigious folly in her to like me."

"Certainly, I do. Go to Julia. I think I see Laura now."

Instead of seeking Julia, Victor wandered aimlessly about the room, addressing a casual word here and there, until he drifted out on the broad piazza, and found himself quite alone. He was standing there when the music commenced. This was the signal of hope to him, for he supposed that the dismal young men would waft their paralyzed spirits into the dance, and free Laura from the necessity of striking sparks out of stocks and stones. Victor concluded he would go and ask her to dance, unless one of the dismal young men, before referred to, had led her off to share his forlorn feelings, in the whirl of the waltz.

Turning to go, his eye took in, at a glance, the interior of a small room, at the end of the house, which had not yet been invaded by visitors. But it was not empty; for Laura, having escaped from her death-heads, was there. She was gazing at a picture of himself, which hung on the wall; it was only a large photograph, but it was singularly accurate as to likeness, and happy as to its view of his face.

Victor, standing in the shade, could see in her upturned face, on which the light fell freely, its expression of passionate admiration, intermingled with something like pity. That fond, cherishing love seemed to set him on a rock, and sweep round him in a sea of unspeakable tenderness. Never had he seen a look on any face, in which self-suppression and yearnings that could not be uttered, were so equally blended. It taught him, that her interest in him was neither friendship nor generosity, but a steadfast, implacable love, and that the depth and the breadth of that love, no human means could ever measure.

He flew round into the room, discovered her in the very act of caressing the picture of himself, with her fond, ardent eyes, and immediately entreated her—to dance.

Just before supper, in order that the flow of soul might ante-date that of the punch-bowl, the folding-doors of an inner room were thrown open, and the audience invited in to feast upon a work of art, to wit, the marble gift of the morning.

Victor, who felt very much as if he were in a dentist's chair, for the sake of having a full-length figure extracted from him, was forced in by Mrs. Middleton, to receive the tribute Society was about to render unto Cæsar.

Exclamations of "how beautiful!" "exquisite!"

"charming!" "what a pose she has!" "what majesty!" "never saw anything so lovely!" were tossed about among them, some of them keeping two or three on the alert at the same time, as the juggler manages to keep a half-dozen balls flying in the air.

In the midst of these meaningless eulogies, Victor began to see, more acutely than ever, the faults of his work. A morbid sensibility devoured him alive, till his only desire was to take the senseless piece of stone and dash it to pieces before their eyes.

The thought occurred to him, while suffering from this feeling, "what does Laura think of it? she has said nothing."

His eyes wandered searchingly through the chattering groups, till they seized upon her, standing a little back of the statue. Laura, and not Laura, for she had ceased to be herself, and become the sublimated spirit of the figure. She had fallen insensibly into its position, which was intended to be drooping, but not despondent. Her head was poised precisely like its head; every feature, as to position, was the counterpart of its feature; but in the expression of the face, lay the superiority of the living to the inanimate statue. For, whereas, in his marble image of "Resignation," that state of mind was represented by a heavy, sullen, sodden look, by a lack of feeling, rather than its control; in her, it was expressed by a soul disciplined, but not crushed, which accepted its fate because it had explored all experiences and sounded them to their depths; a soul not dark with hopeless, helpless defeat, but one whose failures were holier than the successes of others, and whose illumination was the light from the divinest sanctuary of sorrow.

This was the ideal which flitted before his imagination, when he had striven to summon forth his image of "Resignation" out of the block of marble; this was the winged ideal that fluttered its plumage about him, but ever eluded his grasp, when he stretched forth his eager hands to clutch it. Touched, at last, by him, it had seemed to die and leave only its senseless body there, in that distracting piece of stone; but before his eyes its resurrection was completed in the soul of the woman who loved him. It was sown in corruption, it was raised in incorruption; it was sown in dishonor, it was raised in glory.

When the whole armory of light compliments had been discharged into the air, Mrs. Middleton felt it was the hour to break up that practice of small arms, and open the doors of the supper-room. With an alacrity which betokened intense relief of mind, the room was vacated, like a cloud of its electricity, and the company swept supperward with an enthusiasm, not much more intense than had been excited by the work of art.

Victor looked about for Laura, to take her to the banquet; for, by a natural paradox, he felt as if he had committed such a blunder in marble, he was ashamed to show his face to any one, but the only being who knew it. But Laura was gone with her sister, Agnes, and two gentlemen; so, he came down to the table alone, his mind equally divided between hunger and self-depreciation.

It was in vain he attempted to attract Laura's attention; Agnes had secured her, and was monopolizing her, with all her might. She had interesting news to impart—the conversion of Willister into a gentleman. He neither swore, pushed, grumbled, nor got into debt now, and he had secured a situation as clerk in a fashionable hotel. And, indeed, he possessed the most requisite quality for fitting that position, as it is generally filled, namely, *bounce*. He could seem more intensely absorbed in the contemplation of his own thoughts when it was necessary to attend to the demands of a guest; he could take longer to hear any one speak; he could look more surprised when a new comer asked for a room, and more disgusted when a visitor inquired for a resident of the house, than any man out of the whole army of swaggerers. Why, the dexterity with which he could hoist a party up into the dim recesses of the attic, when a whole lower floor was vacant, alone would have made him chief among ten thousand, and altogether clerkly.

Perhaps his hotel life was a good vent for his superciliousness and impertiness; perhaps, having tried the novel experiment of playing the gentleman at home, under Laura's tuition, he liked it. At any rate, he was a decent, peaceable, and harmless Willister, under the shadow of his own roof. It was proved by the happy, sportive manner of his Agnes. She had returned to the ardent ways of her youth, when everything enthused her, threw her into raptures, and she went into ecstacies over a carpet-tack. Laura rejoiced with her so much, at the return of the prodigal Willister to domestic kindness, that she killed her fatted prejudice, and quite took him into her sisterly regards. Besides, dressed as he was to-night, in simple black, with no florid cravat nor gush of pretentous watch-chain, he was not exactly to be ashamed of, and formed rather an agreeable contrast to that party of dismal young men, whose mighty natures seemed to flow in but two channels—low spirits and lisping.

Laura was very cordial to Willister, joking him about his dignities as a public officer, and hoping, if she ever came to that hotel, as a room-seeker, he would, in her honor, sacrifice the wand of his office, that is, divorce himself for a moment from his tooth-pick, to attend to her.

On the next day, Victor saw Laura only for a few moments, before leaving, as his morning was occupied by receiving a formal dismissal from Julia. The latter was tired of waiting for him to throw himself once more at her feet, that she might have the pleasure of walking over him, and concluded to notify her intention to withdraw from the engagement, while he at least remembered that one existed.

Laura informed him she would be in town on Friday night, the one before her departure, and would come to see him play. "And look you, please me," she added, "for it will be long, perhaps as long as my life, before the dramatic art will have any meaning to me again."

"I shall play for *you*," he answered; "you may consider my performance that night, strictly as a confidence between us."

## CHAPTER XIII.

The moon was at its full on Friday night, and Victor, according to his own previous determination, played before an audience of many hundred people, confidentially to one, which two facts together might have accounted for the eccentricities of that night's performance. There were moments when he seemed almost delirious, succeeded by others in which a dull, sluggish stupor hung over him. He laughed when he should have been sad; and his voice wept tears of intonation, where the exigencies of the text exacted a gay and sportive manner. He gazed on the actors and actresses who filled the other parts of the play, with a curious, uncertain look, as though he had never seen them before, and more than once interrupted the most formal speech, with flashes of hysterical laughter.

The party in the prosceneum box, accompanying Mrs. Middleton, knowing him best of all persons in the house, were most struck by the peculiarities of his manner. Julia indulged in a faint hope that he might be afflicted with some anguish, by reason of her dismissing him as a suitor, two days previously. But that amiable hope died out of her mind when, his wandering gaze drifted into their box, and was at once perceptibly anchored on the anxious face of Laura.

The audience endured the eccentricities of their favorite tragedian with a Spartan patience, and his fellow-laborers adapted themselves to them with the meek deference, which insignificant members of the dramatic profession are so ready to show to its great lights. But the members of this company would have been ungrateful indeed, if they had not been willing to bear much unevenness of manner from Victor. If he was peculiarly favored as to popularity, he was peculiarly agreeable as to temperament. He never feared being "played down" by any body; and the better the action of those who supported him, the more pleased he was with it. He went upon the scene in his own way, made pliant to himself every one on it, and was never obstructed or thrown out of balance by any of those little inaccuracies of business, which occur even in the best regulated companies. Whenever stupidity or forgetfulness clipped off an edge of the dramatic figure, his own elastic genius flowed into the cavity, and rounded it into perfect proportions again.

Victor had, in its rarest degree, that exquisite quality of genius—simplicity. Applause was as dear to him as it could be to any sensitive, strongly approbative temperament; but he never strove to absorb that which was given to the members of the stock company. He seemed willing to accede to them the full honors of re-calls before the curtain, and advertising advantages, not out of generosity, but because no other course of conduct ever occurred to him. He was a star in the true starlike sense, not to dim and cloud, but to sanctify all the heaven about it, with its own effulgence and intrinsic beauty.

As for the audience, they bore with him readily enough, for there is no patience, no indulgence, like that of a polished audience toward a well established favorite on the stage.

The first act was over, and the second, wherein the interesting instance of modelling takes place, had commenced. The artist was perched on his step-ladder, the unloved girl was distracting herself on the customary foot-stool, and the newly-adored one, the fair "Colombe," was slowly perambulating the supposititious lawn at the back of the stage. The artist trifled for a moment with his mass of clay, looked with an ominous glance at the model for the occasion, with her round, short face, up-inclining nose and narrow brow; then his eyes leaped for a moment into the box at his right hand, and his fingers began to flutter like birds over the clay. He no longer answered the questions of his despised adorer, from her foot-stool below; he forgot the scorn, indifference and sarcasm which the text of the drama exacted of him, and fixed all his soul on the work progressing under his swift fingers. The audience gazed on him with suspended lives, for the figure growing before them, was rapidly taking on a new meaning and impress.

But where was the retrouseé nose, and the short neck, and high forehead of the visible "Colombe?" certainly not in that oval, down-drooping face, in that finely-cut nose, in that firm, but tender mouth? No, nor did the sculptor deign to cast one glance to the back-ground of the scene, where she still vainly wandered; but all at once his eyes leaped again towards the stage-box, and the audience following them, saw whence the inspiration had come, and the improvisation in clay, stood confessedly before them, an image of Laura Milsland.

The marked resemblance between the head in clay, and that of Laura, was more clearly seen from the proximity of the two, for, forgetting all about herself and the audience, when she saw that something unusual was happening in the scene, Laura leaned eagerly out of the box, instead of concealing herself within it.

Fearing there would be some expression of displeasure from the audience, and not desiring to be involved in it, both the heroine of the back-ground and the one of the fore-ground, beat hasty retreats from the stage. Victor, on the contrary, who had the most reason to dread that displeasure, exhibited an utter indifference to it. He put a few more finishing touches on his work, stroked the head softly, as though he were soothing living hair; then came down from the steps, seated himself on the lowest one, folded his arms on his breast, threw back his head and burst into a long, hollow laugh. In the midst of it the curtain quickly descended, shutting him from the sight of the audience. Immediately after the house was wrapped in one unbroken "hum" like a vast hive of bees. Every body was eager to compare opinions on the subject of Victor's extraordinary conduct; but no audible sounds of dissatisfaction were heard. Only the lively spirits of the upper gallery, made derisive calls for "*Colum,*" and appeals to have that figure "heaved" out again, together with loud screams for Victor.

After a few moments, a sudden movement of the curtain betokened an explanatory appearance, and instantly allayed the commotion. It was the stage-manager, inconsistent as to dress, incoherent as to speech, and confused as to ideas. He begged the indulgence of the ladies and gentlemen; continued, that the sudden and peculiar termination of the act, was in consequence of Mr. Doria's being afflicted with the neuralgia—here he was interrupted by derisive interpolations from the gallery, of " Old juniper," blended with responsive howls of "Old rye, old rye." The speaker paused for silence, then went on to say as Mr. Doria was quite unable to appear before them again that evening, the company had kindly volunteered the delightful farce of " Out of his Head."

The speaker made his exit under a perfect hail-storm of cat-calls, jeering plaudits, and shrill interrogations of " How are you, *new*-ralgia ?"

Behind the scenes the storm was equally raging. The instant the curtain fell, Victor dashed into his dressing-room, and began washing his face, and tearing off his stage garments, like a juvenile Lear. In the midst of this, in came the manager-in-chief, and perceiving the disrobing process, demanded wildly the meaning of it.

" God bless my soul, sir, what are you doing ?"

" Undressing to go home, as you see."

" Go home ! Do you mean to ruin this theatre, sir ?

Don't you know that you belong to me for this evening? You are pledged to appear before the public, and the public have a right to demand the fulfillment of that pledge."

"Suppose I were dying, or dead?"

"But you are neither, though I think you have been drinking. I have a great mind to knock you down, sir."

"I wouldn't advise you to try," said Victor, and he threw up his flexile wrist, with a motion that reminded his antagonist that, notwithstanding its apparent delicacy, it had managed to acquire the texture of iron.

Then it was that the great man had sent his stage-manager before the audience, with the apology of the neuralgia, and the compensatory offer of "Out of his Head."

Victor, in the mean while, went on tearing off his clothes, throwing his shoes about, and demanding his street garments, in a manner that almost made a maniac of his dresser.

Before the curtain rose for the farce, Victor was out, prepared to tear through the streets in the same reckless manner in which he dispossessed himself of his theatrical appurtenances. But he was stopped at the door by an acquaintance of his, a young man of "means" and fashion.

"Hallo, Doria! What does all this mean? Miss Milsland is gone home."

Victor was about to rush past him without a word; but that name at once arrested him, and he asked eagerly—"Did you see her—how did she look?"

"Oh, pale, and tremendously interesting, of course; poor little girl. I would like to make love to her myself; but then, you know, 'twould be inconsistent with my principles, to cut out a friend. What's the matter with you, Doria?"

"Why do you ask?"

"Because you look as if you had been on the top of a windmill, turned round by an equinoctial storm. You like Laura Milsland, what's the use of denying it?"

"I am not called on either to deny or confess it, that I am aware of; who made it your affair?"

"Oh, one must be confiding with one's friends, you know. And let me tell you one thing; I know women, if anybody does, and I just threw my eye over Laura to-night, when you were kneading up that brown dough on the stage, and I found out one thing—she loves you like old gooseberry. If you return it, the affair is easy enough, nobody to make a nuisance of himself by interfering; no absurd father or brother, or anything. Just make your own terms, and she'll be sure to accept them; hold out your arms, and she'll jump off of a church-steeple to get into them. You're a lucky fellow to get things so easy; don't I know her?"

"You know her, as a cursed, conceited fool can know a woman so far above his comprehension as she is above your's. If you say she has no one to protect her from the insolence of such puppies as you are, you lie. She has me. Take this, to prove it."

As Victor followed up his words, by knocking him down and walking over him, it is to be supposed that the proof was perfectly logical and exhaustive.

Laura went home with her kind friend, Mrs. Middleton, without showing any trace of emotion, but her extraordinary paleness; but she refused all offers of refreshment, and retired to her own room. The window of this room commanded a view of the street; so there she sat, watching for the coming footsteps of one lithe figure—sat and watched in an agitation so profound, that it left her as quiet as stone; as the furious storms of the Indian seas, in the acme of their intensity, lash the waters into a white and boiling calm.

The long streets resounded with many footsteps, the flitting to and fro of manly feet—but, oh! not the echoes of that light, nervous footfall, not the graceful shadow of that supple figure, wherein the world's meaning was concentrated for her.

The steps came less frequently, and finally died out altogether, and the great moon slid slowly up the sky; yet still she watched and waited. Still she said to herself, "He will come, if but to say one word to me; he will not let this last night pass away without speaking one word to me, when to-morrow I am to leave him, perhaps, forever."

And thus she watched and hoped, till the night faded quite out of the heavens, and the first symptoms of daylight began to appear—daylight creeping grey, ghastly, and puny, out of the arms of the vast, majestic night. Then her poor, vain hope gave way, and, leaning her face upon her arms, she burst into a spasm of bitter, senseless weeping, giving way to such an indulgence for the first time since she had entered her new life.

Not unseen, however, was she in her hours of waiting, for he she looked for, stole noiselessly by, and, unnoticed, watched that patient vigil, which his faithful love kept for him. In the light of the moon, he could just trace the outlines of that tender, plaintive face, which needed but his presence to make it bright with unearthly joy. In that moment he thought of the light, contemptuous words which the love of that fond heart had called upon her from impure lips to-night, with a sensation of remorse that was new to him. But why think of one man's words? Had she not been set up, as a target for malicious words and thoughts, during the whole period of her love for him? If that love had made her ridiculous and contemptible to himself, how could he expect it would find a softer judgment from others? Something like tears gathered in his eyes with the thought of his own past hardness of heart. It was through this mist he took his last look of her pale, lovely face, and went away, looking very proud and handsome.

## CHAPTER XIV.

LAURA came down to breakfast next morning, with the traces of her last night's agitation scarcely perceptible in her face. She had neither slept nor attempted to sleep, and therefore she was less wearied, both as to look and feeling, than if she had fallen into a fitful doze to be broken off just as it was passing into slumber. A feverish, fictitious strength sustained her body, and her high estimate of justice and delicacy sustained her mind. It was to cheer, solace, and amuse Mrs. Middleton, that she accompanied her on this voyage; therefore, to set forth with the emblems of her own sorrow about her, seemed clearly to her a breach of faith. To go drooping, desponding, grieving, would have been unjust as well as cowardly to her mind; and Laura was as brave as she was loving. So she assumed a manner that was lively, encouraging, and energetic. If that strange, plaintive pallor, which the scene of last night had dashed into her face, still clung to it—who could blame her for that?

Many friends and acquaintances went to witness their departure, and the deck of the barque was covered with the gayest and most brilliant assemblage it had ever accommodated. Every one whom they expected came. Agnes was there, drowned in tears and enthusiasm, and Willister accompanied her, leaving his bounce and his tooth-pick on his clerkly desk. Mr. Middleton was the ruling spirit of the occasion, superintending the bringing in of an incredible number of boxes, arm-chairs, and articles of comfort, and giving so many orders, that they could only be computed by the number of his premonitory fees.

By one of those movements of nature, which sometimes flings off extraneous life unexpectedly, the last hours of intercourse between Laura and Julia displayed an unexpected tenderness. They had been rivals, they had both steeped themselves to the lips in worldliness, and they had wrangled away the last month of their proximity; but they were old schoolmates, linked together by all the ties of early frolics, lessons, battles, and adventures. They had been foes, but they had also been sworn friends. They had drank out of the same cup, devoured apples from the same tree, torn their gowns on the same briers, excavated the same clay, "committed" to memory their lessons from the same book, and frequently slept on the same pillow. Happily these associations are sweeter and stronger than those merely of fashion, flirting, and millinery. So, when the hour came to part them, for an indefinite time, nothing but the most affectionate feeling welled up in their mutual bosoms. When the moment came to clear the ship, in despite of Agnes, Julia was the last one to hold Laura in her arms and press loving kisses on her lips.

Then the "tug" seized hold of the ship and whisked

her off into the bay, and they gradually lost sight of the wharf, and no Victor had appeared, even to wish them a courteous " good-bye." Yet Laura, instead of experiencing that depression of spirits which she had expected, found herself gayer of heart than she had been for many a day. Perhaps this circumstance was owing to the free and breezy atmosphere of the ship; perhaps to the eradication of that hope whose throes had been such anguish to her; perhaps it was simply a physical light-headedness, caused by the reaction of last night's excitement and total loss of sleep. Prudently, she selected the last as her reason to act upon, and went down to rest in her state-room. There were but three other passengers aboard, a lady and gentleman with their son, a youth of sixteen. Mrs. Middleton, who was determined to be ill, lay, still quite well, on the sofa, attended by her maid; so Laura retired to her berth, and in a short time went to sleep. Dinner she refused, and, turning herself in her narrow bed, slept again until tea, when she arose, well rested and very hungry. No one came to table but herself, the other passengers lay around on sofas, and partook of nourishment like strange birds in a granary, who snap up a grain of corn, and then, frightened at their own motions, retreat from the feast until their courage has been restored by the absence of disaster. The captain, an amiable, lazy, good-humored sailor, looked with surprise on the apparition of this fine young lady, evidently in an excellent sanitary condition; but when he found her vivacious, sweet-tempered, and hungry, his surprise was converted into delight. He was a kind-hearted man, but his sympathy with nausea had been so perpetually played upon, that, like a worn string to a violin, it had become flaccid and irresponsive. But all the strings of that well-seasoned instrument, his heart, gave out their hearty welcome to a congenial young lady, whose intelligent face indicated a character more ready to enjoy, and conciliate than to repine, question, and fidget.

When, after tea, she asked him to take her up on deck, he assented to it with marked pleasure, evidently regarding her less as a charge than a comrade. They strolled up and down the deck, exulted in the fine breeze on the "quarter," which kept them so steady and even in their course, and finally, when the striking of two bells indicated nine o'clock, the captain thought it about time for him to "turn in," as it was necessary for him to be on the alert before day-break. Laura retired to her state-room, but having arisen only two hours before, of course it was impossible for her to sleep. She lay and tossed about for a couple of hours, and then, seeing how radiantly the moon was burnishing the waters, resolved to dress and quietly steal up on deck for another hour. No sooner thought than done, and in less than ten minutes she was steeped in moonlight and balmy breeze and sweet quietude. Nothing could be seen on the deck but the man at the helm, whose arms, as he slowly swung the obedient wheel, moved like an automaton, and took nothing from the lovely loneliness of the scene. For a moment, Laura sat watching the sails, which, swaying with an occasional strain and flutter, seemed like the great white wings of a bird in motion; then she began to drift idly up and down the deck. Back and forth she wandered, so lost in dreamy thoughts that she scarcely noted where she was, till, all at once, in turning to retrace her steps, a new sight shook all her drowsy senses into a transport of agitation, and her whole soul rushed into her wondering eyes.

What figure was that which, in the shadow of the

great sail, stood intently looking towards her? Of what avail to question herself, when, as soon as her eyes took in that form, her heart recognized it? for, though the face was drowned in shadow, something in the attitude of the head and the whole spirit of the figure, revealed the truth to her, by a light of instinct stronger than the noonday sun.

A moment's hesitation, and she sped quickly on, and the figure started out from the shadow of the sail, and opened its arms, and she came into them—and was silent

No explanations were uttered, not one word, not a laboring breath broke the mute intensity with which they were clasped in each other's arms, strained to one another's souls, in an embrace in which passion was but one ingredient, and in which was equally blended sympathy, respect, faithfulness, consonance of temperament, and every sentiment which can endear one human being to another.

The great summer moon hung like a vast censer, breathing out clouds of golden incense through the sky; the soft winds of the tropics streamed by them like invisible caresses; the strident sails leaned forward on the ambient air; the winged minutes sped past them, and the man at the wheel raised his automaton arm and struck the half-hour on the resonant bell; and still they rested mute in one another's arms, in a clasp so full of speechless emotion, that it seemed like Death, rather than the very concentration of Life, in one intense and almost awful joy.

## CHAPTER XV.

Mrs. Middleton was so "wonder wounded" by Victor's sudden appearance and its effects on Laura; she quite forgot to be sea-sick the next day, and went through the routine of marine life in an entirely living manner. The relations of these two as plighted lovers, were not in the least concealed from her, and though she saw in that fact the downfall of her brother-in-law's hopes, she wholly sympathized with the pair.

In her mind, Laura, weighted down with doubt and disappointment, was an object of deep respect and esteem; but Laura, adorned with the beauties of happiness, was an object of the fondest friendship.

Now, that the fine temper of Laura's soul was no longer qualified by sorrow, a thousand little artless graces began to climb like flowers over the sturdier virtues, which had borne themselves like rocks against the storms of evil fortune. She reflected her own happiness continually on those about her, and the atmosphere of the ship thus became one of exceptional peace and harmony. Fortunately there was such a tone of gladness among them, for the voyage was any thing but a favorable one. Head winds were succeeded by dead calms, and these again by obstinately adverse winds. The captain began to fear the longest passage on record of that route, for they had already been out a week, and had hardly made more than a good day's run.

Laura was not in the least disturbed by the delay, it would have troubled her little if the voyage had extended itself through the whole of her natural life. For the continents were emptied of interest to her, and all her rivers of life had flowed into the sea.

In the pristine simplicity of ship life, there was safety for her. She doubted the great cities and their allurements; she doubted still more her own attractions,—and in defiance of her efforts to the contrary, her imagination frequently pictured to her the time when she should be past by and forgotten. Her belief in her own happiness was bound to her heart with but a frail thread,——meanwhile the sea was an Elysian field, out of which there was no gate to desertion, but the awful shore.

The old discords which had been frequent between Victor and Laura, even in the earliest days of their acquaintance, existed no longer; they were not exceeded in compatibility of temperament by the Siamese twins, and were only less inseparable than that closely affiliated pair. But the record of unbroken happiness is drowsily monotonous—it has no history. Let them then, pass over to that time, when untoward fortune made their lives memorable again. They had been at sea thirty-seven days, and were at last nearing the island for which they were destined. During the last ten days, they had been fully under the influences of the tropics, and basked in them as most sensitive temperaments do.

The master of the ship looked for a landing in one day or two, or still earlier, if the profuse wind-clouds which were then scudding over the face of the sky, brought them any thing like a fair wind.

By the time night fell, the wind was fair and abundant—an hour afterward it was still fair, but in decided excess. The sails were reduced in volume, and after a while began to be taken in, one after another. By eleven o'clock in the night, there was a gale which, from its very ferocity, promised to be short-lived. The passengers in the cabin were so busy in holding on to any thing that came in contact with them, in order to keep from being rolled about like billiard-balls, that they had little energy to give to mental fear. As for Laura, ready as she was to anticipate spiritual dangers and distresses, she had no disposition to presuppose physical ones. Thus she was unusually composed for the circumstances, while Victor, who had not had her experience in battling with mental suffering, was pale with undue agitation. It was Laura's task to soothe and reassure him, and fate had not entrusted its work this time to unskillful hands.

In less than two hours from the moment of its greatest violence, the gale began to sensibly subside. No one was more rejoiced at this than the captain, for he knew well the barque was not a thing to resist successfully many heavy shocks. The passengers revived visibly, and though the storm was just beginning to abate, it seemed to them already at an end.

Not one hour after that, while they were all congratulating themselves on their good fortune, something suddenly struck the ship with a tremendous jar. Every timber in her was strained and wrenched as if by the rack. The lights were dashed out, and in the midst of the shuddering darkness came the ominous sound of gurgling waters. After the first cry of terror, the little band in the cabin were for a moment paralyzed into silence, and then there was a general rush for the deck. There were only three or four steps to ascend to reach it; but before they could find their way out, the captain appeared, and ordered them all in again. In a few moments the first mate came to them, bringing with difficulty, a lantern, and then their agonized curiosity, at least, was satisfied. They had colided with a large ship, and sustained heavy damages. The ship had been tacking at the time, and came across their bows with enormous force and speed. Either she had passed them by, unable to come near them, in the darkness and storm, or else she was wilfully abandoning them to their fate. Perhaps when the daylight broke, which was not many hours off, she would be found in their proximity, ready to aid and succor them. This was the tenor of the mate's consolation, which was meagre at the best, and in the meantime, the barque was sucking in water like a maelstrom.

Some one suggested the propriety of gathering together, each one, their most valuable possessions, so as to be ready to disembark at any moment. The advice was sound, but difficult of execution; for though the wind had greatly fallen, the sea was full of long, throbbing swells, which not only struck the barque with giant blows, but ploughed her about in a distracting way. Thus, when one was able, with the greatest difficulty, to keep from being shot like an arrow from one side of the cabin to the other, it was somewhat impracticable to accomplish any careful and select packing of portmanteaus. But the attempt was made by every one, and in a short time, one person might be seen suddenly bursting through a state-room, brandishing a hair-brush, like a tomahawk, in ineffectual efforts to keep from being dashed against the cabin side; or another staggering under a treacherous armful, would fall a wreck beneath a billow of bottles and dressing-cases.

Laura crawled lithely to her room, but very soon returned; Victor asked her what she had taken, and for answer, she silently carried his hand up to her throat, and laid it on a slender gold chain. He knew well enough that it bore with it the long-treasured likeness of himself. After a moment she returned, and again emerged from her room, with a small bag in her hand.

The usual means to aid a ship in her distressed condition were taken, and the working of the pumps was prosecuted with the utmost energy, but the insidious waters gained with an ascending ratio of progress upon them.

The passengers' cabin being on deck, was longest preserved from the encroaching element, but after awhile the waters began slowly to rise within it, indicating the necessity of its speedy abandonment.

The great rent in the barque was widening and increasing with the perpetual onslaughts of the waves, like a torn garment subjected to a too vigorous process of washing.

With the faintest tinge of daylight along the sullen skies, the boats were prepared to receive the ship's crew and passengers. The arrangements were characterized by a spirit of disorder and feebleness. The captain, though an excellent man for fortunate circumstances, was not the man for an emergency. Before the attacks of misfortune, he crumbled away into dust. Hitherto he had been a man of happy chance; in the many years of his sea life, never had disaster fallen to his lot. Short voyages, fair weather, or at worst tedious calms, had been his fortune; now, when he was required to face danger and conquer it, when his name was read from the roll-call of those summoned to the test of evil-fortune, his courage fainted away, and he answered, "not here."

His mate was far more energetic, but his was the uneven courage of illiterate minds. Fortunately their proximity to the island-coast, and the great number of vessels continually passing back and forth, gave them a reasonable hope of being speedily picked up, if only they could live until the subsiding of the heavy sea. That, too, was steadily falling; it might be expected to be tolerably quiescent in the course of a few hours, if no winds arose to harrow it up again.

At last, after what seemed weeks of waiting, the reluctant, ghastly daylight quivered along the heavens, and the boats were at once lowered. There was no time to be lost, for the wounded barque was sinking down, and making ready for a final plunge into destruction.

There was little confusion, owing to the small number to be disembarked; but every one seemed to take his own way of accommodating himself. Water and provisions had previously been prepared for the boats, and at last they were lowered, and the human beings transferred from the ship into them.

The captain had intended to locate all the cabin passengers in the boat under his care; but somehow, Victor managed to get into the one under charge of the mate, and so of course Laura followed him.

For a short time they were cheered by the anticipation of being soon discovered by that ship which had wrought their ruin the night before; but after an hour or so, that hope began to lose its force. The captain still clung to it, but the mate, less sanguine, at once dismissed it from his mind. The boats now began to make for shore, hoping to meet ships going in and out of the populous harbor, for which they were bound. The wind was fair, what there was of it, but by accidents of management, etc., the two boats soon parted company.

When the rays of the sun began to take on their full force, it was first discovered in the boat where Laura and Victor were, that not a soul had thought of bringing a hat; for in the damp, chilling night air, the coming heat of the noonday sun was entirely forgotten.

Victor, from his extremely delicate nervous organization, was the first to suffer from the heat of the sun. Laura made a turban of her handkerchief, and wetting it in the sea, placed it on his head. It acted as a temporary relief; but he soon began to complain of a racking headache, such an one as generally accompanies all forms of sun-stroke.

Laura sought in her little satchel for something to relieve his pain. It contained articles of toilette use; a necklace of large, pale coral beads; a lock of hair enclosed in an old worn note, with a masculine superscription upon it; two bottles of perfumery; and other little things scarcely calculated to mitigate the horrors of an open boat on the sea.

She offered him the most spicy of the perfumes, which she thought if it afforded no real relief, might at least interest his senses, and call their attention away from the contemplation of his physical pain. It succeeded better than she hoped; it made him drowsy, and finally put him to sleep. This was succeeded by slight delirium. Then again he sank into a dull, restless sleep, lying heavily upon Laura's knees. In that position, an expedient occurred to her for protecting him from the sun. She unbound the great, massive braids of her hair which were coiled round her head, and carefully loosening them, till they fell in a shower of ebon waves past her knees; she spread them out over Victor's prostrate form, sheltering him completely with a roof of native luxuriance. The rough sailors, charmed with the sight, looked on with gestures and words of admiration and wonder; but *he* could not admire nor even take cognizance of it, for he lay quite sundered from the world, and all the charms with which it can allure.

Long after noon-day the occupants of this boat began

to feel the knawings of hunger; in the sharpening of their mental anxieties, the claims of the body were quite deadened before. An attempt to make a general meal, resulted in a horrible discovery—they had not a particle of food aboard. In the confusion and want of management, all the provisions were put into one boat, and the water into the other. So, unless a quick termination to their trials should ensue, before them was the gaunt shadow of hunger, and before the other, the burning fiend of thirst.

After a long, uneasy slumber, Victor awoke, parting with his shaking hands the waves of hair which draped him in; putting it aside like a curtain, he raised himself, and for a few moments could not understand the unusual circumstances in which he found himself. As soon as they became clear to him, he complained of the usual reaction of a nervous headache, sharp hunger. Then it was that a new pang, to her who had endured so many, slid swiftly to Laura's heart—he was hungry, and she must see him hungering, and not be able to help him. Oh, heaven! would not He who had the power to die for the world He loved, help her, give her the power to save him! She lifted up her soul to Him in the extremity of her supplication, asking only the happiness of dying for him she loved. But no answer, no, no, no answer!—only the gently-waving waters, and the lovely stars climbing up their twilight way, and the summer airs that blowing from the shore, came tinctured with the breath of tropic trees, and told of happy lovers wandering beneath them, and in their own happiness justifying the creation of this great, mocking world.

No, God was not wantonly torturing her, but He had forgotten her. He had forgotten His creature, made in all the extremest capacity for suffering, human in power, and infinite in desire, and He was leaving her alone to struggle with that sea of vast and speechless anguish, which was rushing up to beat down and overwhelm her!

## CHAPTER XVI.

FORTY hours had elapsed since the boat had been left in the vast solitude of the waters, and no hope had dawned for them in the leaden monotony of their horizon. Most of the men in the boat, immured to hardships, and having access to an abundant supply of good water, had not given way much under the privation of food. But Victor, whose superbly sensitive organization was as easily deranged as the finest-stringed instrument, lay quite broken and helpless on Laura's breast, which was now his only rest and refuge. The sharp pangs of hunger had passed from him; feebleness, fever, and occasional delirium possessed him now. It was easy to see that he was steadily sinking away. The perfect outlines of his face had fallen in; his features were drawn and narrowed, and his eyes dull and lifeless in expression. All the color had faded out of his lips, which, like his eyes, were surrounded by dark, blue circles; and his hair blown unresisting about over his brow, added an additional shade to the wan, haggard look of his face. When he slept—as he did three-quarters of the time—it was scarcely possible to know whether it were sleep or death; for his eyelids had so far lost their vitality, they were seldom entirely closed in sleep, and the strip of sad, lightless eye glimmering between the lids, continually fed the awful fears of the woman whose love for him neither life nor death could appease.

His voice, that lovely, sonorous organ which, in its time, had stirred the hearts of multitudes to their depth, now in its childish, broken whispers, only upheaved one agonizing soul. Indeed, there was little left of this chief darling of nature, and that little Laura was cherishing with the last strength of her own poor, happy, loving, breaking heart.

Sometimes, in his lucid moments, he would converse with her in his low, tired voice. Then she learned how well he had known all the devotion of her past years to him. He had never seemed to see it, or believe it, when it was brought to his notice; yet, it was all written down on the tablet of his memory, even to the last atom. He told her—

"Of course I was aware of my power of pleasing women. I knew I could charm, fascinate, mislead them; but, upon my soul, I never thought, in the widest sense of the word, any woman could love me."

"Why not?"

"Because it never seemed to me I could love any woman. I know now more depends on the woman's capacity for loving, than the man's for deserving it."

"You knew that I—loved you?"

"Yes, and I was sorry for it."

"I know that—but why?"

"Because I had chosen for myself a life of pleasure, a life in which I should skim over all the flowers of existence, tasting only their sweets. I was too lazy to love you. To be admired, followed, caressed, petted, enriched, committed to no opinions, and perfectly self-centred, was the ideal life of my desires. But who could live such a life, loving and loved by you? It would have been signing the death-warrant of lightness, and pledging myself to earnestness and distinct meanings in life. I could not have erred innocently then; I should have gained that spiritual insight, by means of which I had erred with a heavy conscience. Principle, not pleasure, must have been my guiding-star, and all the relentless angels would have stood by to see that I did not dash my foot against one stone of reckless self-indulgence. I only desired those loves which, like the flowers of a day, perish in the declining sun. But to love you, was to go down into the great, mysterious waters, through which there was neither pathway nor guide. To love you, was to take a leap in the dark; it was toil, it was self-government, self-abnegation, regeneration—it was belief in immortality, in God—and so I loved you not!"

"So much for one poor, fond, foolish heart like mine."

"I warred against all feeling for you; trampled it down, and trod it into the dust, till the time came when it stole, ere I knew it, like the Holy Spirit in form of a dove, into my inmost heart, and folded its soft wings to rest in its sanctuary. And it shall never be cast out on the waste waters. When, upon the yet happy ship, I opened my arms to take you in, it was never to let you go—unless you wish to leave me."

"I wish to leave you!" and then the tender, fathomless depths of her eyes gleamed out a language her lips could not utter.

After such converse, he would seem quite exhausted, and sink away to the death-like slumbers which freighted her heart so heavily with fear. He ceased to complain of headache, but often of a whirring in his ears and a mist before his eyes. From these swoon-like sleeps, he always awakened half-unconscious, and would gaze around him like a frightened child, until Laura's face aroused his full consciousness.

Often, when too feeble to speak, he would gaze up to her with those dim eyes, which seemed to be full of a mute supplication, as an infant torn with uncomprehended pain, dumbly implores the help of its mother. Sometimes his hands would be raised slowly to her neck, and would feebly stroke her face, until they dropped back helpless again.

Often Laura remembered the time, she had offered herself such wrong, as to suppose she loved this man for his personal beauty. Now how much greater was her love, when all that matchless beauty was quite blotted out, when that exquisite combination of attractions through which, for so many years, her heart was killed all the day long, lay worn and helpless at her feet!

It was strange, how all the personal fascinations, for which he had been unrivaled, melted away from him under the influence of two days of mental and bodily anguish; all the beauties of his face seemed blown out, like lights on twilight and stormy seas.

Often his eyes were fixed wonderingly on Laura, as she sat erect, sheltering him in her arms, never seeming to tire or to sleep, with the scarlet glare of fever flaming on her lips and cheeks, and her wide, lustrous eyes burning like beacon fires over the waters. Then he wondered, what mysterious power sustained her? why was she not tired, and fretful, and frightened, like others? Had she no fear to blanch her cheeks, nor sorrow to bow her head?

He knew not that she sorrowed without ceasing; but not as one without hope; but as one with an angel hope in her heart, and whose strength was the might of an intolerably longing love.

She was strong with the strength to comfort, to sustain him, to bear his griefs, to lift him up, to rescue him from despair, and to carry him over the agonizing gulf of death.

The third twilight which had swathed them in its shadows was drawing on, when he suddenly opened his eyes, and asked—

"Laura, am I going to die?"

Her soul shrank within her, at being chosen to deal that blow to him; but instantly it rose again in its full spiritual courage, and she replied, in a quiet, calm voice—"I could not quite know, Victor."

"What do you think?"

In the same unnaturally, quiet tone, she answered—"I think you will die."

"Ah, my Laura, I am afraid."

"Afraid?"

"I am not ready to die. I have misused my opportunities, trifled with my talents, forgotten all interests but selfish ones. Shall I be forgiven? My whole life witnesses against me. My treatment of you alone may condemn me."

"Do I condemn you?"

"Out of your goodness, sweet one, not because I did not deserve it."

"And will you make Him, who died for us, less merciful than I am? Will you insult His loving kindness, by esteeming it less than that of a creature like me?"

"Pray for me, then, Laura—pray for me."

"I do. Oh, I never cease to pray for you."

"Do not leave me, Laura. Are you tired? Can you hold me a little longer?"

"I could hold you forever."

"Keep close to me; hold me to your soul—and I think I will sleep."

He closed his eyes, and then opening them again,

said, "Do not let me go—hold me fast; if I seem to die, never think I have ceased to need you—keep close to me;——and, Laura, do not let me die in my sleep; let me be looking into your eyes at that moment."

He closed his eyes, and fell into a painful sleep, for his weary breath seemed in travail as it struggled through his lips. This troubled breathing was mingled with low moans and heavy sighs.

Laura, leaning over him, asked, "What is it, Victor —are you in pain?"

"No, not in pain; but there is something so awful in this tearing away of the soul from the body."

He slept again, and Laura was left to rend her already bleeding heart with the thought that his death by exposure, sun, starvation, torture, was due to her; he was drawn into them through following her;—but she flung that thought away from her speedily, if she was to be any consolation to him in his last hours, she felt, "let me shun that thought, for that way only, madness lies."

She was steadily watching the play of a pulse in his wasted throat, whose flutterings were pitifully visible. All at once, that pulse began to make quicker beats, and then it sank altogether. She raised his head eagerly on her breast, fearing his position was no longer comfortable, and at the moment he opened his eyes again.

"Laura, are you there?—do not leave me."

"I will never leave you."

"Oh, my own poor, poor little girl, it is I who must leave you. I had thought to make amendment for your years of wasted love to me; but that hope is blasted. I am to die—and go from you. And you, my poor child, you have nothing for your sacrifices but the added burden of my death. To the last you give all. For your years of unanswered love; for your faith, your truth, I have nothing left to give you, but my dying sigh."

Was it so little then, was it so little for her, who had panted for one smile, one word, one frown, if only so she might see him, longed for these as the shipwrecked long for light in midnight seas, and was that last sigh of his parting spirit nothing? Had she not murmured because she never had been permitted to serve him, that an evil fate had elected to chain her outside of his needs, and now her arms were chosen for his dying bed, and up to her was to rise the last breath of that precious, priceless life.

She looked down on his face, and seeing water-drops gathering upon it, believed there was rain from the heavens; but holding out her hand, she found the air dry, and then touching her face, saw that rain had fallen from her own unconscious eyes. Not a tear yet had she shed in all that strain of bitter anguish, which, for the last few days, had been tugging at her heart, and even now she quenched them with a mighty effort of will.

A languid breeze came creeping across the waters, reviving her after the excessive heat of the day, and she even hoped it would be reviving to him. At first he did seem to breathe more easily, as it rippled gently across his death-like face; but after a moment the labored breathing returned, and every instant he drew his breath more painfully and strangely. She feared even that little breeze to be too strong for him, and drew his face round into her bosom, and sheltered his head with her arms. But his breath seemed to be struggling to escape from him altogether, and remembering his fear of dying in his sleep, she cried out in a low but heart-rending voice, "Victor, oh, Victor, do not die till you have spoken to me once more, once more."

He opened his eyes once again, and a poor, pallid smile fluttered over his face. His lips moved faintly, and she dropped her's down and pressed upon them one breathless kiss. She could feel his feeble mouth tremble in the effort to respond to it, and faintly cling with passive tenderness to her's. With one last effort he clasped his hands about her neck, and his eyes lighted up for a moment with a look of intolerable pathos. Then the light faded out of them, and his hands dropped helpless from her neck, and plucked feebly at her breast, as though striving to grasp something. She caught them both firmly in her own, and they seemed to rest in her's, as though they were never to have another asylum. The quick, strange breathing came on again; the veins in his throat began to swell, and his breathing changed into gasps. In the midst of these gasps he said, "Laura, my eyes are dying; I can see nothing but you. I seem to be changing into air. Can you see me still, or is it dark?"

"It is never dark where you are; you are my light forever."

He moaned again, and again.

"Can I do anything for you?" she cried; "can I help you?"

"Love me! oh, love me! oh, love me with all your might!"

"Forever; while my soul lasts. I loved you from the first, and love you on forevermore."

He seemed to hear her, though there was no more speech for him in all this world; but his fast glazing eyes answered unspeakable things.

No more! for her the end of the earth was come—the third planet was sweeping on to join the extinct worlds. Not a flutter stirred her marble breast; her face was transfixed like a dead angel's. An awful calm settled upon her—she knew what was come, and said to her soul, "be still!" Gasps growing still fainter, hands fluttering within her grasp in feeble convulsion, dying lips sighing up towards her's, dying eyes swimming upon her own with their last life; a sob, a sigh, and——nothing more

Dead! dead love! dead world! dead everything, but the unseen life he had sank away into. Yet she gazed calmly, and with awful patience upon him. Oh! pale, wasted, sorrow-stained face, with what a tragic stillness you buried yourself in that utterly paralyzed breast! hands, how you stiffened in her despairing grasp! unclosed eyes, with what a deadly gleam you reflected back to her's the rays of the rising moon!—and yet she never quailed; her heart stood proudly up, and chose you dead, gainst all the living world!

\* \* \* \* \* \* \*

During the last hours of this time, sounds had come to Laura from the other occupants of the boat, signs of excitement and anticipation. But she heeded them not, because for her, speech, sight, sound, hope, and all meanings lay drifting to death from her arms. But now the glad cry of the sailors shattered her quiet with the words—"The ship is upon us; she will take us in a moment."

A ship? Oh, God, a ship! A thing come to tear her from him; to leave him down in his vast, lonely grave; to drag her back to a sepulchre, to a dead world! At that thought her soul, which had been crouching in deadly quiet, like a crushed, tortured thing, sprang up erect and defiant, and gave forth one long, low, wailing cry—a cry that rang over the waters, and echoed far along the waves, till it died away like the shadow of a sigh.

The ship bore immediately down on them, a boat was lowered, and first of all its occupants sought to give aid to the only female among the wandering strangers. Some one spoke to Laura, but she answered not, nor moved, but continued to lie in the strange position in which they found her, with her arms folded close about another form, and her head leaning partly over the water. Concluding her to be fainting from weakness and exhaustion, they raised her, and then, in the clear moonlight, a dark-red stream was seen to be flowing from her lips.

Not a flutter of life stirred that lion's heart. To feel her pulse was like touching a stone.

Both of the lifeless bodies were lifted into the other boat, and silently conveyed into the ship, from which they were given back into the sepulchral sea next day.

### EXTRACT FROM A LADY'S JOURNAL.

*Sunday.*—"Met with our first exciting incident (yesterday) since we sailed. We picked up a boat, containing the crew and two passengers from a barque wrecked last week. The crew seem to be already recovered from their sufferings, but both passengers were dead. Our physician says the man's death was caused by sunstroke, the woman's by aneurism of the heart. I spoke with one of the sailors this morning, and he tells me, he never saw such devotion as she showed to him, during their three days of suffering; that she seemed not to know what fatigue, or hunger, or anxiety was, till he died, and then all her strength gave way with a sudden shock. He will have it, she died of a broken heart; but, then, the faculty declare there is no such thing in existence. The doctor pronounces it an aneurism, an accident to which she was liable under the most tranquil circumstances, and I presume science must be justified of her words.

We laid them side by side in the cabin below, and I

cannot tell what fascination led me to steal in, time after time, and gaze at them. They had a look of supreme calm; I might almost say, of visible joy on their faces. Who were they? what were they to each other? I find myself wondering within myself a dozen times a day. Was she his bride? But then I thought I detected a likeness between them. Perhaps they were brother and sister. The girl has been of a darker skin than the man, but much loss of blood has bleached her face to undue whiteness, and there was but one tint of pallor on each cheek. As the sunbeams crept fitfully over their faces, the same tender smile seemed to illumine them. Ah! surely they were closely alike!

Found dead in one another's arms, we had not the heart to separate them, but committed them together to the tomb of the great sea.

\* \* \* \* \* \* \*

*Sunday.*—A week has passed since we met with our hapless boat, and since then nothing has occurred worth speaking of. I still find myself speculating upon those two whom we only rescued in death. Nor, often as I gazed upon their two faces, can I separate, in memory, the one from the other. No sooner does memory recall his face than her's blends with it, the features of the one melt into the other, mingle, and are transfused.

Try as I may, I can only remember them as one."

END.

CPSIA information can be obtained
at www.ICGtesting.com
Printed in the USA
LVHW10*0735180918
590492LV00010B/71/P